T0293082

MAKE THE DEAL

MAKE THE DEAL

Negotiating Mergers & Acquisitions

Christopher S. Harrison

BLOOMBERG PRESS
An Imprint of
WILEY

©2016 The Bureau of National Affairs, Inc. All rights reserved.
Published by John Wiley & Sons, Inc., Hoboken, New Jersey.
"The 1st edition of *Make the Deal* was published by Bloomberg Press in 2014."
Published simultaneously in Canada.

For general information on our other products and services or for technical support, please contact our
Customer Care Department within the United States at (800) 762-2974, outside the United States at
(317) 572-3993 or fax (317) 572-4002.

Wiley publishes in a variety of print and electronic formats and by print-on-demand. Some material
included with standard print versions of this book may not be included in e-books or in print-on-demand.
If this book refers to media such as a CD or DVD that is not included in the version you purchased,
you may download this material at http://booksupport.wiley.com. For more information about Wiley
products, visit www.wiley.com.

Library of Congress Cataloging-in-Publication Data:

ISBN 9781119163503 (Hardcover)
ISBN 9781119163657 (ePDF)
ISBN 9781119163602 (ePub)

Printed in the United States of America
SKY10050741_070823

Contents

About the Author

Christopher S. Harrison currently serves as Chief Investment Officer of The Falconwood Corporation, a financial management firm and research laboratory that has incubated and operated numerous highly successful financial and technological ventures.

Having managed billions of dollars in successful investment transactions, including debt, equity, and real asset ventures, Mr. Harrison earned a reputation as a superb negotiator and business strategist. During his eight years at Cravath Swaine & Moore, one of the world's most prestigious law firms, he handled numerous high-profile debt, equity, and M&A deals. As co-head of the market-leading asset management M&A practice at Schulte Roth & Zabel, the premier investment management law firm, he ran some of the most sophisticated public and private deals and facilitated the strategic growth of several prominent financial services and asset management businesses.

Mr. Harrison teaches popular courses at NYU School of Law on the financial and legal aspects of negotiating and investing in business transactions. He is a regular speaker at industry conferences and webinars.

He holds a JD degree, cum laude, from NYU School of Law, where he focused on law and economics.

CHAPTER 1

Introduction to Deal-Making

Deal-Making in Practice

Looking back, I have come to realize that careful attention to transaction details played a critical role in the businesses I founded over the course of my career. Thinking strategically about potential outcomes—and setting the stage in the contract to navigate them in the future—was critical to my success.

—Dr. Henry G. Jarecki

My proposal turned the tables. I had conveyed it cautiously. Sound legal advice had been hard to come by. None of the lawyers I had hired could do more than follow technical instructions. As the clock was working against us, I followed my intuition on what our legal rights were. As desperate as things stood for our company, I figured that I could not possibly make things worse.

The effect was stunning. Triumphantly smug a moment before, the guys on the other side backed down. Perhaps they had known the weakness of their position all along and played hardball to get the better of us. After all, they were a large national player with a reputation for running over minor league players like us. Perchance I surprised them. Or had they not thought seriously about our side of the issue, let alone the business implications of their own legalese? At that moment, I realized how crucial legal knowledge was to running a business.

From that conference room, I took the shortest way to law school—only to find in my subsequent career that corporate practice is effective only if business judgment and legal expertise coincide.

That is the impetus of this book. It brings business, finance, and law together, showing how legal form configures the economic outlook, and how to support a business strategy with a legal framework. More specifically, it is designed as a tool for individuals in both business and law—in-house, in practice, or in training—to understand how merger and acquisition (M&A) deals are negotiated and how acquisition contract terms impact economic outcomes. It analyzes current techniques and mechanics used in acquisition agreements and shows how to design deal terms to meet the needs of your particular transaction.

In the larger scheme of things, this book may be a small step further down the road of commoditizing and quantifying legal advice. But I hope this book will also caution against overdoing it. As the review of actual deals will show, each is different. There is no "one size fits all" solution. Effectively combining different elements, applying the law to a specific situation, and calculating the economic effect of contract terms requires skill, intellect, and often a good dose of ingenuity that is not inherent in any commoditized form of legal advice.

Creativity (among other human faculties) does not come in a box. If, in that conference room, I had not been able to find a new perspective, to think outside and beyond the paradigm that the legal experts—including my own counsel—had presented me, the company I managed would have ended up like the other small fry. It is innovation that, more often than not, will give you an edge.

What makes M&A practice such a rich experience is that almost every deal is distinct in its facts, the business issues at stake, the economic trends in play, and the personalities and negotiating tactics involved. Given the number of variables, a deal can take on many different forms. It is crucial to understand that these different forms will invariably produce different legal and economic results. Structuring to solve business issues—and sorting out business issues resulting from the structure—is what M&A is all about.

The art of negotiating has been much dwelled on, but it is absolutely useless when the reasons for having a provision are not understood, when the follow-on implications of winning or not winning a point escape the players, or when they come to the negotiating table without any idea regarding their company's or client's backup positions. How will you know when a point is worth the fight, when to give in, and when to walk away? How will you know what to ask for in the first place? Before getting cute at the negotiating table, you have to understand your business goals and your options—including the legal terms with which to achieve them. Otherwise, your art will backfire: "In my many business negotiations, I have always been amazed that the other side will ask for something that is less advantageous to them than the deal they already have," notes one of my clients.

This book starts by examining the various agreements that practitioners have to negotiate before actually sitting down to talk about the acquisition agreement. These include confidentiality agreements, standstill agreements, exclusivity agreements, and letters of intent or memoranda of understanding. These agreements protect the parties from economic disadvantage due to the deal process, set rules for the negotiations, and define preliminary objectives.

Separate chapters of this book show how the core elements of an acquisition agreement—that is, purchase price mechanics and adjustments, representations, covenants, conditions, material adverse effect clauses, financing contingencies and reverse breakup fees, fiduciary outs to top a public deal and indemnities—function within the context of a deal. Each chapter explains how a component is negotiated in real life with the purpose of creating value for and balancing risks between the parties. Comparing various strategies for solving business problems, some methods to provide for "rough justice" while other approaches are more refined. Transaction techniques often make a difference—and sometimes all the difference. The chapters include war stories to demonstrate potential pitfalls and bring out the relevance of certain techniques. In addition, statistics on how deal terms are negotiated in practice give an overview with regard to the prevalence of certain provisions and thus a sense for the market. Finally, sample provisions from actual contracts model the language that make a particular deal work.

This book next analyzes the overall framework of an acquisition agreement. It examines the different deal structures—that is, stock sales, mergers, asset sales, and complex structures—and lays out the criteria according to which practitioners choose (or should choose) between them.

War Stories

War stories from practice bring home the flavor of what is at stake in actual deals. Highlighting why drafting matters, the crux of each story elucidates the problems the parties grappled with, sidelined, or simply overlooked. Their successes and failures show the lessons learned. After all, to understand—and laugh at—the mistakes of others is the best way to appreciate why a point is important.

War Story ══

Thirty war stories reveal the workings of deal terms by way of example. The core issues at stake are conceptually "based on a true story," but they are all works of fiction.

Each mistake and problem described in those sections has happened in practice. The stories that go with them, however, bear no relationship to actual transactions. Any correlation to any real parties or lawyers—especially those who made mistakes or ended up on the wrong side of unexpected events—is purely coincidental.

The Market

Lawyers have been slow to quantify their expertise. But with the passage of time, and the continuously improving ease with which lawyers can gather and crunch the numbers on other deals, a more quantitative mind-set is filtering into practice.

This book uses quantitative analyses to see how deals fit into observable patterns of the marketplace, while, at the same time, cautioning against a simplifying, precedent-oriented approach to deal-making. After all, a weighted-average set of terms would, in fact, suit no one. And the examination of any one deal point in a vacuum can lead the parties to overlook the interactions among deal points or the specific needs of the parties at hand.

Nevertheless, as quantitative studies of transaction terms begin to proliferate, deal-makers will more frequently be pushed by the force of precedent into standardized provisions, paving the way for majority terms to become more and more dominant. As time goes by, the average may become the norm, whether or not the average fits the facts of a particular deal. Knowledge of what constitutes "market terms" (i.e., terms that have become commonplace in transactions) has become critical to arguing a position and can be a helpful tool for convincing the other side that a position is fair.

THE MARKET

Nearly 100 "The Market" sections are culled from studies of deals in which the author participated, as well as from a variety of other publicly available studies. As such, the data represent a generalized meta-analysis derived from numerous independent sources.

Quantitative analyses vary meaningfully from study to study. Different results are generated by:

- *Sample size.* The smaller the sample, the more they can be influenced by outlier deals.
- *Sample selection.* Rarely do studies consider all available data. How they pick and choose affects the results.
- *Period reviewed.* Trends change, by definition. The period studied matters.
- *Mix of deal types.* Different deal types constitute their own market. More or less of one type skews the results.

To help avoid the illusion that quantitative analysis of deal terms is a precise science, all results in this book have been rounded to the nearest 5 percent, or to thirds or halves, depending on the context.

Sample Provisions

Sample provisions illustrate model wording and key drafting choices. Frequently, these examples represent "form" language, or wording a practitioner would use as a starting point before changing it to fit a particular deal.

Sample Provision

Over 140 "Sample Provisions" are based on formulations used by the author as well as actual public deal precedents.

[Bracketed text] usually indicates a drafting choice. It shows an issue buyers and sellers may negotiate, or a provision that is more or less aggressive. Brackets are also used to summarize missing text, in order to focus an example on the primary topic.

Underlining is used to emphasize key words or phrases.

Litigation Endnotes

Good contracts are negotiated in the shadow of litigation. Rules of contract construction tell us that the court's primary job is to interpret the intent of the parties, who are relatively free to draft any provision they wish.

Courts do this by first giving a plain-English interpretation to the words on the page. In doing so, courts often assume the lawyers understand the underlying case law. Practitioners, in contrast, often draft as if the dictionary rather than case law provides the primary resource for giving meaning to the words they draft—and the topics they decide to avoid and be silent on. Case law provides the backdrop for lawyers to determine when silence works for them or against them, and when they should try to clarify ambiguity.

Some of the cases that elucidate these issues are interspersed throughout this book in approximately 100 litigation endnotes. They are not intended to provide a definitive statement of case law in any particular jurisdiction. Instead, they highlight the kinds of issues that must be dealt with in drafting, to avoid your client's falling into similar litigation.

CHAPTER 2

Setting Up the Deal

Overview and Confidentiality Agreements

Overview of the Predeal Process

Deals start in many different ways but progress along a relatively standard track. After one party introduces the concept of a deal to the other side, the predeal process kicks in.

If there is sufficient interest in a serious discussion, the first step is to negotiate a confidentiality agreement. This agreement protects the target's sensitive business information, and requires the deal talks to be kept secret. A confidentiality agreement can also include other key transaction process terms. Those can include:

- A "no-poach" provision (also called "no-hire" and nonsolicitation provisions) that restricts the bidder from trying to hire away the target's best employees, and
- A "standstill" that prevents the bidder from taking potentially hostile moves against a public company if a friendly deal cannot be negotiated.

If a deal is potentially worth the diligence effort, the bidder may ask for exclusivity. An exclusivity agreement prevents the target or sellers from working with competing bidders during a limited period of time. This gives the bidder breathing room and comfort that the sellers are not negotiating with another bidder in the room next door.

In many cases the parties next go into full contract negotiations. If the deal is complex, they may first lay out the key terms in a term sheet, or in the more narrative form of a letter of intent. Such documents provide a deal summary and make sure the parties are generally on the same page before going into detailed, full transaction documentation. Term sheets and letters of intent are almost always nonbinding summaries of where negotiations stand; they do not represent a binding contract, but are merely a road map for the more formal contract to be drafted.

Each of these agreements is discussed separately in the next chapters.

Confidentiality Agreements

In almost any deal, a potential buyer will require access to nonpublic information regarding the target. This so-called "due diligence" review attempts to ferret out unexpected information regarding the target, its structure, liabilities and its prospects, and to refine the buyer's financial analysis.

Although a buyer may often propose an indicative price or price range before completing its due diligence review, the buyer normally needs extensive private information before finalizing the binding deal price.

Depending on the target, some public information may be available. Very little public information will be available to the buyer if the target business is privately owned, which makes the buyer heavily reliant on the diligence process.

If the target is a public company, basic information will be available under the Securities and Exchange Commission's (SEC's) disclosure requirements, including historical financial statements. If the target business is a division or part of a public company, its SEC filings would not be specific enough for a buyer, especially if there are no separately reported "segment" financials for the target business. Whatever the situation, more information is always necessary.

To accommodate both the buyer and the seller, the target normally provides diligence information, but on the condition that the buyer agrees not to disclose it to third parties or use it for any purpose other than to evaluate the deal at hand.

Targets have good reason to avoid sharing information unnecessarily. Competitors may exploit the information for competitive advantage, or potential start-ups may strategically use the data in determining whether to enter the market. A target may also suffer in its commercial dealings with customers if they learn the target's internal profit margins.

The core restrictions in a confidentiality agreement and how they operate are summarized below. This chapter also discusses the scope of what has to be kept confidential and several exceptions, the obligation to "return or destroy" information and the end of the process, and when and how confidentiality agreements terminate.

This chapter focuses on confidential information. However, the parties frequently enter into two-way agreements. For example, the target may conduct some diligence on the buyer, if any of the consideration will be in the form of buyer stock, and the buyer will want the target to keep the deal talks quiet.

Due diligence

There are several reasons for due diligence. One derives from the fiduciary duty of care that a corporate board has under corporate law. In addition, under securities laws that govern the offer and sale of stock, the issuing company and its board of directors (and others) can be held liable for material misstatements or misleading omissions made in connection with that sale. Under these same securities laws, the board can invoke a defense that relieves it of liability: it needs to show that it exercised due diligence in carrying out its responsibilities.[1] Conducting a thorough business and legal diligence review has become a central part of creating that due diligence defense.

Due diligence, however, is about more than avoiding securities law liability. It goes back to the Roman law doctrine of caveat emptor, or "let the buyer beware." Under that doctrine, the buyer could not recover from the seller for defects that rendered an asset unfit for ordinary purposes unless the seller actively concealed latent defects. As discussed in the indemnity chapter,[2] the buyer's ability to recover for losses is limited in several ways. Because of these limitations, the rule of caveat emptor still applies. Sales are relatively final exchanges, and it is the responsibility of the buyer to ensure that it is satisfied with the bargain before entering into the contract.

War Story

A strategic investor was looking to buy a stake in a particular Asian venture that had been brought to its attention. The deal was small for the buyer, but the prospects looked great. Given the transaction size, the buyer thought that the diligence budget had to be kept small.

The sellers presented due diligence documents claiming that the target held a long-term, exclusive license to intellectual property rights to music in important markets outside of its home country. The diligence documents were all in English. They had been officially translated, all the way down to the stamped and sealed certificate from the state-owned music company.

It all looked good to the U.S. lawyers and diligence team. The buyer and target signed an exclusivity agreement and started negotiating a deal. As the transaction progressed, the buyer also engaged local counsel in the target's home jurisdiction.

When local counsel reviewed the underlying (local language) diligence documents that had been "translated" into English, they were shocked. The target did not have an exclusive license to intellectual property at all—the target merely acted as an "agent" in marketing the intellectual property rights of others. There was no license, and their agency relationship could even be terminated at will at any time.

With a little more digging, it turned out that the local official who provided the official English translation was related to a board member of the target.

The buyer simply walked away, without pursuing fraud charges that could be embarrassing. The buyer lost its investment in time and legal fees, but close due diligence protected it from a much larger loss. The buyer never investigated whether the target gave up after that, or simply went shopping for a less careful buyer.

Restrictions on disclosure

Confidentiality agreements restrict the buyer from disclosing confidential information to third parties. This is the core element of the contract.

While this restriction may seem simple enough, it begs the question of who exactly counts as a third party and who does not. Normally, an exception allows confidential information to be disclosed to "representatives" of the buyer. Representatives include the bidder's internal personnel, and external agents such as the financial advisors, accountants, and lawyers. That leaves everyone else as a third party.

Sample Provision

Recipient shall keep all Confidential Information received by it confidential and shall not disclose such Confidential Information, in whole or in part, to any person, except that Recipient may disclose Confidential Information to those of its Representatives who need to know the Confidential Information for the purposes of evaluating the Potential Transaction, provided that such Representatives are informed by Recipient of the confidential nature of such information and are bound by contractual or professional confidentiality terms substantially similar to those set forth herein.

The exception for representatives permits disclosure only to those who "need to know" the details in order to play their role in the transaction. The result is a kind of working group disclosure concept. The deal team gets the information it needs, but outside of the deal team, the data flow is cut off.

Restrictions on use

The use of confidential information by the buyer is also restricted by confidentiality agreements. While the restriction on disclosure defines the working group allowed to receive confidential information, the restriction on use determines what they can do with it.

Consider what a potential buyer could do with the target's information if there were no restriction on its use. For instance, the potential buyer could use it to compete against the target in the future. Targets often express concern that strategic bidders may start negotiations merely to gain access to such data. Some targets view providing data to potential competitors as a necessary evil to get a deal done. Restrictions on use are one of the ways to help limit the potential damage from confiding in a competitor. Actually enforcing a restriction on use, however, is challenging.[3]

War Story ───

There was great interest in the auction, since the target had made quite a name for itself as an innovator in a stodgy industry. It was almost viewed as "one of a kind."

A large potential strategic buyer sent an entire deal team of 25 people from various departments for a week of in-person diligence sessions with the target. They sat through meetings with key management of each division, talked through the target's projections, and chatted about the prospects for the target's latest and greatest ideas. They were serious. They negotiated hard, as would be expected, and they stuck out the process until quite late in the game.

Eventually, the target selected a private equity buyer and finalized a deal. The private equity buyer wanted to consolidate the target into one of its existing portfolio companies in the industry and was willing to pay a hefty price.

For four months, the target and the new private equity buyer worked through the process of obtaining antitrust approval, securing the buyer's financing, and obtaining target shareholder support. After that, they had an integration job ahead of them, which would distract their best management talent for yet another few months.

Once the target was ready to get back to business and continue their push to change the marketplace, they discovered a new competitor—the same strategic buyer that had lost out in the auction!

As far as the target could tell, none of the actual confidential information had been misused. They had no evidence of a breach. But they could not shake the feeling that they had just trained the competition and then given them over half a year to catch up while the target was distracted by the minutiae of closing and integration.

The customary restriction on use is a simple statement confirming that the target's confidential information will not be used for any purpose other than evaluating the deal at hand.[4] As a practical matter, it is difficult for a target to know how information is used by a bidder. And it may be impossible for a buyer to avoid indirectly or implicitly using what it has learned.

Sample Provision

Recipient shall not use any Confidential Information for any purpose other than to evaluate the Potential Transaction.

So much rides on the meaning of the three-letter word "use." Relying on the word "use" in this context is an example of the drafting style that puts enormous weight on interpreting inherently vague terms in a variety of unpredictable contexts. Other examples include the concepts of "reasonableness" and "reasonable best efforts," and notions of "materiality" and the term "material adverse effect." At the same time, acquisition agreements also include inflexible and potentially arbitrary rules in other contexts, such as a defined expiration date or "drop-dead date."

War Story

A start-up mining company struck a good deal and acquired rights to a rich set of mineral deposits. It promptly went looking for capital to develop a large mine. Obviously, it required all its potential investors to sign a standard confidentiality agreement.

One potential strategic investor decided the price was too high. After spending a lot of time focused on the region, that investor thought the small mining company had overlooked untapped surrounding areas. Rather than do a deal with the start-up company, that investor started buying up mining rights nearby, on the cheap.

It turned out that the investor was right: those nearby rights were in fact more valuable than the target's location. The investor started putting money into the development of substantial mining operations, and the start-up company soon found its fledgling operations dwarfed by larger operations all around it.

The start-up company sued. It claimed that the big mines were developed only because the investor used the start-up company's confidential information to discover how rich the region could be.

The investor countered that the start-up company had provided no data whatsoever on the surrounding land. The start-up company was actually trying to lay claim to the spark that shined light on the prospects of the region. That kind of claim, the buyer argued, went beyond the realm of protective intellectual property rights.

Eventually, a state court judge with little experience in commercial matters had to decide. It found for the underdog, and awarded the investor's entire mining operation to the small company as compensation for the breach.

Confidential information exists not only on paper but also in the minds of the bidder's management team. Assume the bidder knows how high the target's projections are, and assume the bidder has spent a lot of time talking to the target about the catalysts that will determine its success. How could the bidder ignore those facts when making strategic decisions? How would the target or even the bidder know which catalysts the bidder would have focused on if they had not been pointed down the path blazed by the target?

Agreements rarely, if ever, attempt to distinguish what types of implicit uses of memory are permitted and which are not. At least the restriction on use does clearly prohibit uses of physical representations of the information, such as the bidder's handing over the target's product design plans to the bidder's research and development team.

Definition of "confidential information"

Use and disclosure restrictions broadly apply to all "confidential information" (or "evaluation material").[5] These terms typically start with a broad definition, covering all information related to the target business provided by the seller (or its representatives) to the buyer (or its representatives), whether or not it is actually confidential. The definition generally covers oral as well as written disclosures.

Sample Provision

The term ["Confidential Information"] ["Evaluation Material"] means all information relating to the Target that is furnished to the Buyer by or on behalf of the Target, together with any summaries, analyses, extracts, compilations, studies, or other documents (whatever the form or data storage medium) that contain, reference, are based upon, or otherwise reflect such information relating to the Target.

In addition to covering raw data provided by the seller, the buyer's internal analysis of that data is also covered. In other words, if the buyer evaluates and summarizes the seller's business prospects using confidential information, the buyer's own work product is restricted the same way as direct confidential information.

In some cases, a narrower concept of confidential information is used. Under that approach, confidential information is defined as all information that is, well, confidential. Since that begs the question of what is confidential, the definition is sometimes further limited to information that is actually stamped or marked as "Confidential." This puts a burden on the target to mark every relevant piece of paper and every e-mail, so is often avoided by targets in the context of deal diligence.

Carve-outs from the scope of confidential information

As previously noted, confidentiality agreements usually start by covering, in overbroad strokes, all information provided by the target. Then, the contract cuts back the coverage through specific exceptions to the definition of the term "confidential information." Information excluded from that definition is, for the most part, generally excluded from all the restrictions under the confidentiality agreement.

"Generally known by the public"

Information that becomes generally known by the public is normally excluded from the definition of confidential information. If the financial press or trade journals report facts about the target's business, there is no longer the same justification for the seller to restrict the buyer from using that nonpublic information in the same way any other competitor or third party could use it.

Of course, other competitors may not have any certainty as to the accuracy of the information and, unlike the potential buyer, may not understand all the related "mosaic" of facts that provide context.

Sample Provision

The term "Confidential Information" does not include any information which: (i) is or becomes generally [available to] [known by] the public other than as a result of disclosure, directly or indirectly, by Recipient or its Representatives [in violation of their obligations under this Agreement], [...].

In some cases the potential buyer may use and disclose information that is "generally available" to the public, even if it is not actually "generally known" to the public. Neither standard is well defined. It may not be clear in any particular instance whether information is sufficiently public to meet these exceptions.

On its face, "generally available" means that public accessibility is all that counts, rather than actual public dissemination. The phrase "generally known" does not present the same issue, but does beg the question as to how broadly understood any particular piece of information needs to be before the exception applies.

If the potential buyer leaks confidential information and causes it to become publicly available, the potential buyer cannot profit from its own breach. The exception would not apply in that case. Theoretically, if the potential buyer's representatives inadvertently disclose confidential information, all of its competitors could freely use the data, but not the buyer.

Already in the buyer's possession or received from an appropriate third-party source

Information already in the buyer's possession, or which it later receives from a third party, is often excluded from the definition of confidential information. If the buyer already has details about the target before it enters into deal talks, the buyer can continue to use that preexisting information. If the bidder learns information about the target through legitimate means outside of the diligence process, then that information stays outside of the reach of the confidentiality agreement. The bidder will not lose the ability to use data merely because the target reproduces a copy of what the bidder already has free use of.

Sample Provision

The term "Confidential Information" does not include any information which: [...] (ii) was within or comes into Recipient's possession on a nonconfidential basis from a source (other than the Target or any of its Representatives), [provided that Recipient is under the reasonable belief [after reasonable inquiry] that such source is not bound by a confidentiality agreement with or other contractual, legal or fiduciary obligation of confidentiality or secrecy to the Target [or any other party] with respect to such information].

In other cases, the seller wants to lock up the buyer from using and disclosing any confidential information—even if the buyer already had that information before signing the confidentiality agreement or separately obtains it afterwards. In that case, the seller would delete this exception.

Usually, this type of exception does not apply if the buyer receives the information by inappropriate means—for example, if the buyer received it from a source, such as a former consultant to the target company, that passed on the information in violation of the source's own obligations to the target.

What constitutes an "inappropriate" source varies from agreement to agreement. Sometimes, the buyer cannot use this type of exception if the source violates a duty of confidentiality to the target. Sometimes, the exception does not apply if the source breaches any duty to any party, even if not owed to the target. Sometimes, even if there is such a breach of duty by the source of the information, the buyer loses the benefit of this exception only if it actually knew (or, sometimes, if it should have known) that it was provided in breach.

Independently developed by the buyer

Information that the buyer separately develops without using the target's confidential information may also be excluded from the definition of confidential information. For instance, if the buyer's M&A team learns about a business technique from the seller, while the buyer's internal research and development team is busy independently developing the same or a similar technique, the fact that the buyer's M&A team also learned it from the seller will not stop the buyer from using its own, internally developed, version of that technique. The buyer would argue that it should not lose the benefit of its own product development as a cost of evaluating a deal with the seller.

Sample Provision

The term "Confidential Information" does not include any information that: [...] (iii) is developed by Recipient or its Representatives independently of and without reference to any Confidential Information, [provided such independent development can be reasonably proven [by Recipient] [by Recipient's written records]].

Enforcement of this exception is challenging. Targets often fear that it would be impossible to prove that the buyer's internal development teams used the target's ideas. Sometimes this leads the target to avoid the independent development exception altogether, particularly when as a practical matter the information in question is unlikely to be independently developed.

Sometimes the target adds language that shifts the burden to the buyer to prove it did not misuse confidential information in its development process. Proving a negative is difficult for a buyer, however.

The best way for the target to protect its innovative ideas is to simply withhold the most sensitive information until a later stage of negotiation, if it discloses the ideas at all before closing.

War Story ═══

The target's law firm developed a transaction technique that, in its view, would allow a new class of deals to be done on a tax-free basis. Others had struggled with, and generally avoided, that type of transaction because of all the thorny tax issues.

The investment bank that was hired to provide a fairness opinion on the deal wanted its counsel to confirm that the transaction would be tax free. Otherwise, the after-tax proceeds would be relatively small and the price would not be as fair as it seemed.

The target's law firm refused to disclose their tax theory. After some push-back, they agreed to explain the tax structure, but only if the investment bank's counsel signed a confidentiality agreement without an "independently develops" exception. The target's law firm was afraid that the investment bank's lawyers would use the exception by seeking out an opportunity to independently develop and recreate the technique.

The investment bank's lawyers were dumbfounded. Their tax experts were convinced that they, too, could easily come up with the newfangled tax structure on their own if needed for a particular deal. They did not want to be locked out of working on a whole class of transactions for fear of being sued over misappropriating the tax technique.

The target's lawyers insisted on protecting their big idea. The investment bank's counsel refused to yield. Since neither side would budge, the investment bank ended up giving the fairness opinion without diligencing the tax-free nature of the deal.

Disclosures required by law

Confidentiality agreements permit the buyer to make legally required disclosures. For instance, the buyer may need to disclose information regarding the seller's business in a court proceeding relating to the deal, or could be compelled by securities laws and stock exchange regulations to disclose that it is engaged in talks for a potential transaction.

Sample Provision

Notwithstanding paragraphs [restriction on disclosure of Confidential Information and deal information], either party or its Representatives may disclose Confidential Information to the extent required by law [or requested by a governmental authority] [...].

The parties may expand this exception to also include information requested by a governmental authority, even if not required to be disclosed. Regulated entities, in particular, will frequently keep their regulators apprised of confidential deals as they are proceeding. And they may want to provide information requested by the regulator, whether or not legally required to do so, in order to maintain good relations with that governmental authority.

Of course, if disclosure is required by law, the buyer will have to make the disclosure, whether or not doing so violates a contractual obligation to the seller. Since this exception applies, the buyer will not put itself in breach by making legally required disclosures. In other words, this exception shifts the risk of such disclosures to the seller, in the sense that the seller bears the loss of control over the information without recourse.

Procedural rights protect the target from inappropriate decisions by the buyer about what is required to be disclosed. The first line of protection is to require the buyer to give the seller notice of required disclosures. This provides an opportunity for the seller to pursue formal protections from a court, such as a protective order or limits on the scope of information disclosed. In order to make protective filings or challenge the buyer's conclusions, the buyer would need prior notice.

Sample Provision

[...] provided that such disclosing party shall, to the extent permitted by law [and to the extent reasonably practicable], provide the other party with prior written notice and an opportunity to make any protective filings or requests.

Prior notice of required disclosures is not practicable or permitted by law. For instance, particular European anti-bribery laws require a bidder to inform the authorities if it discovers bribery on the part of the target, but make it illegal to inform the target that the bidder has made such a report.

On occasion, actions of the bidder itself give rise to the legal requirement to disclose—which in turn triggers the exception under the confidentiality agreement that permits such disclosure. In some cases, the target has argued that the buyer should not be allowed to cause the disclosure requirement and then take advantage of the exception.[6]

Return or destroy

After a deal has died, the potential buyer no longer needs confidential information about the target. The target can require the potential buyer at any time to return to the target or destroy all physical and electronic forms of confidential information held by the potential buyer.

The potential buyer may prefer to destroy—rather than deliver to the target company—the buyer's own internal reports that evaluate and comment on the target's confidential information. Those evaluations (including, for instance, the embedded market and synergy assumptions) are proprietary information of the buyer.

Sample Provision

Upon the Target's request, Recipient and its Representatives will promptly return to the Company or destroy any and all Confidential Information (whether in written or tangible form, or in electronic or any other form), all summaries, analyses, extracts, compilations, studies, or other documents that contain, reference, are based upon, or otherwise reflect the Confidential Information.

Many targets require an officer of the potential buyer to sign a certificate confirming the destruction or return of the target's confidential information. Although the officer may have no personal liability, as a practical matter, the officer is unlikely to put his or her own signature on the certificate if it were not true. Requiring a certificate is often a helpful technique; otherwise, it may be easy for the potential buyer to let things slip and not bother to destroy all the data, especially since the destruction cannot be practically monitored by the target company.

Sample Provision

Recipient will provide the Target with the certification of an officer of Recipient's organization [and that of each of its Representatives] certifying that such destruction has occurred.

The obligation to return or destroy is triggered by the target sending a request. This usually occurs when the target decides that it is no longer going to work on a deal with the potential buyer. This requirement leads to the potential for a foot fault: once the deal is dead, it is easy for the target (and its lawyers) to forget to send out the return or destroy request.

War Story

The target ran a tight ship and led a successful auction. It included both strategic and private equity bidders in the process, casting a wide net.

Through successive stages of the process, the target had narrowed down the list of potential bidders. Eventually, it settled on a buyer and signed the deal at a nice premium. Exhausted from seemingly endless nights without adequate sleep, the lawyers on both sides collapsed. They were proud of the success of their clients, which, in some small way, they attributed to their own abilities.

When a competitor launched what appeared to be a copycat product a year later, the winning private equity buyer set out to investigate. It could not prove whether the competitor used any confidential information in the process but stumbled over a set of mishaps on its own end.

The target's business and legal teams had not thought to send out instructions to the broad array of bidders in the auction process to require them to return or destroy their confidential information. All the bidders had retained the full sets of information—even after the term of the confidentiality agreement (and its restriction on use) had ended.

Such archived data can be hard to delete. For instance, it may be difficult as a practical matter for the recipient to destroy disaster recovery archives. Since virtually all critical information is exchanged by e-mail, there is very little destruction that actually occurs under the "return or destroy" provision. No longer do boxes of documents need to be taken to the shredder.

To deal with this, the potential buyer may carve out those archived files from the return or destroy obligation. Such electronic archive exceptions have become commonplace. When these "archive" exceptions were first crafted, electronic backup copies of files were something to which only information technology specialists had access. Nowadays, many people regularly archive all e-mails, and those may be immediately recallable from the regular e-mail interface.

Sample Provision

[...], provided that Recipient may retain an electronic copy of Confidential Information in accordance with its general electronic archival procedures, it being understood and agreed that (i) such Confidential Information shall remain subject to the provisions of this Agreement for so long as it is maintained by Recipient, even after termination of this Agreement, and (ii) no personnel of Recipient shall access such Confidential Information other than information technology personnel in the ordinary course performance of their duties.

If the archive exception is included, the target may wish to clarify that the retained records may be accessed for only limited purposes by information technology (IT) personnel, and that the information remains subject to the restrictions on use and disclosure—even after the confidentiality agreement terminates. Otherwise, on its face, the potential buyer would be entitled to recover and use the archived information after the primary term of the confidentiality agreement expires.

War Story

Early in the diligence process, the potential buyer discovered serious legal compliance issues at the target company. After an extended delay necessitated by the target's attempts to fix its problems, and after negotiations to craft a remedy to those issues, the parties could not reach agreement.

Eventually, the deal was finally called off. The buyer's electronic e-mail archive system was set to put all e-mails into an (easily accessible) archive after 90 days, unless manually deleted by the user. So by the time the deal process ended, details of the target's compliance issues were in the potential buyer's archives.

Obviously wanting to prevent this sensitive compliance information from leaking while the target continued to clean up its act, the target promptly issued a "return or destroy" request to the potential buyer.

The buyer had very few printouts of the data, and those were promptly tossed in the trash can. After reviewing the archive exception, the buyer concluded that it did not need to delete all the old e-mails from its backup system. The buyer signed the "return or destroy" certificate and sent it back—without deleting a single e-mail.

Boundaries of how much confidential information can be provided

Even after the potential buyer signs on to the confidentiality agreement, the target may still not want to share all of its sensitive information for a number of reasons, both practical and legal.

As a practical matter, the target may not be confident that contractual restrictions on use and disclosure sufficiently protect its data. For instance, a target normally should not provide its trade secrets under any circumstances. To reduce its risk, the target may stage delivery of the most sensitive information until later in the diligence and negotiation process. Sellers often establish progressively greater access to sensitive information as the diligence and negotiation process moves forward, as the number of bidders shrinks, and as the seller becomes more confident that a transaction with that potential buyer will actually be signed.

As a legal matter, the antitrust rules against collusion among competitors limit the information that can be provided in diligence. Until the buyer closes the deal to buy the target, the buyer and target are still separate companies that are not allowed to collude with each other. For that reason, competitively sensitive information may be restricted to a "clean room" to which only outside counsel has access. Sometimes, access is granted to the buyer's in-house counsel.

If some of the buyer's other employees also have access, then only those who are not active in business functions such as marketing, pricing, and product development will be allowed to review those documents. The participating employees may be asked to individually agree not to share that information with others inside the buyer's organization.

The target may have contractual confidentiality obligations to third parties that restrict how much information it can provide to a potential buyer. Commercial contracts between the target and its business partners frequently prohibit disclosure about the contract in broad strokes, with no carve-outs to allow disclosure to a potential buyer. Sometimes, those provisions cover only sensitive contract terms, such as a royalty rates and other pricing details. In other cases, they restrict disclosure of the existence of the commercial agreement itself.

There is no obvious solution to this dilemma in the context of an acquisition. The buyer does not want the target to breach its obligations to its business partners—the buyer will, after all, inherit those relationships. Nevertheless, the buyer needs diligence before committing to a transaction. In some cases, the buyer and the target simply breach the confidentiality provision, usually at the end of the diligence process.

Disclosure may be limited to a small number of the buyer's representatives and may be completed in person or with other electronic restrictions

that give more protection to the information (for instance, no ability to print or download). In other cases, the buyer reviews the information only after signing. Even though such post-signing diligence may still technically breach the restrictions in the underlying commercial agreement, at least, at that point, the target is certain that it has a signed deal. In some other cases, the target is able to get the buyer comfortable that the buyer does not need to review the information.

Enforcement

It is difficult for targets to enforce a confidentiality agreement. All but the most blatant violations occur without the knowledge of the target. In particular, inappropriate "use" of confidential information in some indirect form is difficult for a plaintiff to establish. Explicit use of the target's documents is unlikely, since the potential buyer would have returned or destroyed them, and may not have had the ability to print or download the most sensitive information in any event. Information "in the heads" of buyer's experts and management, though, cannot be destroyed.

Indirect use by the potential buyer could come in many forms, from decisions as to which research projects to fund, to how aggressive a party can be in commercial negotiations (due to having a better sense for the position of its rival), and to simply knowing what questions to ask.[7] All commercial decisions are complex. Attempting to show that confidential information drove a decision to take or delay an action can become an exercise in speculation.

Nevertheless, there are many notable cases of parties being awarded significant damages for a counterparty's breach of a confidentiality agreement.[8] A court may also grant specific performance, ordering a party to stop using or disclosing confidential information or making that party take corrective actions.

War Story ▬▬▬▬▬▬▬▬▬▬▬▬▬▬▬▬▬▬▬▬▬▬▬▬▬▬

The target had few options. Its industry was small, but it wanted to partner with the right buyer. After spending a good deal of time negotiating a deal with its first potential buyer, the talks turned sour. The buyer would have been a great strategic match, but it had played hardball on price and continued to stall. The target had cut its price several times, but eventually could go no lower.

Between a rock and a hard place, the target finally decided to move on. Then the first potential buyer became upset that it was left hanging after it spent resources to pursue a deal. Wanting to teach the target a lesson, or simply to get revenge, the first potential buyer engaged the new candidate in conversation and gave a detailed account of its negotiations with the target—including how low the target had been willing to go on the purchase price.

The next day, the new candidate unexpectedly cut its price. The target was perplexed, but, without any meaningful alternatives, moved ahead with the deal. When the target eventually learned of the conversations that explained the price cut, the target sued the first potential buyer. The court awarded substantial damages—resulting in the first potential buyer basically having to make whole the actual buyer's drop in price.

Liability for representatives

Many of the restrictions in a confidentiality agreement bind by their terms not only the buyer but also its representatives.

Some confidentiality agreements affirmatively state that a breach by a representative of a party will be treated the same as a breach by the party itself. In other words, each party has strict liability for its representatives. This is designed to ensure that the buyer takes a sufficient amount of care in overseeing its representatives.

Many buyers want to avoid direct liability for breaches by its advisors. The buyer may not perceive itself to have any meaningful control over its advisors. Instead, the buyer may agree to inform its representatives that the target's information is subject to a confidentiality obligation (which should be obvious to the advisors in any event).

In some cases, the target will want to ensure that the buyer's representatives owe a confidentiality obligation to the target directly, not just to the buyer. This allows the target to directly enforce the obligation against those representatives. For many service providers, such as lawyers and accountants, their own professional obligations are normally viewed as sufficient—and those parties would not likely accept direct liability to the buyer in any event. For third-party agents, such as debt financing sources, the target may require the advisor to sign a separate confidentiality agreement.

Sample Provision

[Each party shall be liable for breaches of this Agreement by its Representatives as if such breach were committed by such party itself.]
   —OR—
[Each party shall use commercially reasonable efforts to cause its Representatives to comply with this Agreement as if party hereto.]

As noted above, the term "representative" is defined quite broadly. It includes lawyers, bankers, and accountants, as well as affiliates and employees. A key function of the term "representative" is to define who may receive information from the buyer. As a result, the potential buyer will want to make sure the term is sufficiently broad.

Sample Provision

The "Representatives" of a party include the officers, directors, equityholders, employees, agents, and affiliates of such party (and the officers, directors, equityholders, employees, and agents of any such affiliates).

Expiration of the confidentiality agreement

Most confidentiality agreements expire after 2 to 5 years and, in rare cases, in as little as 6 to 12 months. This means that the key restrictions on use and disclosure no longer apply after that time.

The potential buyer may be concerned that it cannot effectively monitor its various confidentiality obligations for prolonged periods of time. It will have destroyed or returned the physical representations of the information prior to the end of that period, so the knowledge in the heads of the buyer's employees is what is at stake.

The buyer will argue that, over time, it is simply not possible for its employees to distinguish what they learned from which sources and, since that task is impossible, the buyer cannot be held responsible for the consequences. The buyer will also argue that the target's business information will lose its sensitivity over time in any event, which may make the target more comfortable with early expiration.

Expiration provisions are a blunt means to address these concerns. For example, the distinction between confidential business information and deal process information is typically lost.[9] After the term of the confidentiality agreement expires, most confidentiality agreements would allow bidders to disclose that they were part of an M&A process and how the process was conducted. If the target does not successfully complete a sale, it may be shocked to learn that within a year or two all bidders can openly comment on the failed auction—and even reveal what the bid prices were.

Expiration provisions rarely contain exceptions for sensitive information. For example, if the buyer learns trade secrets that (by their nature) are expected to be kept secret, most targets would argue that the buyer should not be permitted to publicize that information a few years after the M&A process began. Alternatively, the target can avoid disclosing any trade secrets in the diligence process.

Occasionally, targets remove the expiration provision altogether or, instead, require information to be kept secret for as long as it remains "confidential," without specifying how long that may be the case.

Process Control through the Confidentiality Agreement

Restrictions on collusion and bidder groups

Confidentiality agreements are used to govern procedural aspects of an M&A transaction, particularly in an auction context.

In an auction, the confidentiality agreement usually restricts collusion by potential bidders. Sellers are concerned that permitting collusion between bidders will reduce the number of competing bidders in the auction, potentially reducing the purchase price.

Absent an anti-collusion provision, confidentiality agreements give buyers broad latitude to disclose information to their "representatives." A buyer may justify sharing information on the theory that the other bidder would be acting as an agent of the first bidder while working together on a bid.

Anti-collusion provisions sometimes work by prohibiting disclosure to equity financing sources. Such language assumes that if two bidders collude, they would do so by having one bidder become an equity co-investor in the other bidder's offer. This is a fairly narrow drafting approach, which addresses only a limited type of co-investment mechanism. Even if technically narrow, however, such an explicit anti-collusion provision is usually sufficient as a practical matter for the bidder to understand that collusion is not welcomed by the target.

Sample Provision

Notwithstanding the foregoing exception [to allow disclosure to Representatives], Confidential Information may not be disclosed to any actual or potential [equity financing source] [or debt financing source] without the written consent of the Target.

Arguably, anti-collusion provisions are not necessary. In confidentiality agreements, the restriction on disclosure to third parties could be read to prohibit collusion, whether or not there is a specific restriction. Under that reading, it is not feasible for two parties to collude without discussing the deal process, and those discussions are prohibited. However, the target is often concerned that, without explicitly prohibiting collusion, a potential bidder may feel comfortable talking to other bidders that are separately subject to confidentiality agreements with the target. The theory is that since both colluding parties have the same information, one bidder is not actually disclosing any relevant facts to the other; thus, they are not violating the non-disclosure provision.

War Story ━━━

A global conglomerate wanted to sell one of its divisions through a multi-billion-dollar auction. The confidentiality agreement was silent on the topic of collusion.

One of the bidders was concerned that it could not raise enough debt capital to make a serious offer and considered joining up with one of the competing bidders through a complex joint venture arrangement. With only a few bidders in the process, this joint venture would have presented a significant loss of competition among bidders—with all the drawbacks for the seller.

After the seller noticed the mistake, its financial advisors sent a process letter to the bidders stating that collusion had been intentionally permitted in the early stages of the process in order to allow efficient bidder groups to form. But, from that point on, the letter continued, collusion would not be tolerated. Any bidders teaming up would both be excluded from the process.

The seller had so much as admitted that there was no prohibition on collusion embedded in the confidentiality agreements. Taking that "face-saving" position was, itself, perhaps a second mistake; it prevented the seller from arguing that the general restriction on disclosure prohibited collusion.

The potential joint venture partners thought that threatening to remove colluding bidders from the auction process made limited sense. They doubted that the seller would follow through and actually exclude both of them from the process. Collusion reduces competition for the seller, since two bidders are combined into one. But excluding the combined bid of those parties cuts competition even further—both are lost to the process.

Fortunately for the seller, the two potential joint venture partners decided that they could not work together for unrelated business reasons. The seller's threat was never tested.

━━

In some cases, collusion is explicitly allowed, as long as notice is given to the target or preapproval procedures are followed. This approach may make sense if a potential buyer has an antitrust problem and needs a partner to acquire a portion of the target's assets in order to satisfy regulatory requirements.

The process terms of a confidentiality agreement may also limit a bidder's discussions with its debt financing sources. The target is usually concerned more about the risk of leaks than the loss of competition. If several potential bidders each speak to multiple banks about the potential transaction, it may not be long before most players in the financial markets are aware of the deal.

On the other hand, bidders cannot put together reliable bids without feedback from their banks. As a result, discussions with banks (unlike collusion) are normally permitted at an agreed point in the process, with prior notice to the target.

Some potential buyers want to lock up their banks so that they cannot finance a competing bidder. The target will want to prohibit bidders from doing so. For instance, a strong bidder could hire several top banks for syndicated financing, conditioned on an agreement from each bank that it will not back any other competing bidder. The target will view this as an uneven playing field, and will not want to see other bidders suffer competitively.

Sample Provision

Without the written consent of the Target, the Buyer will not restrict the ability of any potential debt financing sources of the Buyer to provide debt financing to any other potential counterparty to an alternative transaction with the Target.

Disclosure of M&A process information

Deal information is frequently treated differently than the target's business information. The fact that a deal is being negotiated, the price and the terms offered is given more protection. The carve-outs to the definition of what constitutes confidential information do not normally apply to deal information. In other words, the parties cannot openly discuss facts about the transaction, even if the transaction talks are leaked to the public.

Deal information is not necessarily furnished by the target to the buyer, which is the core of how confidential information is often defined. As a result, a separate confidentiality provision relating specifically to deal information is usually added to the agreement.

Such restrictions on the use of deal information offer protection to both the target and the buyer. The target would be protected from bidders disclosing that an auction is occurring. The buyer would be protected from the target "shopping" its offer to other bidders.

Sample Provision

Recipient shall not disclose to any person the fact that Confidential Information has been made available to it, that any negotiations or discussions have or may occur, the identity of the parties hereto, or any of the terms or the existence of this Confidentiality Agreement, except that Recipient may disclose such information to those of its Representatives who need to know such information for the purposes of evaluating the possible Transaction, provided that such Representatives are informed by Recipient of the confidential nature of such information [and agree to be bound by terms substantially similar to those set forth herein].

Litigation Endnotes

1. Directors may avoid liability under § 11 of the Securities Act of 1933 by showing that "[they] had, after reasonable investigation, reasonable ground to believe and did believe … that the statements therein were true and that there was no omission to state a material fact required to be stated therein or necessary to make the statements therein not misleading." 15 U.S.C. § 77k(b)(3).
2. *See* Chapter 14, "Indemnities."
3. *See, e.g., Goodrich Capital LLC v. Vector Capital Corp.*, No. 1:11-CV-09247 (S.D.N.Y. June 26, 2012). In *Goodrich*, a financial advisory firm approached a private equity firm to be a potential financing source for the buyer of one of the financial advisory firm's clients. The confidentiality agreement prohibited the private equity firm from using confidential information for any purpose other than opportunities involving the financial advisory firm (and its client). After the proposed financing deal failed, the private equity firm itself acquired one of the targets, without involving the financial advisory firm. The court found that the financial advisory firm adequately alleged a breach of contract claim that the private equity firm used confidential information for a purpose that was not expressly permitted under the confidentiality agreement.
4. *See* Chapter 3-B6, Effect of confidentiality agreements on hostile tender offers (discussing how restriction on use provisions can in effect act as standstill provisions).
5. *See* Chapter 2-C2, Disclosure of M&A process information (discussing how information about the existence and terms of a transaction—"process information"—should be treated differently than confidential business information about the target).
6. *See, e.g., Martin Marietta Materials, Inc. v. Vulcan Materials Co.*, 56 A.3d 1072 (Del. Ch. 2012), *aff'd*, 68 A.3d 1208 (Del. 2012). In that case, the buyer made a hostile tender offer, which obligated the buyer under law to make public disclosures relating to the target. *See also* Chapter III-B6 (discussing how the exception for legally mandated disclosure can be drafted narrowly to exclude disclosure requirements that arise due to acts of the buyer).
7. *See, e.g., Sit-Up Ltd. v. IAC/InterActiveCorp.*, No. 1:05-CV-09292 (S.D.N.Y. Feb. 20, 2008). In *Sit-Up*, a potential buyer learned information about the original potential target's confidential sales and cost information during deal negotiations. When negotiations failed, the defendant buyer moved on to pursue a new target and used the original potential target's information to perform a comparative financial analysis. The court stated that it was an undisputed fact that the defendants used confidential information for "a purpose other than considering a transaction with Sit-Up" and, therefore, breached the confidentiality agreement. The court granted summary judgment in the plaintiff's favor. *Id.* at 47.

8. *See, e.g., RRK Holding Co. v. Sears, Roebuck & Co.,* 563 F. Supp. 2d 832 (N.D. Ill. 2008). In *RRK Holding,* a jury awarded $25 million (including $8 million in punitive damages) to the owners of a small tool company as damages for a large retailer's breach of a confidentiality agreement. The tool company, which manufactured a popular spiral saw, entered into a confidentiality agreement with the large retailer to produce a spiral saw to be sold exclusively at that retailer. Negotiations between the parties failed and the tool company never manufactured the saw for the retailer. Instead, the retailer introduced its own spiral saw using technology that the tool company had confidentially disclosed to the retailer during negotiations. The jury found that the retailer breached the confidentiality agreement by disclosing the information to its manufacturer for production of the saw.

9. *See* Chapter 2-C2 (discussing of how to distinguish confidential information about the target from information about the transaction itself for purposes of a Confidentiality Agreement).

CHAPTER 3

Setting Up the Deal
Key Provisions and Agreements

"No-Poach" Provisions

Protecting target employees

Through the diligence process, the buyer will get to know the target's key employees and identify the ones who have talent or have made meaningful contributions to the target business. If the buyer does not get the deal, it may be easy for the buyer to poach choice employees from the target in order to start its own competing business. To address this concern, targets will often include a "nonsolicitation" or "no-hire" provision in the confidentiality agreement.

Sample Provision

Until the date that is __ months after the date of this Agreement, the Buyer and its Affiliates will not, directly or indirectly, solicit for employment or hire any Covered Employee.

These provisions will often last for one to two years. A "no-hire" prohibits the buyer from hiring the covered employees. A "nonsolicit" prohibits the buyer from soliciting them for employment. An exception to the nonsolicit may allow buyer to hire a covered employee who first approaches the buyer (without being solicited) or who has already terminated his or her employment with the target. A nonsolicit also frequently makes it clear that general solicitations are permitted, such as giving a search request to a headhunter that is not targeted at the covered employees.

Sample Provision

Notwithstanding the foregoing, the following shall not constitute a solicitation: (i) general solicitations not targeted at Covered Employees, [or (ii) discussing employment with any Covered Employee who [independently contacts the Buyer or any of its Affiliates without any prior solicitation] [or has previously terminated his employment with the Target]].

Scope of no-poach provisions

The scope may cover anywhere from a few to all of the target's employees. A no-hire is usually narrower, and often limited to key management. A nonsolicit may cover a broader group of employees (e.g., vice president and above) or can be defined functionally (e.g., any person who becomes known to the potential buyer in the diligence process).

Sample Provision

A "Covered Employee" is any [member of [senior management]] [or other employee] of the Target [who was [first] introduced to the Buyer in connection with the Potential Transaction].

Buyers need to make sure the provision is administratively feasible in its organization. Under a limited no-hire, for example, a buyer can give the no-hire list to its human resources group to check compliance before making any hires, but ensuring that no one in its organization informally solicits target employees may be more difficult.

War Story

The deal started with a lot of excitement on both sides, and a drive to move quickly. The first target's CEO instructed its team to negotiate lightly and try to get a deal done quickly. With that guidance, the first target had accepted the buyer's form of confidentiality agreement, without an employee nonsolicit or other employee protections. Soon after, deal talks fell apart. The buyer ended up thinking that the target's CEO was an idiot, but also observed that the target had a strong CFO, and a COO known to be one of the best in the business.

The buyer moved on to look for its next deal. Six months later, it made an offer to another target in the industry—what business folks fondly refer to as a "dog." It had been mismanaged, falling behind its peers in the industry, but it was cheap, and a perfect opportunity for a turnaround effort. And the buyer knew just the team to lead it.

A couple of phone calls and dinners later, the COO and CFO of the first target agreed to work for the buyer. The CEO of the first target called his in-house counsel as soon as he learned of the departures but, unfortunately, they found that they had left themselves exposed to such a risk in the confidentiality agreement.

Standstill Agreements

Standstill agreements prevent a potential buyer from making a hostile bid for a public company target. They also prohibit agitating the board of a public company for change, such as proposing to replace management or undertake a corporate restructuring. Standstills are sometimes drafted as stand-alone agreements, but more often than not they are dropped in as a section of the confidentiality agreement. This chapter discusses how standstills lock up hostile parties, and the various exceptions and triggers that can free up a bidder.

By definition, target boards do not like hostile proposals. Among other things, target boards assert that they are exercising control over the M&A process for the benefit of their shareholders. Targets argue that anyone with nonpublic information has an unfair advantage when pursuing a proxy fight or pricing a hostile bid. More specifically, targets are concerned about the buyer pursuing an opportunistic bid at a time when the board believes its stock is undervalued.

Of course, a majority of the shareholders would have to accept the bid for any hostile tactic to succeed. Targets argue that, even though a bid may be acceptable to shareholders, it may be structured or timed to provide the lowest acceptable premium. Allowing the target board to reject a bid that would be acceptable to a majority of the shareholders creates a bargaining platform with leverage that can also be used for the good of shareholders—to get a better offer in most cases. Target boards argue that by allowing a few deals to be rejected despite the wishes of the shareholders, shareholders as a whole will tend to get better deals.

Bidders argue that target boards too often use standstills to block legitimate proposals that shareholders want to hear about. Nevertheless, most bidders sign standstill agreements as a "cost" that the bidder must pay in order to gain access to confidential information.

There are two primary components to a standstill agreement: the restriction on acquisitions and the restriction on activism. The normal time period for a standstill to be effective ranges from six months to two years.

Restriction on acquisitions

The restriction on acquisitions prohibits the buyer from acquiring equity in the target. It also covers any other target securities that vote, or can be turned into voting securities. The focus on voting instruments is tied to the central concern of preventing the buyer from acquiring interests that could help it influence the fate of the company. This restriction can be expanded to prohibit acquisitions of debt securities of the target. Particularly if the target is in (or comes into) financial distress, the buyer could wield significant influence as a stakeholder of the target's debt.

The restriction on acquisitions typically extends beyond the buyer to also prohibit acquisitions by its controlled affiliates. In some cases, this provision reaches upstream as well and covers all of the buyer's affiliates. It does not cover unrelated acquisitions by representatives of the buyer.

Sample Provision

Until the date that is __ months after the date of this Agreement, the Buyer and its [controlled] Affiliates [and their Representatives [acting on behalf of the Buyer or its [controlled] Affiliates]] shall not, directly or indirectly, take any of the following actions: (i) acquire or [publicly] propose to acquire [any] [more than [5]% of [any class] the] [voting] securities of the Target or any [material] assets of the Target [...].

Deal-specific exceptions to the restriction are often appropriate. In particular, if the restriction prohibits acquisitions by upstream affiliates rather than just downstream, controlled affiliates, the buyer will need exceptions to permit actions outside of its control. One example is an employee pension plan affiliated with the buyer, where independent investment decisions are made by the plan's trustee, which could decide to invest in securities of the target company.

In other situations, a private equity bidder may be affiliated with funds that trade in equity securities. The private equity bidder will frequently carve out those fund activities, but, in doing so, usually agrees not to share information with the funds. To achieve this, the exception may be drafted in conditional language: it only exempts noncontrolled affiliates that have in fact not received any confidential information (or deal discussion information) from the buyer.

Traditionally, standstill agreements have not covered the buyer's acquisition of derivative positions in the securities of the target as long as they do not constitute beneficial ownership of equity or provide voting influence over the target. Standard forms of standstill agreements are being adapted, and some now cover derivative positions as if the holder of the derivative were the holder of the underlying instrument.

Sample Provision

[...] (it being understood and agreed that any instruments or other rights the value of which is derived from or based on [equity] securities in the Target shall be deemed to be [equity] securities subject to this clause, [...].

Since equity derivatives generally do not allow their holder to vote any underlying shares, some practitioners take the position that derivatives should not be covered by standstills. On the other hand, because a holder can frequently convert its derivative exposure into actual equity ownership (e.g., by selling the derivative and buying the equity), derivative exposure often gives a holder roughly the same bargaining power as the equivalent ownership of equity. As a result, management of a target company may care as much about restricting derivative positions as they do about restricting direct equity ownership.

Restriction on activism

The restriction on activism restricts a broad array of shareholder proposals, such as making an offer to acquire the target, proposing a state of directors to replace the target board, and cooperating with third parties to take prohibited actions.

Sample Provision

[…] (ii) [publicly] propose any merger, acquisition, reorganization or other extraordinary transaction involving the Target, (iii) solicit proxies against or otherwise [publicly] propose to influence the policies or management of the Target, or (iv) join or participate in a group with respect to any of the foregoing.

As with standstills in general, there are differences of opinion as to the value of restricting shareholder proposals. Shareholders making such proposals generally believe that they will drive up the stock price of the target for the benefit of all shareholders. Management of the target, in contrast, often views such proposals as serving the particular interest of the activist shareholder over the interest of the activist company and its shareholder base as a whole. With that view in mind, management frequently insists on these restrictions in standstill agreements as a condition to providing the shareholder with confidential information.

Restriction on waivers

The standstill typically prohibits the buyer from publicly requesting a waiver of the standstill restrictions. Publicly announcing that a bidder has requested a waiver of the standstill in order to permit the bidder to make a premium offer to buy the company puts the board under scrutiny from its shareholders. It could also draw the attention of other potential bidders, and effectively put the target company "in play." As a result, targets argue that allowing public waiver requests would defeat the purpose of the standstill in the first place.

Sometimes, private requests that the target board waive the standstill restrictions can have the same impact. Public company targets have disclosure obligations to their shareholders under federal securities laws, so the target itself may feel compelled to disclose that a private waiver was requested—again putting the board under scrutiny from its shareholders, and potentially putting the target company "in play."

Sample Provision

The Buyer agrees to not [publicly or privately] request a waiver of or amendment to any of the provisions of this paragraph.

There have been some legal challenges to tight restrictions that prohibit even private proposals to the board. They argue that the board cannot fulfill its fiduciary duties to act in the best interest of its shareholders if it willfully blinds itself to proposals that may benefit shareholders.[1] However, even when private proposals are restricted, it may still be possible, through indirect and implicit means, to let the board know that the potential bidder would be willing to make a proposal if the board seemed willing to entertain one. This implicit offer is usually vague and conditional, often allowing the target to conclude that it need not publicly disclose the approach.

Release triggers if the target is "in play"

The restrictions on acquisitions and activism sometimes contain exceptions for significant events. For example, the buyer may be free to make an acquisition proposal if the target has already agreed to be taken over by a third party or has become the subject of a hostile bid.

Sample Provision

The foregoing restrictions shall cease to be of any effect in the event the Target [publicly announces that it] has entered into an agreement or discussions with another Person regarding any acquisition of [a controlling interest in] Target.

The bidder may also be freed up if the target proposes a reorganization plan in a bankruptcy proceeding. The buyer will argue that it should be allowed to participate in any deal process on an equal footing with other bidders if the company is otherwise "in play."

"Most favored nation" provisions

In an auction, a potential buyer may want to confirm that the standstill will not put it at a disadvantage relative to a competing bidder. This can be achieved through a "most favored nation," or "MFN," clause. Most targets resist MFNs, not wanting to end up with the lowest common denominator.

An MFN requires the target to give the buyer a better standstill provision if it gives a better deal to any other competing bidder. The MFN can relate to any particular clause, such as duration, or can cover the standstill as a whole. For instance, if the target agrees to no standstill, or to a shorter duration, for a new bidder, any other bidder with MFN protection will be freed up from its own standstill to the same extent.

Sample Provision

If the Target enters into any other agreement relating to a Potential Transaction that includes provisions more favorable to the counterparty thereto than the provisions of this [standstill] paragraph [taken as a whole], then the Target shall promptly notify the Buyer of such provisions and provide the Buyer with a copy of such provisions (without disclosing the identity of the counterparty). Within [five business days] after receipt of such provisions, the Buyer may elect to replace the applicable provisions of this Agreement with [all of (but not a portion of)] [any of] such more favorable provisions.

The better terms sometimes automatically apply, but usually they are offered to the bidder, who can then decide which clause it prefers. The bidder with MFN protection will usually be given the option to take on the new terms or not as a package. In some cases, the bidder with MFN protection gets the benefit of each better term, and need not take or reject the package as a whole.

Effect of confidentiality agreements on hostile tender offers

If the buyer strikes the standstill from the confidentiality agreement, is it then free to make a hostile tender offer? Can it launch a hostile offer after a short standstill expires?

Even if there is no standstill in effect, the target may argue that the bidder inappropriately used confidential information in formulating its bid or in determining its bid price—in violation of the restriction on use. In such a case, the target could ask a court to enjoin the bidder from making the hostile bid. This can be a surprising result for a buyer who fights hard to avoid signing up to a standstill.

In particular, if the confidentiality agreement refers to the transaction at hand as a "negotiated" deal (for example, in the definition of "Potential Transaction"), then the basic restriction on use could, perhaps inadvertently, turn into a standstill. The key exception to the restriction on use allows confidential information to be used to evaluate the deal at hand. If that deal at hand is defined to be a friendly deal, then arguably no information may be used to formulate a hostile proposal.[2]

If the buyer wants certainty that it could go hostile, then instead of simply deleting or shortening the term of a standstill, the buyer should clarify that the restriction on use will not prohibit launching an unsolicited offer.

The restriction on disclosure could also prevent the bidder from launching a hostile offer, because Federal securities law may require it to disclose confidential information it gained during due diligence in the public offering documents for the hostile bid.[3] There is usually a provision allowing disclosures permitted by law, but it is often not clear whether that permits legal disclosures that are only necessary because of the actions of the bidder itself (such as in launching an offer).

War Story

In anticipation of a potential deal to acquire a smaller competitor, the buyer and the target negotiated a confidentiality agreement.

The target insisted on including a standstill provision in the confidentiality agreement that prohibited the potential buyer from making a hostile public offer. The buyer resisted, and eventually won the point. Or so it thought.

The confidentiality agreement was fairly customary, with standard restrictions on disclosure and use. The standstill was the only real sticking point. When the target finally relented, counsel for the potential buyer deleted the standstill, sent around the final copy, and called it success. The target shared its operational plans and projections as part of diligence. The potential buyer was impressed, and offered what it thought was an attractive price.

The target promptly rejected the offer as inadequate, and deal negotiations broke down. But the buyer was determined: it went hostile by making an unsolicited tender offer. The target immediately sued to enjoin the offer.

In its claim, the target pointed to the restriction on use. It argued that the bidder must have used the target's confidential information. It reasoned that the bidder should not enjoy an unfair advantage over other potential buyers to acquire the company on the cheap, although it did not go so far as to propose running an auction and giving all potential buyers an equal opportunity.

Exclusivity Agreements

Exclusivity agreements give the potential buyer time to finalize a deal, during which time the target agrees not to negotiate with other potential buyers. No buyer wants to be a "stalking horse." Buyers invest significant expense and time into conducting due diligence before they are in a position to sign an acquisition agreement. A buyer may be reluctant to risk wasting its investment in this pursuit if it believes the target is actively negotiating with another bidder.

An exclusivity agreement does not guarantee that a potential buyer will get the deal, but it does convince the buyer that it is not merely a backup option to another preferred buyer. Of course, there are many circumstances—such as auctions—in which the buyer is happy to invest substantial resources into a potential acquisition knowing that it faces strong competition to acquire the target. The buyer is most likely to get exclusivity in complicated transactions which take longer to negotiate and require more diligence.

For the target, exclusivity can help or harm its ability to get the best price and terms depending on the circumstances. A target with many potential buyers would normally feel compelled to avoid exclusivity unless the target believes it cannot get a better deal elsewhere. In contrast, if a target has few alternatives, it may grant exclusivity in order to help ensure that it receives at least one acceptable offer.

Practitioners sometimes say that a buyer can only obtain an exclusivity agreement when it does not need one. In other words, if a target has other prospects, it will not sign an exclusivity agreement and may pursue those prospects while negotiating with the buyer. If it does not have other prospects, it may enter into an exclusivity agreement—but, in that case, the buyer would likely be the only bidder anyway.

Although it can show up as a component of another agreement (such as a confidentiality agreement), more often than not, exclusivity can only be agreed upon after initial deal talks, so it follows the confidentiality agreement and is reflected in a stand-alone document. Exclusivity is created by two parallel provisions. One is external, prohibiting the target from doing a deal with another potential bidder. The other is internal, requiring the target to negotiate in good faith with the buyer at hand.

This chapter outlines the content of exclusivity agreements, including the core restriction on the target negotiating with other parties, how and when the restrictions are terminated, and which parts of these agreements are legally binding.

Prohibition on deals with other parties

Exclusivity agreements prohibit the target from engaging in parallel negotiations during an exclusivity period (discussed below). In addition, they go further to prevent the target from soliciting other offers, providing diligence information to other potential bidders, or actually signing up another deal.

Sample Provision

During the Exclusivity Period, the Target shall not, and shall cause all of its Representatives not to, directly or indirectly, (i) solicit or [knowingly] induce or encourage the submission of any Acquisition Proposal, (ii) enter into any agreement or understanding (whether or not binding) with respect to any Acquisition Proposal, (iii) other than informing persons of the existence of this letter agreement (but not the identity of the Buyer) to the extent necessary in response to another Acquisition Proposal, provide any confidential information regarding the Target to any third party, or (iv) otherwise engage in any negotiations or discussions with any third party in connection with any Acquisition Proposal.

"Fiduciary outs" in exclusivity agreements

Exclusivity restrictions closely resemble "no-shop" provisions found in merger agreements with public company targets.[4] No-shop provisions contain so-called "fiduciary out" escape clauses that permit the target's board to exercise its fiduciary duties imposed by corporate law.[5] These exceptions allow the target to—notwithstanding the no-shop restrictions—provide diligence, to negotiate unsolicited offers, and even to terminate the first deal and sign a competing deal (upon payment of a breakup fee).[6] Such fiduciary outs are premised on a target's need to be able to exit a transaction if the fiduciary obligations of the target's board of directors require it to do so. Exclusivity agreements, in contrast, do not usually contain those escape clauses as a matter of practice.

Targets wanting to avoid exclusivity restrictions they regret signing up to have sometimes asked courts to read fiduciary out exceptions into the agreement.[7] Potential buyers who benefit from exclusivity agreements argue that—unlike in a public company merger context—corporate law does not require exclusivity agreements to include fiduciary outs. In public mergers, the fiduciary duty of the board has been judicially interpreted to require fiduciary outs to remain in place until the target's shareholder vote has been held.[8] In an exclusivity agreement, there is no vote to be held, and nothing for the board to recommend to shareholders. An exclusivity agreement does not commit a target to a deal, but instead commits it to not negotiate or sign up a deal with a third party during a relatively short period. Accordingly, buyers argue, there is no need for related fiduciary out exceptions.

The target is usually willing to accept an exclusivity agreement that does not contain a fiduciary out. The exclusivity period is typically short, and the target is not required to actually sign a transaction with the first buyer party to the exclusivity agreement. As a result, exclusivity does not present the same type of "last opportunity" for the target to obtain a control premium as does an actual acquisition.

In addition, if a target informs the potential buyer that the target no longer wishes to pursue a transaction with that buyer—for instance, because the target believes it can obtain better terms from a third party—then the potential buyer will frequently not want to waste its resources continuing to negotiate. The parties simply terminate exclusivity by mutual agreement in most such cases, so the target is not kept out of the market unnecessarily.

Breaching exclusivity may give the potential buyer a damages claim, but it may be worth it to the target in some cases. For a public company target, the damages would, in effect, be paid by the interloper buyer. The interloper buyer would acquire a target that is burdened by potential liability claims against it. In public company deals the value paid to the target's shareholders is typically fixed, so the target's shareholders would still receive the agreed-upon consideration whether or not damages had to be paid.

War Story ══

The target was in dire straits. Desperate for a deal, it finalized a letter of intent and agreed to exclusivity with the potential buyer. The full purchase agreement was expected to follow promptly but had not been drafted yet.

As a public company, the target normally would not have announced an unfinished deal, but it felt the need to convey to the market and its customers that it had found a path to survival. When the handshake deal was announced, a competing bidder decided to jump in. Not knowing when the target might sign up the announced deal, the competing bidder prepared a target-friendly merger agreement, dropped in a premium price, and delivered the signed offer to the target.

The target was caught in a bind. It wanted to accept the better price, of course, but was bound by exclusivity to just sit by and ignore it. The target had not asked for a fiduciary out, or even thought about the issue. It was not bound to sign the first deal, but it felt it could not wait long enough to let the exclusivity period simply run its course and expire—in the meantime, the better bid could be lost. The target could even lose both deals in the process, which could mean financial disaster.

The target took a leap of faith. It signed the new bidder's contract and announced a finalized deal. The target told the original buyer that an unwritten fiduciary out implied by law had excused its breach of exclusivity.

The first bidder was incensed. It asked the court to enjoin the new deal, but the court refused. It asked the court to enforce the target's obligation to negotiate in good faith, but the court again refused. So it sought damages.

Months after the target closed the new deal, the damages claim was settled. The target paid a substantial sum to the original bidder. Since at that point the target was 100 percent owned by the buyer (and the target shareholders had already collected their money), the settlement was effectively paid by the new buyer.

Exclusivity period

Exclusivity expires at the end of a short, defined period. The exclusivity period is designed to be long enough to complete the process of negotiating a deal, while not locking up the target for unnecessary periods of time. The period will often range from two weeks to two months, but it can also be as short as a few days. The period varies depending on the parties' desire for speed and the complexity of the diligence and acquisition documents. Targets may also use tight periods to put pressure on the buyer to complete diligence and negotiations in a timely manner.

Usually exclusivity terminates at the end of the exclusivity period. If the parties want to extend it, they can sign an amendment to extend it. Alternatively, the agreement can be designed to "roll over" into an additional extension period unless one party takes the affirmative step to terminate the agreement (e.g., by delivering a termination notice).

Sample Provision

The Exclusivity Period shall be automatically extended for [10 business days] following the end of the Exclusivity Period or any such extension period, unless no later than 5:00 P.M. on the two business days prior to the end of the then-applicable Exclusivity Period or extension period either the Buyer or the Target provides written notice to the other party that it is terminating this Agreement as of the end of the then-applicable Exclusivity Period or extension period.

The requirement for an affirmative termination can easily be fulfilled as a legal matter, but has practical significance. The act of termination can send a signal to the other side about the target's lack of satisfaction with the process; as a result, an actual termination in such cases is often avoided by the target, resulting in an extended exclusivity arrangement.

If the buyer and target decide that they cannot move forward because of a disagreement over terms, in most cases the parties will mutually agree to go ahead and terminate exclusivity. Although a buyer contractually has the power to keep the target out of the market in most deals even after the buyer stops negotiating, they usually will waive that right if there is no deal to be had. Nevertheless, a target may be wise to provide for this case up front. To that end, a target may add a provision that exclusivity expires if the buyer stops actively negotiating a deal or if the buyer changes the deal (e.g., proposes terms inconsistent with the term sheet).

Obligation to negotiate in good faith

Some exclusivity agreements obligate the parties to negotiate in good faith during the exclusivity period. This is more likely when the parties have already reached a basic agreement on the economic terms of the deal.

A buyer may want to include this provision because it reflects the parties' actual expectations heading into the negotiations—that everyone is prepared to go through the normal process for getting a deal signed. The seller may be concerned that, if it decides not to go forward with a transaction, it could have liability to the buyer for failure to keep negotiating.

Sample Provision

During the Exclusivity Period, each of the parties hereto shall negotiate in good faith definitive documents regarding the Proposed Transaction.

An obligation to negotiate in good faith can be legally binding or may, by its terms, be nonbinding (a so-called "moral" rather than legal obligation). Even if it is binding, enforcing an obligation to negotiate in good faith is difficult. How could the buyer show that the target rejected compromise positions out of bad faith? Is the target not justified in sticking to its economic positions?

In some deals, all the material terms have already been agreed in a term sheet.[9] In those instances, it may be more feasible to enforce an obligation to negotiate to finalize the documentation. Since most all term sheets are nonbinding, even if there is a term sheet that forms the backdrop for negotiating in good faith, the target can always change its mind on what economic terms it is willing to accept.

Specific performance would also be difficult to pursue for breach of an obligation to negotiate in good faith. The target could, theoretically, be required to show up at a meeting and otherwise "go through the motions"—but if there is no obligation to sign an agreement at the end of the process, such a remedy would probably be futile.

No obligation to execute definitive documentation

Even when the target is obligated to negotiate in good faith, it is not obligated to take the final step and actually sign the definitive documentation that it negotiates. In other words, an exclusivity agreement may require the parties to negotiate toward acceptable terms, but does not require the parties to actually agree to those terms, even if they are generally acceptable. In most cases, there is an express provision confirming that the parties are not obligated to enter into definitive agreements, thus avoiding any risk that a court will interpret the obligation to negotiate as implying an obligation to sign the finalized arrangements.

Scope of damages

Some say that an agreement is only as good as its enforceability. When it comes to exclusivity, it is hard to measure damages for breach, which limits to some extent the legal value of the contract. It may still have significant practical value because the target will want to avoid any disruptive lawsuits. Since the buyer is not entitled to a signed deal, what has it actually lost if the target walks away from negotiations?

The amount of damages is not obvious. In some cases buyers have asked for expectation damages calculated based on the profits that the buyer would have earned if it had bought the target,[10] claiming that their damages are the lost value of the deal to the buyer, but that argument seems difficult to sustain. Realistically, if the target was never obligated to sign a deal, the most that the buyer could ask for may be reimbursement of its deal expenses, such as legal and accounting diligence fees. Even then, targets may feel that much of the expense was incurred before exclusivity was signed, and may have been incurred even if exclusivity had not been agreed (or breached).

Some buyers will add an explicit remedy to the exclusivity agreement to avoid this type of dispute over a relatively small amount of damages. The main solution is to explicitly provide for expense reimbursement as a remedy for breach—usually for all deal expenses, not just those incurred since the exclusivity agreement was signed.

Mutual exclusivity

Sometimes a target will also ask the buyer for exclusivity. Usually, the buyer could pursue multiple deals at once without harm to the target so buyer exclusivity is not an issue. In other cases, though, the target fills a particular niche for the buyer. If buying a competitor of the target would mean that there is no more interest or room to acquire the target, then the target may have the same concerns as a buyer normally has about being a stalking horse. For instance, the target may be intended to complement the buyer's business by adding a specialty product or service line. Mutual exclusivity could be used by the target to prevent the buyer from filling that need through another acquisition while negotiating with the target.

Short of asking for mutual exclusivity, the target could also ask the buyer for notice of disruptive events. For instance, the target could require the buyer to provide notice of another deal that could, for instance, create antitrust problems for the buyer to acquire the target.

Term Sheets

Letters of intent (LOIs), memoranda of understanding (MOUs), and term sheets establish the key terms of a transaction. Establishing those terms in a shorthand form reduces drafting time, and allows the back and forth of negotiations to proceed faster. They have the benefit of reducing legal costs at a point when it is not clear whether the parties can reach agreement on the fundamental terms of a deal. They are also written in a form that is easier for the business teams to understand, so they facilitate greater participation by the business teams in negotiations.

As a matter of custom, LOIs and MOUs tend to be drafted in a more narrative format, and tend to have less detail on the specific terms of the deal. Term sheets tend to be more specific as to terms. Each form serves the purpose of generally documenting the outline of a transaction in a simplified format, and the terms "LOI," "MOU," and "term sheet" are used somewhat interchangeably in this chapter.

Term sheets are most common in complex and unique deals. In transactions with ordinary provisions, using a term sheet may not bring speed or efficiency. If the "devil is in the details," a term sheet may even be less efficient than going straight into full documentation; it can delay focusing on the definitive wording, which is where most of the work remains to be done. If not drafted precisely enough, term sheets can gloss over the level of detail that actually tends to present the most difficulty. The parties may build momentum towards a deal without having to work through all the nuances that may in the end not be resolvable.

Nonbinding

LOIs, MOUs, and term sheets are typically intended to be nonbinding. Assuming that is the case, it is critical to explicitly state that the parties do not intend to be legally obligated to sign or close a transaction. Absent clarity on this issue, whether the parties intend to be bound would be a matter of fact to be determined through litigation. There are some high-profile examples of poorly drafted documents under unique circumstances in which it was hard in retrospect to tell whether the parties meant for a term sheet to be binding.

Some courts have enforced term sheets that one party argued were never intended to constitute binding contracts. Most of those cases present unusual facts, such as the parties publicly announcing the deal on the basis of a term sheet,[11] or one party signing a new deal with a different buyer just before the other party could approve the transaction,[12] or one party appearing not to act in good faith.[13]

Courts will look to a number of factors to decide whether an agreement is binding, including the intent of the parties to be bound as manifested by the explicit language of the agreement, any further approvals or actions to be taken by the board or shareholders of one or both of the parties, the need for further negotiations to settle the essential terms of the transaction, or any partial performance on the part of the parties. In practice, lawyers now make it clear on the face of LOIs and MOUs that those documents are nonbinding in order to avoid having to deal with such a fact-based analysis.

War Story

The seller was ready to get rid of one of its underperforming divisions. That division was a drag on earnings, and had a lower profit margin than the seller's other operations. Management wanted to refocus the division on growth areas.

After a multiround auction, the seller was disappointed with the final price. But it had selected its winner and moved forward to negotiate the final documents. The auction resulted in an agreed term sheet, which was, of course, nonbinding by its own terms.

In the middle of negotiating the full deal documents, a new bidder emerged. It was unclear why that new bidder had not participated in the auction. In addition, it somehow knew enough about the pricing to slightly outbid the best price of the auction.

The new bidder was given fast-track due diligence, and was handed the auction winner's almost fully negotiated acquisition agreement (with the names simply changed to the new bidder). The new bidder made very minor edits to the contract, and was ready to sign.

In the meantime, the auction winner was also close to finishing its deal. After one final session of face-to-face negotiations, the seller's lead negotiator stood up, congratulated everyone, and announced, "We have a deal." After a round of handshakes, it appeared as if the lawyers merely needed to input the agreed changes and prepare signature pages. The auction winner expected its final agreement to be distributed overnight.

The next morning, the auction winner was stunned to read a press release from the seller: it had signed with the new bidder overnight!

Though its claim was sketchy at best, the auction winner sued—arguing that the near final documents and the seller's "we have a deal" statement, when taken together, formed a binding contract. The court decided that it was a matter of fact to be determined at trial. That meant the auction winner's claim survived the motion to dismiss—and that it was in for a full trial if it did not settle.

The seller refused to settle. It could not avoid a jury trial. Ironically, because there was no signed contract with the auction winner, there was no agreement containing the standard waiver of the right to a jury trial. The seller slowly recognized that it was in for a long trial or a big settlement.

Eventually the seller settled for an amount that made it wish it had just sold at the slightly lower price to the auction winner. Even more ironic: the target business ended up performing poorly. The auction winner wound up much better off economically with the settlement than it would have if it had actually bought the target.

Required public disclosure

For a public company, agreed deal terms in a term sheet, LOI or MOU can exacerbate difficult disclosure issues under federal securities laws and the rules of the stock exchange on which its securities are listed. Generally speaking, disclosure is required if there is a duty to disclose and failure to disclose the deal would be material to shareholders of the target.

Unlike many jurisdictions, in the United States all material information does not have to be disclosed on a current basis. Instead, only a limited array of specific events have to be disclosed on a current basis. For instance, the duty to disclose can arise from affirmative Securities and Exchange Commission (SEC) filing obligations. Those disclosure requirements include the required annual or quarterly report filings, and the current disclosure requirements under Form 8-K.[14] The Form 8-K rules include, in particular, a requirement to make public disclosure if the target enters into a material contract.[15]

More importantly, a duty to disclose can arise if the target makes a false or misleading statement—requiring the target to disclose the deal in order to correct the error. SEC rules include general prohibitions against material misstatements and omissions (including Exchange Act Rule 10b-5).[16] Those could require disclosure of deal talks if the public company target makes any other disclosures that implicate the deal—or suggest the absence of a deal. Depending on the context, failing to disclose a potential deal that is imminent could make other statements appear misleading. In a few cases, courts have found targets to have a duty to update prior statements, particularly if they were predictive in nature or appeared to have an "evergreen" nature to them.[17]

Case law provides some guidance as to when disclosure of negotiations would be material to investors before a deal is actually signed.[18] Those criteria are based on a general review of all the facts and circumstances. The two primary factors to consider are the size of the deal and the probability of the deal.[19] That leaves the parties to attempt to control the apparent probability of the transaction. For example, if the parties negotiate an LOI, it becomes more difficult to take the position that substantial uncertainty remains as to whether the parties will ultimately come to an agreement. After the parties sign up the deal, it could appear, with "20/20 hindsight," that the LOI evidenced a solid agreement, and that could color a court's judgment as to how probable the transaction was at the time the LOI was signed.

The parties may also be concerned that an agreed term sheet increases the likelihood of a leak. If the deal team members believe that transaction terms are agreed in principal, they may feel more comfortable talking to friends in the industry or members of the press.

Litigation Endnotes

1. In *In re Complete Genomics, Inc. Shareholder Litigation*, the court held that the restriction on a bidder privately requesting a waiver impermissibly prevented the flow of information to the board, which had a duty to "take care to be informed of all material information reasonably available." Transcript Ruling, *In re Complete Genomics*, No. C.A. 7888-VCL (Del. Ch. Nov. 27, 2012). A board has "ongoing statutory and fiduciary obligations to properly evaluate a competing offer, disclose material information, and make a meaningful merger recommendation to stockholders." *Id.* The court enjoined enforcement of the provision. *But see In re Ancestry.com Inc. S'holder Litig.*, No. C.A. 7988-CS (Del. Ch. Dec. 17, 2012) (holding that there is no per se rule in Delaware against the use of such provisions).

2. *See, e.g., Martin Marietta Materials, Inc. v. Vulcan Materials Co.*, 56 A.3d 1072 (Del. Ch. 2012) *aff'd*, 45 A.3d 148 (Del. 2012) and 68 A.3d 1208 (Del. 2012). When acquisition negotiations failed, the buyer launched an unsolicited offer for the target's shares using nonpublic information gained during the negotiations, which provided important insight into the value of the company. Concurrently with the hostile offer, the buyer commenced an action seeking a declaration that it did not violate the parties' confidentiality agreement, which included a restriction on use of confidential information, but not an express standstill provision. The court ruled against the buyer, finding that the confidentiality agreement contemplated the use of confidential information only in connection with a mutually negotiated merger between the parties, not a hostile transaction. Thus, the use of the information in connection with the hostile transaction was a prohibited use under the confidentiality agreement. The court effectively read a standstill provision into the restriction on use. *See also Certicom Corp. v. Research In Motion Ltd.*, [2009] O.J. No. 252 (Ont. Sup. Ct. Jan. 19, 2009). *Certicom* involved a buyer that signed a confidentiality agreement allowing use of confidential information only to evaluate a friendly deal. The buyer proceeded to launch a hostile offer using the confidential information, which the court enjoined as violating the confidentiality agreement.

3. *See, e.g., Gen. Portland, Inc. v. LaFarge Coppee S.A.*, [1982–1983 Transfer Binder] CCH Fed. Sec. L. Rep. ¶ 99,148 (N.D. Tex. 1981). A potential buyer, unable to come to a deal with the target, unilaterally made a hostile offer to the board of the target in violation of the confidentiality agreement, and publicized it. After the target filed suit, the court prevented the offer from taking place until after the confidential information was no longer "material or competitively sensitive." *But see Res. Exploration v. Yankee Oil & Gas, Inc.*, 566 F. Supp. 54 (N.D. Ohio 1983) (declining to enjoin a potential buyer from making a tender offer for a target after the buyer reviewed confidential information under a confidentiality agreement which had no explicit prohibition on hostile offers, and simply required confidential information to be "used in relation to [the buyer's] offer").

4. *See* Chapter 13-A, Overview of "No-Shop" Provisions.

5. *See* Chapter 9-C, Change in Recommendation & Fiduciary Out.
6. *See* Chapter 13-B, Types of Restrictions in No-Shop Provisions; Chapter 13-E, Fiduciary Out Breakup Fees.
7. *See Global Asset Capital, LLC v. Rubicon U.S. REIT, Inc.*, No. C.A. 5071-VCL (Del. Ch. Nov. 16, 2009). The court rejected the target-defendant's contention that the fiduciary duties imposed on the target's board of directors permit the board to violate an exclusivity agreement that did not contain a fiduciary out. The court noted that the existence of a fiduciary duty does not give rise to an inherent fiduciary out; instead, fiduciary outs must be bargained for to ensure that a contract does not restrict the exercise of fiduciary duties.
8. *See In re Mobile Commc'ns Corp. S'holder Litig.*, No. C.A. 10627 (Del. Ch. Jan. 7, 1991) (holding that the board's duty to entertain potentially superior offers for the sale of the target extended up until the date stockholder approval was secured, but not beyond the date of stockholder approval).
9. *See* Chapter 3-D, Term Sheets.
10. *See, e.g., Wavedivision Holdings, LLC v. Millennium Digital Media Sys. LLC,* No. C.A. 2993-VCS (Del. Ch. Sept. 17, 2010) (holding that, because the target breached exclusivity by signing a separate deal with a new third-party buyer, the original buyer was entitled to damages for the target's breach). In coming up with a formula for expectation damages, the court in *Wavedivision* reasoned that the original buyer was entitled to the value it expected to realize from the agreement, minus (i) any cost avoided by having to perform (such as the purchase price), and (ii) any mitigation that the original buyer was able to achieve by purchasing another target. *Id.* at 43–44.
11. *See Texaco, Inc. v. Pennzoil, Co.,* No. 84-05905 (Tex. Dist. Ct. Dec. 10, 1985), *aff'd in part,* 729 S.W.2d 768 (Tex. App. 1987), *cert. dismissed,* 485 U.S. 994 (1988), *appeal dismissed on agreement of the parties,* 748 S.W.2d 631 (Tex. App. 1988) (applying New York law). At trial, the jury in *Texaco* found that a binding agreement existed between Getty Oil and Pennzoil on the basis of a signed, but conditional, Memorandum of Agreement between the entities and identical, simultaneously issued press releases announcing the agreement "in principle," which contained other conditional language.
12. *See, e.g., Am. Cyanamid Co. v. Elizabeth Arden Sales Corp.,* 331 F. Supp. 597 (S.D.N.Y. 1971) (holding that, under New York law, a letter of intent could constitute a binding agreement, based on the level of detail in the LOI and its wording, which provided that if the parties were unable to execute a definitive purchase agreement or obtain the necessary shareholder/board approvals, neither party would have any obligation to the other). In *American Cyanamid,* the buyer's board had not yet met to approve or reject the deal.
13. *See Global Asset Capital, LLC v. Rubicon U.S. REIT, Inc.,* No. C.A. 5071-VCL (Del. Ch., Nov. 16, 2009) (granting the plaintiff's motion for a temporary restraining order, ruling that a letter of intent which is "sufficiently definite" may give rise to enforceable obligations, and finding that an agreement to negotiate

contained within a letter of intent gave rise to a duty to negotiate in good faith because "radio silence is not negotiating in good faith").

14. In addition to federal securities laws, state laws can also impose a duty of disclosure. *See, e.g., Alessi v. Beracha*, 849 A.2d 939 (Del. Ch. 2004) (finding a duty to disclose under state law where the target engaged in a buy-sell program for small shareholders during merger negotiations and rejecting the target's argument that the deal talks were not material because the merger was actually signed and announced a little more than a week later).

15. *See* SEC, Form 8-K: Current Report Pursuant to Section 13 or 15D of the Securities Exchange Act of 1934, at 4 (Item 1.01: Entry into a Material Definitive Agreement) (requiring a U.S. reporting company to disclose the entry into a material definitive agreement).

16. *See* 17 C.F.R. § 240.10b-5.

17. This occurred in *Weiner v. Quaker Oats Co.,* where a buyer had announced its debt-to-equity capitalization ratio, and had gone on to make a prediction regarding its future ratio. 129 F.3d 310 (3d Cir. 1997). The acquisition was financed in part with debt, which raised the debt-to-equity ratio. The circumstances led the court to conclude that the buyer had a duty to update its debt-to-equity ratio predictions once they became unreliable. *Id.* at 318 (citations omitted). Of course, doing so would have been difficult without disclosing the pending deal. *But see Levie v. Sears Roebuck & Co.,* 676 F. Supp. 2d 680, 687–88 (N.D. Ill. 2009) (concluding that the failure to disclose deal talks was only misleading if it related directly to or was otherwise sufficiently linked to the arguably misleading statements in question).

18. *See Basic Inc. v. Levinson,* 485 U.S. 224 (1988) (holding, in part, that merger negotiations must be disclosed if the potential transaction is material and if nondisclosure would be misleading).

19. *See id.* at 250 (discussing how the analysis of materiality turns on the deal size relative to company size, and the likelihood the transaction will be consummated).

CHAPTER 4

Architecture of the Acquisition Agreement

Key Elements of the Acquisition Agreement

Acquisition agreements are made up of several core building blocks or components. Each has its own function in the agreement, and each interacts with the others to build higher-order structures. In a typical acquisition agreement each is segregated into its own article. Complex deal components—such as financing contingencies and breakup fees—are implemented through multiple provisions that cut across several different parts of the agreement.

The first part of this chapter provides an overview of those key components and how they work together. It shows all pieces of the puzzle at once. The second part of this chapter compares and contrasts how they operate and when they are most or least useful in a deal. After that, each component is discussed in detail in its own chapter.

Structure

The acquisition structure is defined in an initial section of the acquisition agreement.[1] At the most basic level, deals take one of the following forms:

- A stock sale (or a tender offer in public company deals);
- A merger; or
- An asset sale.

In a stock sale, the buyer acquires the stock of the target company. If the target is a small, privately held company or a wholly owned subsidiary of a larger company, the stock can be purchased in a simple, private sale directly from the shareholders. If the target is a public company and its shares are widely held, the stock sale would take the form of a public tender offer to buy shares from all those shareholders and would be subject to the tender offer rules under the federal securities laws.

In a merger, two companies join together to form a single entity with combined assets and liabilities. Often, the entity on the buyer's side is a special purpose vehicle (an empty shell); there is no true merging of assets and liabilities, because the target is the only party that brings an operating business to the merger. In practice, it is another mechanism for the buyer to acquire the stock of the target and own it as a subsidiary. Among other things, the target is required to obtain shareholder approval. If the target is a public company, the shareholder vote takes the form of a public proxy solicitation subject to proxy rules under the federal securities laws.

In an asset sale, the assets and liabilities of the target business may have to be teased apart from the other business activities of the target before they are sold to the buyer. If the target is selling all or substantially all of its assets, approval by its shareholders will be required. These structures can also be combined into more complicated, multistep transactions.

Initially, it may appear that different structures should lead to fundamentally different types of acquisition agreements. However, acquisition structures can be thought of as simply one among many deal components. Perhaps surprisingly, most of the other components do not change significantly across the key types of structures.

Public and private deals will usually have some different key components. The defining characteristic of a private deal is the existence of a known, identifiable seller that will be available to indemnify the buyer and stand behind any other post-closing obligations. For instance, a family may be selling its wholly owned business, or a corporation may sell one of its divisions. In a typical private transaction, the contract typically is negotiated directly with the owners of the target and no subsequent shareholder vote is required. That eliminates the uncertainty of public transactions arising from the need for a shareholder vote or shareholder acceptance of a tender offer.

In a public transaction, ownership of the target entity is usually widely dispersed, and there is no readily identifiable party to stand behind the obligations of the target after closing. As previously noted, in a public transaction shareholder support is still needed after the deal is signed, which creates a level of uncertainty not present in private transactions. A public company is also subject to ongoing disclosure requirements established by the Securities and Exchange Commission (SEC). This leads to a significant amount of information regarding the company in the public domain that is available for analysis as part of the buyer's initial due diligence.

Deal consideration

How the buyer pays for the target business can take different forms.[2] The buyer may simply pay cash or it may offer equity in the buyer or one of its affiliates as consideration. In a public transaction, equity or other securities issued as deal consideration would have to be registered under the securities laws. Alternatively, the buyer can issue a note payable to the seller over time. Cash, equity, and notes can also be combined.

Regardless of its form, the purchase price may be fixed at the time of signing or may be subject to adjustments measured at the time of closing. For example, the purchase price may fluctuate depending on the amount of working capital left in the target business on the closing date or based on the market value of any securities issued as consideration.

In addition to adjustments that apply as of closing, changes in the purchase price can be measured based on post-closing performance or hurdles. For example, earn-outs (in private deals) and contingent value rights (in public deals) provide additional purchase price payments if the target company meets performance hurdles after closing. The measurement period for earn-outs or contingent value rights may extend several years into the future. For instance, an earn-out may pay out based on performance over a span of three to seven years.

Representations and warranties

Sellers or target businesses use representations and warranties (referred to simply as "representations" in this book) to confirm important facts.[3] Representations describe the target in detail, as well as relevant aspects of its ownership and corporate structure. They are usually written in an affirmative form, often subject to knowledge and materiality qualifications. Target-specific exceptions are placed in a separate disclosure schedule. The process of working through and reviewing the disclosure schedule is an important part of buyer diligence.

Other components of the acquisition agreement provide the buyer with two key remedies for breaches of representations. A closing condition (and related termination right) gives a buyer the right to walk away from a transaction without closing if the representations were not sufficiently accurate. This right usually exists if representations were not sufficiently accurate at signing or became inaccurate by the time of closing.

If the target is privately held, the seller usually backstops the representations with an indemnity that allows the buyer to close and then sue to collect damages for breaches of representations. As a practical matter, if the target is a publicly held company with a large number of shareholders, an indemnity is difficult to implement and requires holding back part of the deal consideration. Public company deal indemnities have not been done in practice outside of a couple of various instances.

Covenants

Affirmative covenants require a party to take actions.[4] This includes a general requirement to use an agreed level of efforts to obtain governmental approvals and to otherwise satisfy the closing conditions and get the deal closed. The covenants include an obligation to operate the target business in the ordinary course between signing and closing. Negative covenants prohibit the target business from taking specific types of actions before the closing, such as incurring debt, making material acquisitions, or selling material assets.

Closing conditions

For a variety of reasons, most transactions cannot be completed on the date the acquisition agreement is signed. For instance, after signing the parties may need to secure shareholder votes or governmental approvals. Conditions describe the events that must occur and facts that must exist before a party is required to close the transaction.[5] Conditions typically include a requirement that the representations and warranties of the other party be sufficiently accurate, and conditions that both the other party has complied with its covenants and required governmental approvals have been received. In addition, buyers usually have the benefit of a condition that there has been no material adverse effect on the target business.

Closing conditions are occasionally referred to as "outs." They are "free" to exercise. In other words, if a condition for the benefit of the buyer has not been satisfied, the buyer is not required to close the transaction—and the buyer is not required to pay any fees or damages to the target company when the buyer refuses to close on that basis. This stands in contrast to some termination rights that require payment of a reverse breakup fee before they can be exercised.

Termination rights

Termination rights permit one or both parties to terminate the transaction agreement.[6] Under the "drop-dead date" termination provision, once a specific date has passed (for instance, five months after the signing) either party can terminate the acquisition agreement if the transaction has not yet closed. Other termination rights can be thought of as "early" termination rights, in that they permit a party to stop waiting for the "drop-dead" date to pass. Early termination rights reflect the fact that parties normally do not expect to be required to comply with covenants, including the covenant to try to satisfy the conditions, for an indefinite period of time.

Early termination rights mirror closing conditions. If a party is not required to close because a particular condition has not been satisfied, that party may want to terminate early if it is no longer feasible to satisfy that condition. For instance, if the representations are not sufficiently true to meet the closing condition standard, and have not or cannot be brought into compliance during a cure period, the buyer can terminate. If a public target holds a shareholder vote and shareholders vote down the deal, then the buyer can go ahead and terminate.

Like conditions, some termination rights are "free" to exercise. This applies to terminating for breaches of representations or covenants, or, because the target has suffered a material adverse effect (MAE). If the target in a public company merger terminates to accept a better deal, the target usually has to pay a breakup fee. Exercising financing-related termination rights, in contrast, often trigger payment of a breakup fee by the buyer. If paid by the buyer, this is referred to as a "reverse" breakup fee, such as a financing failure reverse breakup fee.

No material adverse effect protection

Almost all acquisition agreements have a condition that allows the buyer to refuse to close if a material adverse effect on the target has occurred. Sometimes, these are referred to interchangeably as "no-MAE" (material adverse effect) or "no-MAC" (material adverse change) provisions.[7] They protect a buyer to some extent from having to close the deal and pay full price when the target company is worth substantially less than it was when the deal was signed.

No-MAE protections are weak for a few reasons. Courts have generally concluded that no-MAE provisions are intended to allow a buyer not to close only in the event of very substantial adverse effects on the target that are likely to have a long-term impact on its business. Further, the definition of a "MAC" typically excludes a variety of adverse effects; common exclusions include changes in the economy or the target's industry. As a result, the most common causes of decline in a company's value—broad industry and economic trends—are ignored, and the buyer is not protected by the no-MAC provision against those types of adverse developments.

Some buyers use quantitative measures to obtain more definitive protection against a downturn in the target business. Closing conditions in favor of the buyer tied to minimum earnings before interest, taxes, depreciation, and amortization (EBITDA), revenue, number of customers, or the like are referred to as "quantitative MAC" clauses. The thresholds for triggering a quantitative MAC normally provide some buffer zone below the base case expected results. Quantitative MAC clauses usually do not contain all the various exclusions for adverse effects (such as those attributable to changes in the industry or the economy) that general MAE clauses contain.

Financing risk

What happens if a buyer cannot obtain the debt financing it needs to pay the purchase price? This can be addressed in several ways.[8] The acquisition agreement could include a financing condition, permitting the buyer to terminate or not close the deal (without having to pay any fees) if it does not receive debt financing. Financing conditions are extremely rare, though they are occasionally still used in tender offers.

A reverse breakup fee is the most common alternative, under which the buyer is permitted to terminate the transaction upon payment of a negotiated fee if it is unable to obtain its debt financing despite having used sufficient efforts to do so. A few deals give the buyer a "walk right," under which the buyer can terminate the agreement for any reason (not just for a debt financing failure) upon payment of a reverse breakup fee.

Financing contingencies and related breakup fees are accomplished through several components, including conditions (if there is a related condition), termination rights (to permit termination that triggers the reverse breakup fee), remedies that determine whether the buyer is subject to specific performance (i.e., whether a court is permitted to force the buyer to close the transaction), the provision that governs what claims survive termination, a related cap on damages, and protective wording that prevents the target from skirting around the cap on damages by suing buyer's employees or other buyer entities up the ownership chain. These provisions must work together seamlessly to obtain the desired result.

Topping a public company merger

In public deals (transactions in which the target is a public company),[9] the acquisition agreement will include a "no-shop" provision and a "fiduciary out." The no-shop prohibits the target and its advisors from soliciting alternative transactions or otherwise engaging with another potential buyer. The fiduciary out exception allows the target to engage with a potential alternative bidder—despite the no-shop—as long as the bidder approaches the target first on an unsolicited basis. The fiduciary out also allows the target company to terminate the acquisition agreement with the initial buyer in order to sign a transaction with a competing bidder offering superior terms.

So-called "go shops" delay the implementation of the no-shop for a month or two in order to allow the target company to "shop" for a higher-paying bidder. After the go-shop window ends, the no-shop provisions apply.

Indemnities

In public deals (where public stockholders receive the sale consideration), the buyer is not entitled to an indemnity in practice. In private deals (where the target is a private company), the acquisition agreement normally includes an indemnity.[10] If a seller's or target's representations prove to be inaccurate, the indemnity compensates the buyer for its damages. Indemnities for breach of representations mostly protect the buyer against the unexpected or unknown; any known issues would be disclosed by the target in the disclosure schedules and, thus, would not constitute a breach. The seller may separately indemnify the buyer through a special indemnity for a risk or liability that is known and fully disclosed.

An indemnity typically includes the right to recover actual losses as well as related expenses (e.g., defense costs in litigation), while also placing several limitations on recovery—such as a cap on the aggregate amount of the indemnity, a deductible or threshold amount of damages that must be incurred before an indemnity claim can be successfully pursued, and restrictions on seeking punitive or speculative damages.

The indemnity may provide recovery for breaches of representations as they are written, or may provide recovery based on a special reading of the representations in which the parties ignore "materiality" qualifiers. In other words, in those cases the buyer can recover if the representation had been written on a "flat" basis without any such qualifiers—even though it was actually written in a qualified form. If the indemnity is based on such a hypothetical reading of the representations, it will often, in exchange, give the target the benefit of a deductible before the buyer can recover damages.

Solving Problems and Managing Risk: Comparing Techniques

Much of deal-making is an exercise in addressing risks and solving business problems faced by the buyer or seller. Deal-makers use several tools to address these situations, which can be combined in different ways in a deal. For example, if the target faces a potential liability, the parties may adjust the purchase price for the risk, draft closing conditions or related termination rights tied to successfully fixing those matters, or provide a special indemnity to protect the buyer from losses related to that liability. If a risk triggers termination of a deal, the termination can be without cost, or the parties may agree to a breakup fee payable by the target company, or a reverse breakup fee payable by the buyer, in order to align incentives to avoid the termination.

Each problem-solving technique has its own set of characteristics, and they differ along several lines. For instance, as discussed below, these tools vary in the timing of the protection and underlying loss (e.g., pre-, at, or post-closing). Some techniques provide economic recovery for a loss, while others do not. Some attempt to make the buyer whole for the amount of the relevant loss, while many simply provide "rough justice."

This section compares and contrasts these tools and reviews, at a high level, how they can be used to solve problems. The questions below illustrate how these provisions function. For simplicity, most are written from the buyer's perspective, but many could also operate as protections for the seller.

Is the buyer compensated for its losses?

Some problem-solving tools operate to make a party whole for losses or damages it has suffered; some do so in part; and some not at all. Indemnity is, by nature, designed to make the buyer whole for damages it has suffered. Although it is subject to limitations on the buyer's recovery—such as a cap on recovery and a deductible—the indemnity is generally designed to match the size of the solution to the size of the problem.

A purchase price adjustment is also designed to make the buyer whole, though the adjustment may not, in fact, compensate for all related losses. For example, a working capital adjustment compensates a buyer for a shortfall in working capital at closing. If the shortfall is due to a general decline in the business, the buyer is not compensated for the shortfalls it will experience in the future.

Closing conditions and termination rights provide no compensation for losses. Instead, by allowing the buyer to refuse to close or to terminate the deal, it helps the buyer avoid the loss in the first place. Breakup fees and reverse breakup fees provide some compensation, but the amount may or may not match the scope of actual losses. The amount of the fee is fixed in the acquisition agreement at signing and does not adjust for the actual amount of the damages.

Does the buyer have to close?

Some provisions apply only if a deal closes; others let the buyer avoid closing. Indemnity protection only applies after closing, requiring the buyer to close in the face of the problem, and then seek recovery. A purchase price adjustment also requires the buyer to close the transaction in order to benefit from its protection. By using a closing condition and/or termination right, a party may avoid closing. Breakup fees apply only in the event of a termination.

Does the buyer have to continue to work toward closing?

Between signing and closing a deal, the parties are usually required to use reasonable best efforts to satisfy the closing conditions. The termination right allows a buyer to stop working toward closing; the other problem-solving methods do not.

Closing conditions do not permit the buyer to stop working toward closing. They are conditions to closing—not conditions to a party's obligations to comply with its covenants. Although the buyer may refuse to close once the time for closing otherwise arises, the buyer is, perhaps paradoxically, not excused from continuing to use its efforts to achieve closing in the meantime.

Termination rights, in contrast, allow the buyer to stop complying with its covenants once the provision is exercised, so they excuse the buyer from continuing to work toward closing the deal. Termination rights often, but not always, mirror key closing conditions, allowing the buyer to terminate the deal early when it would not be required to close the transaction in any event.

As noted above, indemnities and purchase price adjustments only provide benefits if the buyer closes despite the problem. Breakup fees and reverse breakup fees apply only in the event of termination, but they have no effect on the obligation to work toward closing in advance of a termination.

Does the buyer take risk in exercising its protections?

For some solutions, the buyer takes risk if it tries to exercise its remedy and the target shows that the buyer was not entitled to the protection it claimed. For others, the only risk to pursuing a claim is wasted effort and legal cost.

Making an indemnity claim poses no risk to the buyer (other than perhaps damaging the ongoing relationship with the other side). If the claim is too high, the parties will work through the dispute resolution process and arrive at a final amount for the loss. The purchase price adjustment, likewise, does not put the buyer at risk for claiming an adjustment, even if it ultimately does not prevail.

Exercising a closing condition or termination right, in contrast, presents risk. If a buyer claims that it is not required to close or permitted to terminate—and refuses to close or tries to terminate on that basis—the seller can challenge its conclusion. If the challenge is successful, then (in retrospect) the buyer may be shown to have breached its obligation to close. That breach can subject the buyer to significant damages. For instance, damages could be measured by comparing the premium value that the buyer offered to pay in the deal to the value of the target's equity after giving effect to the failed transaction.

Breakup fees and reverse breakup fees themselves do not present risk (although the related termination may be challenged, as discussed above).

Rough justice or a refined solution?

Some solutions are intended to measure and make the buyer whole for its actual losses. Others provide a remedy that may or may not match the significance of the problem, and thus, provide a type of "rough justice."

An indemnity is generally designed to be a refined solution. It compensates the buyer for its losses, subject to limitations on recovery (such as deductibles and caps). A purchase price adjustment is also designed to make a party whole for the actual amount of shortfall or loss as measured as of the closing date. This mechanism does not compensate for future losses.

Closing conditions and termination rights act more by means of "rough justice." They are "on/off" switches, which cannot provide any refined solution in between. A failed condition or a termination right can be the basis for the parties to negotiate a revised deal that better reflects economic reality (which may be a more refined solution), but repricing the deal is not required by the condition itself.

What is the timing of the protection?

Some provisions address risks that occur pre-closing, some are measured at closing, and some address post-closing risks. Indemnity for breaches of representations usually protects a party from breaches that occur at signing and closing. Although payment on the indemnity occurs after closing, the indemnity does not cover breaches that arise after closing. However, a special indemnity can be negotiated to cover losses that arise before or after closing.

Purchase price adjustments provide pre-closing protection. Adjustments are given effect as of the closing, though calculating the adjustment and tru-ing up the amount may extend into the post-closing period. Earn-outs and contingent value rights, in contrast, measure post-closing performance. They protect a buyer from the target's failure to meet future projections or mile-stones for a meaningful period of time into the future.

Closing conditions and termination rights address pre-closing problems only. If an event happens before closing, a party may terminate or refuse to close. If the same event happens the day after closing, no protection is provided. Sometimes forward-looking wording can be written into the trig-gers for these protections. For instance, the closing condition could cover a specified event, and be triggered by a reasonable expectation or likelihood of that even occurring in the future (i.e., the level of potential future risk as of closing can be measured, but post-closing events themselves are not measured).

Breakup fees and reverse breakup fees are triggered by termination and, thus, only protect against pre-closing matters.

Litigation Notes

1. *See* Chapter 16, "Structuring M&A Deals."
2. *See* Chapter 5, "Purchase Price."
3. *See* Chapter 6, "Representations and Warranties."
4. *See* Chapter 7, "Covenants."
5. *See* Chapter 8, "Closing Conditions."
6. *See* Chapter 9, "Termination Rights."
7. *See* Chapter 10, "Material Adverse Effect."
8. *See* Chapter 12, "Financing Risk."
9. *See* Chapter 13, "Topping a Public Merger."
10. *See* Chapter 14, "Indemnities."

CHAPTER 5

Purchase Price

In a sense, no term of the transaction is more important to the buyer and the seller than the price to be paid. This chapter introduces the forms of consideration that may be offered and paid in a deal, and how those payments can vary or be adjusted based on facts that exist at closing or even performance that occurs after closing. This chapter also discusses the incentives that purchase price provisions give the parties, and how to control for and counterbalance those incentives.

Types of Consideration

Cash or stock

The purchase price can take different forms. Cash consideration is the simplest form of payment. The seller can also be paid in equity of the buyer. Equity consideration raises additional issues, such as whether the issuance of stock by the buyer must be registered under the securities laws, and the extent to which the seller will need to conduct due diligence on the buyer, and ask for (and receive) representations from the buyer.

> **THE MARKET**
>
> The percentage of public deals involving stock consideration fluctuates from time to time. From around one-quarter to around one-half of public deals used some form of stock consideration.

Fixed or contingent

The consideration may be fixed or contingent. If the purchase price is contingent, it can be adjusted as of the closing date or can be subject to a post-
closing adjustment. An adjustment for matters that exist as of the closing
date is referred to simply as a purchase price adjustment or a closing date
adjustment. An adjustment for matters that exist post-closing typically takes
the form of an earn-out in private deals or a contingent value right (CVR) in
public deals. These contingent forms of consideration allow the parties to allocate the risk of business performance between signing and closing, and after
closing in the case of an earn-out or CVR.

Stock Deals

The purchase price structure is determined at signing, when the parties enter
into the deal. It does not get paid until a later date (closing), however. If the
consideration is to be paid in stock, the parties must figure out how to deal
with the fluctuation of stock prices during the period between closing and
when the deal was signed. The parties can decide to fix at signing the number
of shares to be issued as consideration at closing. This is referred to as a fixed
exchange ratio. In that case, the value of the shares being issuer will fluctuate
with changes in the price of the buyer's stock.

Alternatively, the parties can decide to fix at signing the value of the
shares to be issued at closing and let the number of shares fluctuate as needed
to achieve that total agreed value. This is referred to as a fixed price structure.
A so-called "collar" is a hybrid between these two options. A collar can start
by fixing at signing the initial number of shares of stock or the total value, but
then only allow the other end (the value or number of shares, respectively) to
fluctuate within bounds. These are all described in more detail below.

Fixed exchange ratios

In a fixed exchange ratio, the target's shares are purchased in exchange for a
fixed number of shares of the buyer. This gives the target shareholders both
the upside and the downside of changes in the value of those fixed number of
shares of the buyer's stock being used as consideration. The value received on
the closing date can be more or less than was originally expected at signing. It
gives the buyer comfort knowing that its dilution is capped, in that the buyer
cannot be required to issue more than the agreed number of shares to close

the deal even if the buyer's stock price falls. On the other hand, if the buyer's stock price goes up, the buyer may feel that it is overpaying for the target because that fixed number of shares will have more value than expected at the time of signing.

Sample Provision

Each share of the Target's common stock issued and outstanding immediately prior to the Effective Time (other than Excluded Shares [shares held by the Buyer and subs, appraisal shares, etc.] will be canceled and automatically converted into the right to receive [1.0] [exchange ratio] fully paid and nonassessable shares of the Buyer common stock.

Fixed exchange ratio deals are more common in strategic transactions between players in the same industry, since each party is already subject to industry-related and market-related price risks. In those cases, a rise or fall in the buyer's stock price may well imply a similar change in the value of the target shares being sold. Fixed exchange ratio deals are also more common among similar-sized companies. In such deals, there should not be many cases in which the value of the target increases or decreases where the value of the buyer's shares do not increase or decreases in proportion—making it less likely either party will regret having fixed the exchange ratio. For players in different industries, in contrast, the target's shareholders (and the target's board) may be less interested in taking industry-related risk related to the buyer's equity.

Fixed price

In fixed price stock deals, the value of the stock consideration is fixed. The number of the buyer's shares to be issued to the target shareholders is not fixed—the number will be adjusted at closing to ensure that the agreed value is delivered. This can result in more or less buyer stock being delivered at closing than would have been anticipated at signing. It gives the target shareholders the comfort of knowing that the value of the deal cannot decrease, but also takes away the upside to the target's shareholders if the buyer's stock price should rise. The buyer is at risk of having to issue more shares than expected, resulting in more dilution to its existing shareholders; but the buyer is protected from potentially having to pay more in value to be received by the target's shareholders than it bargained for.

Sample Provision

Each share of the Target's common stock issued and outstanding immediately prior to the Effective Time (other than Excluded Shares [shares held by the Buyer and subs, appraisal shares, etc.] will be canceled and automatically converted into the right to receive the number of fully paid and nonassessable shares of the Buyer common stock determined by dividing [$10] [the deal price per share] by the Average Closing Price of the Buyer's common stock.

The number of shares of the buyer's stock is based on a formula, which divides the agreed deal price to be paid for each share of the target's stock by the value of the buyer's stock. If the buyer has agreed to pay $10 per share for the target's stock and the average trading price of the buyer's stock at closing is $5, then the buyer must deliver two ($10 ÷ $5 = 2) buyer shares for each target share. The average closing price is usually based on the trading price of the buyer's stock over an agreed number of days prior to closing (such as the last 10 trading days).

Collars

Collars act as limits on the extent to which the value can fluctuate (when applied to fixed ratio structures) or the extent to which the number of buyer shares to be issued can fluctuate (when applied to fixed value structures). A collar has a "floor" and "ceiling," which are usually (but need not be) symmetrical. The collar range is often 5 to 10 percent above and below the current trading price of the buyer's stock (fixed ratio structure) or the agreed deal value (fixed value structure). The collar concept can also be adjusted by using only the floor or ceiling concept, or by making the range for one larger than the other.

Fixed exchange ratio structure

In a fixed exchange ratio structure with a collar, the target shareholders take the ups and downs in the buyer's stock price within the collar, but not beyond. The collar ensures that the target will not be paid "too little" and that the buyer will not have to pay "too much" (potentially giving the target's shareholders a windfall benefit). In a fixed exchange ratio deal, the value of the consideration to be paid to the target's shareholders will fluctuate up to the edge of the collar, but the collar will cause the ratio to nevertheless slip (start adjusting) if the value to be received by the target's shareholders swings too far.

For example, if the value of the buyer's shares falls by 15 percent between signing and closing, and the collar is 10 percent, the target's shareholders will take the reduction in value down to 10 percent. But rather than the target's shareholders suffering the drop in value from 10 to 15 percent, the exchange ratio will be adjusted to ensure that the value received by the shareholders does not fall further than 10 percent.

Sample Provision

[…] provided that, (x) in the event that the Average Closing Price of the Buyer's Common Stock is greater than [$11] [deal price per share plus collar percentage], then such shares of the Target's Common Stock will be canceled and automatically converted into the right to receive a number of fully paid and non-assessable shares of the Buyer's Common Stock determined by dividing [$11] [deal price per share plus collar percentage] by the Average Closing Price of the Buyer's Common Stock and (y) in the event that the Average Closing Price of the Buyer's Common Stock is less than [$9.1] [deal price per share minus collar percentage], then such shares of the Target's Common Stock will be canceled and automatically converted into the right to receive a number of fully paid and nonassessable shares of the Buyer's Common Stock determined by dividing [$9.1] [deal price per share minus collar percentage] by the Average Closing Price of the Buyer's Common Stock.

Fixed value structure

In a fixed value structure with a collar, the buyer takes the ups and downs in the buyer's stock price within the collar, but not beyond. The collar ensures that the buyer will not suffer "too much" dilution or capture "too much" of the benefit from a run-up in the buyer's stock price. In a fixed value structure, the exchange ratio will fluctuate; the collar will cause the value to be paid to the target's shareholders to nevertheless start adjusting in extreme circumstances. It allows the ratio to fluctuate within a band as needed to keep the value constant.

Because the ratio cannot go outside of the collar band, if the value of the buyer's stock being offered as consideration swings too far up or down in value, the initial ratio adjustment will not prevent further change in value. For example, if the value of the buyer's shares falls by 15 percent between signing and closing, and the collar is set at 10 percent, then the buyer will have to issue more shares to make up the price decline for the first 10 percent. But rather than the buyer suffering the drop in value from 10 percent to 15 percent, the exchange ratio will become fixed at the band provided by the collar, and the value of the consideration offered will decline by 5 percent.

Sample Provision

[...] provided that (x) in the event that the Average Closing Price of the Buyer's Common Stock is greater than $__ [value plus collar percentage], then such shares of the Target's Common Stock will instead be canceled and automatically converted into the right to receive __ fully paid and nonassessable shares of the Buyer's Common Stock and (y) in the event that the Average Closing Price of the Buyer's Common Stock is less than $__ [value minus collar percentage], then such shares of the Target's Common Stock will instead be canceled and automatically converted into the right to receive __ fully paid and nonassessable shares of the Buyer's Common Stock.

Closing Date Purchase Price Adjustments

In many private deals (but not public deals), the purchase price will be adjusted based on the financial state of the target business at the instant of closing. These adjustments allow the parties to change the purchase price to account for positive or negative developments between signing and closing.

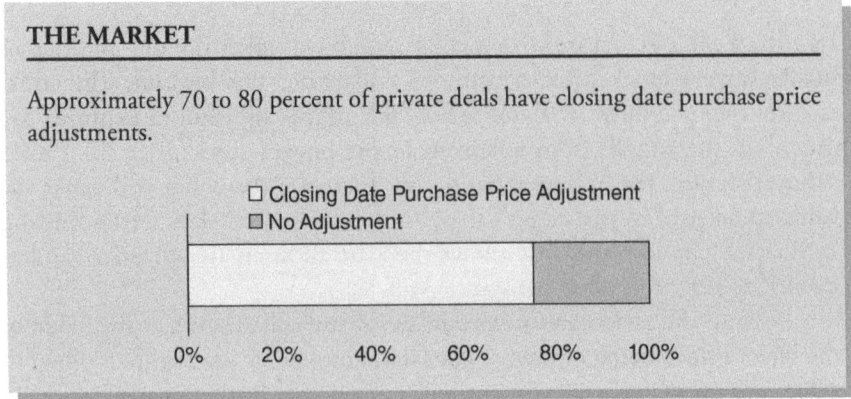

THE MARKET

Approximately 70 to 80 percent of private deals have closing date purchase price adjustments.

☐ Closing Date Purchase Price Adjustment
☐ No Adjustment

0%   20%   40%   60%   80%   100%

Adjustments can be "two-way" (up or down). They can also be "one-way"—for instance, adjusting only downward for negative developments, but not upward for positive developments. There are various types of adjustments. The most common adjustment in private deals is for working capital.

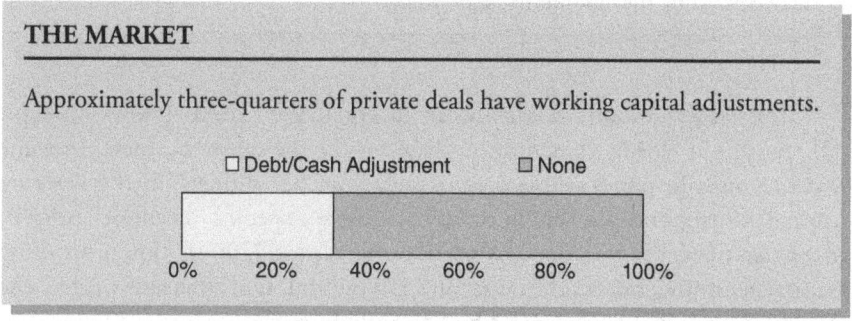

Many private deals also have separate adjustments for debt of the target and/or cash on hand.

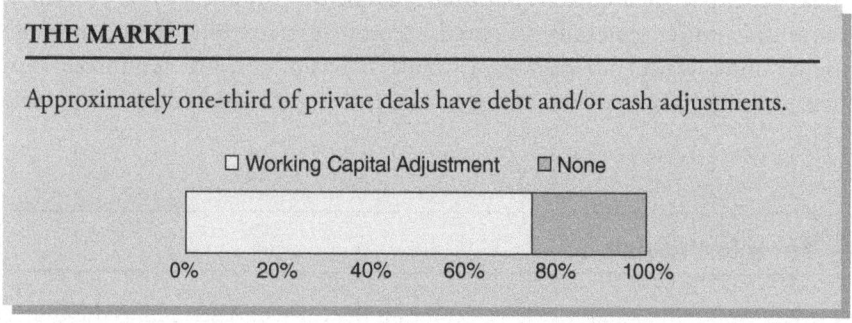

Some private deals adjust for inventory levels. In asset management transactions (e.g., acquisition of a hedge fund), the assets under management on the closing date can also be used to adjust the purchase price. In a working capital adjustment, the parties may increase or decrease the purchase price to the extent that the amount of closing date working capital of the target business is higher or lower than an agreed (expected) target amount.

Sample Provision

To the extent that the Closing Date Working Capital Amount exceeds the Target Working Capital Amount, then the Purchase Price will be increased by the amount of such excess. To the extent that the Target Working Capital Amount exceeds the Closing Date Working Capital Amount, then the Purchase Price will be decreased by the amount of such excess.

The target amount is usually set to equal the expected working capital amount at closing, based on projections for the target business. In some cases, a built-in purchase price adjustment can be "hidden" in the working capital adjustment, possibly in order to achieve a specific "headline" price in the agreement. For instance, the parties may expect $200 million in working capital at closing, but set the target at $250 million. If all goes as expected, the purchase price will be decreased by $50 million at closing.

Working capital is typically defined to mean the current assets of the target, such as cash and receivables, minus its current liabilities, such as its accounts payable. Debt and fixed assets are not considered "current" assets and liabilities, though an interest payment due on debt within the next year may be a current liability. The parties should also be careful to note that under generally accepted accounting principles debt flips from being noncurrent (not working capital) to being "current" (counts against working capital) when its maturity date is one year or less after the closing date.

Sample Provision

The "Working Capital" of the Target means the Current Assets minus the Current Liabilities. "Current Assets" means all consolidated current assets of the Target and its Subsidiaries, determined in accordance with generally accepted accounting principles (GAAP) (applying consistent principles, practices, methodologies and policies as set forth in the Audited Financial Statements), [other than current tax assets]. "Current Liabilities" means all consolidated current liabilities of the Target and its Subsidiaries, determined in accordance with GAAP (applying consistent principles, practices, methodologies and policies as set forth in the Audited Financial Statements) [other than current tax liabilities].

Tax assets (such as a right to a refund) and tax liabilities (such as accrued taxes due) are sometimes excluded from the definition of working capital, particularly when there is a separate tax indemnity. In such cases, the parties may agree to exclude taxes from the definition of working capital, in which case the purchase price is not adjusted at closing for tax matters. The target would still have to pay all indemnified taxes when due under the tax indemnity. The parties could have a tax indemnity and nevertheless still agree to include taxes in the definition of working capital. In that case, an adjustment for taxes is built into the working capital adjustment at closing, and the tax indemnity will protect the buyer from any additional taxes not reflected in the closing date accruals.

Innovative closing date purchase price adjustments include a "ticking fee" that adjusts the purchase price based on how long it takes to close the transaction. For instance, the purchase price may be fixed if the deal is closed within three months from signing, but increase by an agreed amount per day for each day the closing is delayed after a target date of say three months. A ticking fee of that type would motivate the buyer to accelerate the closing timing to the extent within its control.

Deals may have more than one type of adjustment, such as both a working capital and a debt adjustment. When more than one adjustment is used, the drafting needs to take into account any overlap. For instance, the current portion of debt (i.e., the amounts due within the next year) may be covered by both the working capital and any debt adjustment. Also, since time passes between signing and closing, some items that are not "current" (i.e., one year out or less) at the time of signing may be current by closing, leading to unexpected overlap.

Indemnities and purchase price adjustments can also inadvertently overlap, leading to the buyer's potentially receiving double recovery. Current taxes that are due is an example of a current liability, which may be the subject of both a tax indemnity and an obligation accounted for in working capital. The parties can easily regulate through drafting which adjustment and/or indemnities cover which types of assets and liabilities, as long as they are focused on the issue.

War Story ▬▬▬▬▬▬▬▬▬▬▬▬▬▬▬▬▬▬▬▬▬▬▬▬▬▬▬▬▬▬▬▬▬▬▬▬

The target had $400 million in seven-year debt that was due to mature in a year and a half. Under a typical change of control clause in the loan agreement, that debt would accelerate and become due at closing.

As part of the M&A deal, the sellers agreed to a low purchase price, as long as the buyer agreed to assume the debt. Rather than the buyer paying off the debt at closing, the buyer agreed to guarantee the debt, and the lenders agreed to waive the change of control clause so that the debt would stay in place after closing. Although the original maturity date stayed was unchanged, the buyer negotiated the right to extend it for one-year periods at increased rates, if needed. The purchase agreement had a customary working capital adjustment, which reduced the purchase price dollar for dollar for all current liabilities in excess of current assets.

Just prior to closing, a little more than six months after signing, the accountants were asked to prepare the working capital statement. Since at that point the entire principal amount of the debt was due within less than one year, it was deemed to be a "current" liability at closing. It all had to be included on the official working capital statement. As a result, the working capital statement technically called for the purchase price to be reduced by $400 million.

The sellers balked—obviously not intending to reduce the purchase price by $400 million! Fortunately for the sellers, the buyer did not try to take advantage of the drafting mistake on the sellers' part.

Regulating Incentives

Closing date adjustments regulate the incentives of the parties and how benefits and risks are shared among them in the period between signing and closing. The interaction between purchase price provisions and other parts of the acquisition agreement, such as covenants, has to be carefully considered. Purchase price structures create and modify incentives, which covenants often need to control.

For example, a deal structure may effectively provide that the seller will keep the benefit of cash on hand as of closing. That would be the result, for example, in an asset sale if cash is not included in the transferred assets. It would also be the case if a purchase price adjustment gives the seller the economic benefit (increase in purchase price) of excess cash on hand at closing, such as an adjustment for cash or working capital.

If the seller receives the excess cash on hand at closing, then it will have an incentive to spend less investing in the future of the business than it would have if it were expecting to be the owner of the business in future periods. The seller could decide to build less inventory than usual, postpone significant capital expenditures, or spend less on long-term marketing, and so on. The savings will accrue to the seller, since, at closing, it will keep the cash it did not spend. The future business may suffer, but that deficit will be borne by the buyer.

In some cases, adverse incentives created by the purchase price structure can be dealt with through other specific purchase price adjustments. For instance, a separate adjustment for inventory can be added to the agreement, so that the seller will no longer have an incentive to underspend on inventory. If the seller spends $10 million less on building inventory, it would not be allowed to keep the $10 million in savings. Instead, the seller will see the purchase price reduced by $10 million, offsetting any advantage of having saved on inventory buildup.

In other cases, adverse incentives are best dealt with through covenants. For instance, a covenant may require the seller to spend on marketing according to an existing marketing budget or continue capital projects on a pre-agreed schedule.

Post-Closing True-Up

Most purchase price adjustments are based on facts as they exist at closing. On the closing date itself, however, it is not possible to have an exact, agreed determination ready and agreed as to how much the adjustment should be. There is no time for one party to calculate and the other party to review the calculations. In those cases, the purchase price paid at closing is based on an assumption that there will be no adjustment, or is based on the good faith estimate of one party (usually the seller or target). After closing, the books can be examined, and a true-up will put the parties in the position they would have been if the closing date purchase price had accurately reflected the correct adjustment.

For example, a day or two before closing the seller may make a good faith estimate of the closing date inventory or working capital. Often, there is no formal right for the buyer to challenge the estimate (because the buyer is expected to rely on post-closing true-up mechanisms to protect itself if the estimate is wrong). Of course, if the buyer believes the estimate is too far off, it will try to work things out with the seller before closing so as not to pay on the basis of a bad estimate. After closing—often 30 to 60 days after closing—the buyer usually prepares a formal statement of the inventory or working capital as it existed on the closing date. Then the sellers are given an opportunity to review the statement.

If the reviewing party finds any errors in the preparer's statement, a general dispute mechanism is triggered. Although the acquisition agreement may generally contemplate access to courts to settle disputes, purchase price adjustments typically have a separate mechanism for resolving differences, designed to ensure that the true-up process will work efficiently. The parties are required to work together in good faith to agree on the correct amount of the adjustment for a period of time, such as 30 days. If the parties do not agree, they are required to submit the dispute to an accounting firm, which will be asked to make a determination within a short period of time (e.g., another 30 days). This process ensures a quick resolution by an accounting expert, rather than by a court or arbitrator.

The accountant's decision is binding on the parties. In some cases, the agreement will specify that the dispute resolution mechanism for the adjustment is enforceable as an arbitration award and is the exclusive remedy—ensuring that the parties cannot create an end-run around the agreed process and bring the matter to the courts.

Earn-Outs

Purchase price adjustments can be determined by post-closing events. In a private deal, this kind of post-closing adjustment is generally referred to as an earn-out.

Under an earn-out, the seller usually pays a portion of the anticipated purchase price at closing. The up-front portion of the purchase price can vary widely—from a small percentage to nearly all of the purchase price. The remainder of the potential purchase price is "at risk," depending on the performance of the target business after closing. Typically, if the business performs poorly, the total purchase price will be less than if the target had been acquired for a flat price at closing. If the business performs well, the total purchase price will be more than it would have been if a fixed price had been agreed.

Earn-outs can help bridge valuation differences between parties. A seller may project that its earnings will grow substantially in the following two years, but the buyer may not be confident enough in those projections to pay a premium for the expected growth. To close up the valuation gap, a portion of the purchase price could be made contingent on growth or on another financial measure of performance.

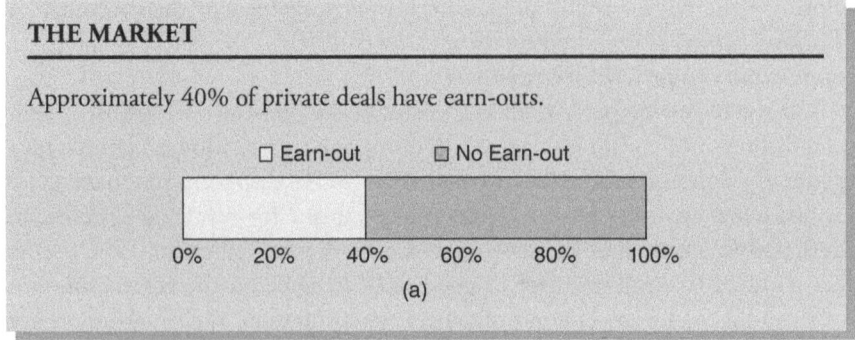

THE MARKET

Approximately 40% of private deals have earn-outs.

☐ Earn-out   ☐ No Earn-out

0%   20%   40%   60%   80%   100%

(a)

The prevalence of earn-outs varies widely based on the industry of the target. Acquisitions of pharmaceutical businesses and asset management businesses tend to have earn-outs in 80 percent or more of deals.

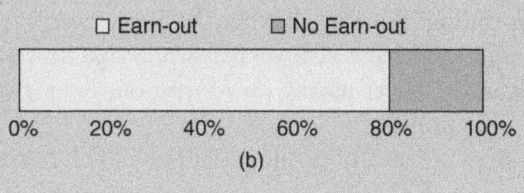

(b)

The measurement period for an earn-out depends on the circumstances the parties are trying to address. Four- or five-year measurement periods are quite common, but shorter and longer periods are also used. Sometimes, there are multiple earn-out payment triggers along the way, so that the sellers do not have to wait for (or condition all the payments on) events over extended periods of time. For instance, earn-out payments could be triggered at the end of each year for five years after closing, rather than one payment at the end of the entire period.

THE MARKET

The length of the earn-out measurement period varies widely. Around 80 percent of deals have earn-out measurement periods from one to three years (roughly equally distributed among those periods).

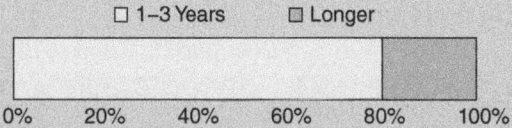

In deals in which the seller's management team continues to run the business, the measurement period may extend for five or more years.

Any earn-out needs to be based on some measure of the target's economic performance after closing. Earn-out metrics often focus on revenue. An earn-out based on revenue incentivizes the sellers to expand sales. However, since a pure revenue measure ignores the business expenses required to achieve that revenue, the parties will have different incentives about expenses. If the seller has remained with the business as management, the buyer will have to worry about the seller overspending. If the earn-out is based on revenue and thus does not take expenses into account, the seller does not have to worry about the buyer overspending. But the seller may be concerned that the buyer will spend too little on the business. A buyer may worry that a revenue based earn-out could result in the buyer paying on an earn-out even if revenue growth results in little or no profit.

In some deals, a measure of earnings such as EBITDA is instead used to measure the earn-out. EBITDA is a measure of earnings before taking into account certain types of expenses and deductions (earnings before interest, taxes, depreciation and amortization). Unlike revenue, it does generally take into account the expenses of the business. When an earn-out is triggered by a financial metric that takes into account expenses, then both the seller and the buyer have an incentive to keep expenses down.

However, the seller may be concerned that the buyer will spend too much. It forces the seller to take an interest in controlling the buyer's decisions as to the appropriate level of expenditures to be made. This desire for the sellers to control the expenses of the company post-closing can create difficult governance negotiations. The seller wants some ability to ensure that the company meets the earn-out targets, and the buyer wants freedom to run the business they just purchased.

Some deals use objective milestones that are not tied to revenue or earnings to measure the earn-out. Such triggers can be the approval of a new drug by the applicable governmental authorities or the manufacturing launch for a new product. To be effective, such measures need to be objective and able to be confirmed by a third party. Otherwise, there is a higher likelihood of disputes arising in the future.

THE MARKET

In deals that use earnings or revenue (as opposed to milestone) to measure the earn-out, revenue is used in roughly two-thirds and earnings is used in roughly one-third.

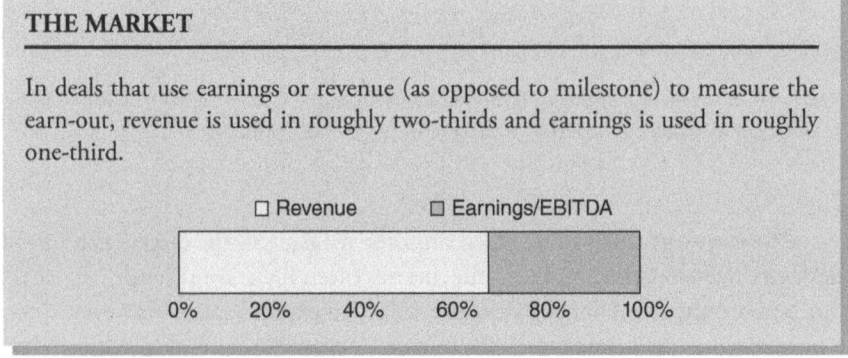

In an earn-out, although the ultimate purchase price is based on post-closing performance of the target, equity control of the target shifts to the buyer at closing. To help address this conflict, the buyer often gives the seller some degree of continuing contractual control of the day-to-day operations of the target until the earn-out measurement period is over. In that way, the buyer keeps a management team that is highly incentivized to make the business perform. The seller ensures that the business they are relying on is well managed. The seller will also need to make sure that the buyer is committed to making decisions needed for the business to thrive.

In some cases, when the buyer is in control of the business after closing, a seller will accuse the buyer of managing revenue growth so that it shows up only after the earn-out deadline has passed. For instance, the buyer may invest heavily in the business, but focus on those areas with long-term payouts beyond the earn-out measurement period.[1] To help address these concerns, the seller may require control rights over decisions that impact their ability to meet the earn-out hurdles. These are all highly deal-specific matters that must be dealt with in light of the buyer's actual ability and incentive to drive and manipulate results of the target business.

To address the different incentives of the parties, the buyer is sometimes required by covenant to operate the business during the earn-out period consistent with past practice. In other deals, the buyer is required to run the business to maximize the earn-out. As the owner of the business, the buyer will resist limitations on its ability to adapt operating decisions to changing market conditions.

THE MARKET

Approximately 10 to 20 percent of earn-out deals require the business to be operated consistent with past practice during the earn-out measurement period. Another 10 to 20 percent require the buyer to run the business in such a way as to maximize the earn-out.

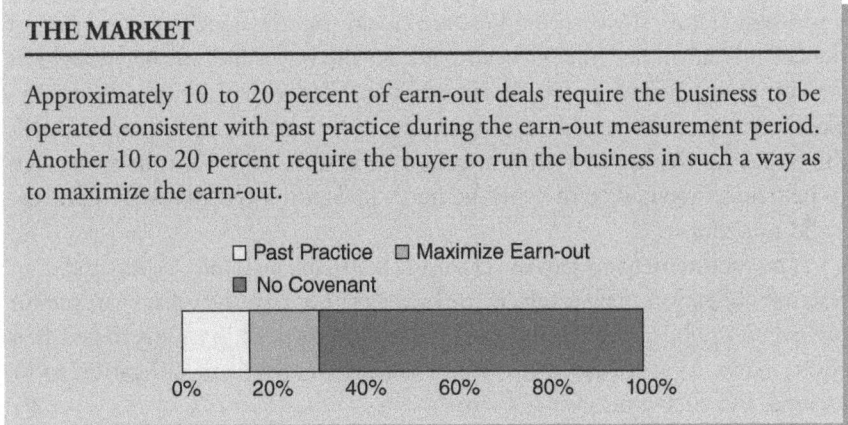

Even if a special covenant by the buyer is not included in the acquisition agreement, many state laws imply a covenant of good faith and fair dealing into contracts. Those may be interpreted to prevent the buyer from "playing games" to manage the business in a way that is designed to impair the earn-out, at least in the most egregious cases.

War Story

A small company found itself in the position of having an extremely hot product and a number of interested buyers. It had the technology, but needed a sales force larger than it could afford.

Believing heavily in the product's future potential, the small company negotiated a deal that promised a rich purchase price if the business was successful, but placed the vast majority of the value in a long-term earn-out.

Shortly after closing, the buyer's existing enterprise began to suffer. Negative publicity and unfavorable economic conditions took their toll. The buyer, strapped for cash and with a negative view of the economy, cut funding for the small company's once highly successful product and put its sales force to work in other areas. The small company's business failed to meet the criteria for the earn-out.

The seller sued, arguing that the buyer was at least required to provide a minimum amount of marketing for the product after closing. The court concluded that the contract did not set out any affirmative obligations for the buyer. Despite the belief that the earn-out was a win-win situation for all parties when the deal was cut, the seller—with no covenant protection to rely on—obtained very little value.

Earn-outs can be thought of as creating a type of joint venture. While the buyer will technically own the business at closing, the contingent portion of the consideration has not yet been paid. So the buyer has, in that sense, not yet completed its full purchase, leaving the seller with a continuing equity-like interest in the business. Consequently, if the buyer turns around and sells the target (or the buyer itself is acquired), the seller will want their earn-out to be paid immediately, to avoid being locked into a venture with a partner it did not choose.

The requirement to pay the earn-out is usually a simple, unsecured contractual obligation. As a result, if the buyer cannot pay, the sellers can sue for the payment obligation. But the sellers have no ownership claims to get their equity back. In some cases, the sellers ask for the payment obligation to be secured, but such a provision is rare.

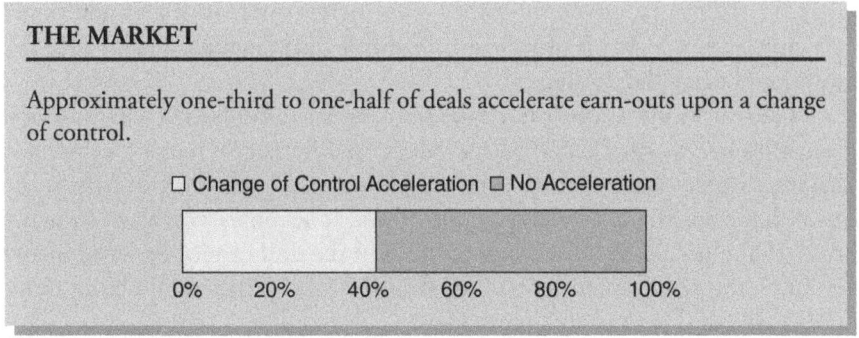

THE MARKET

Approximately one-third to one-half of deals accelerate earn-outs upon a change of control.

Contingent Value Rights

In public company transactions, a purchase price adjustment based on post-closing events is called a "contingent value right" (CVR).[2] A CVR is an instrument delivered at closing to the target's shareholders as part of the consideration. It obligates the buyer to pay additional cash consideration if specified events occur, or if specified financial performance is achieved. As with earn-outs, CVRs represent one-way adjustments—they only increase the purchase price paid. CVRs are rarely used.

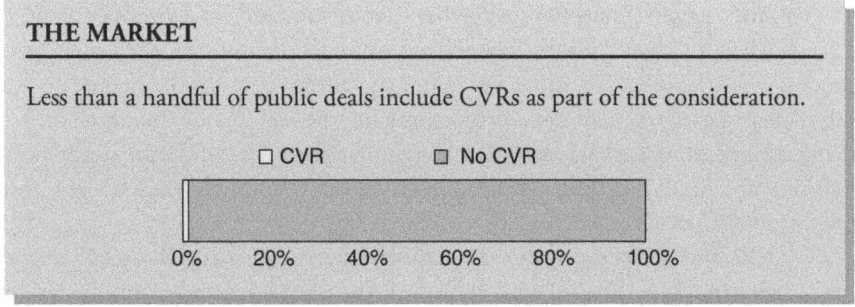

THE MARKET

Less than a handful of public deals include CVRs as part of the consideration.

The CVR is sometimes tradable on the market, so shareholders can sell them and receive current value from other market participants who view them as a good investment. However, if the CVR is a tradable security, its offer and sale to the target's shareholders as part of the deal must be registered under the securities laws. A unique instrument such as a CVR will take time to work through the registration process. If the deal needs additional time to close for regulatory or other reasons, the securities law registration process may be of little consequence (other than incremental work and additional expense). But if a deal is otherwise on the fast track, including a CVR in the mix could delay the timing.

Like earn-outs, CVRs can be used as a means to bridge the gap for tough valuation issues—particularly if the valuation difference is based on each side having to guess as to whether concrete future events will come to pass. If the event happens, the CVR will pay out. If not, it becomes worthless. In many cases the valuation gap is too substantial and the deal cannot be saved in any event. Some practitioners have noted that, once the parties start talking about CVRs, the deal is almost certainly dead.

Occasionally, CVRs have been used for purchase price protection, to ensure that the merger consideration received by target shareholders has a minimum value at a future date. This is a different type of use for a CVR. Such CVRs are not tied to the performance of the target itself, but are tied to the value of the buyer's equity. In other words, if the sellers receive buyer stock as consideration and plan to hold on to the buyer's stock, then the sellers may want to know that the buyer's stock price will remain somewhat stable.

If the value of the buyer's stock collapses shortly after the closing date, then the value received by the sellers will be dissipated. A CVR can be structured to deliver additional value to the sellers in the event that the buyer's stock depreciates in value during a defined period after closing. This kind of price protection is rare, since buyers are usually not comfortable providing a guarantee against market movements that are beyond the buyer's control.

CVRs can have a number of other features. For instance, they may have redemption features, to allow the issuer to redeem at a fixed price or at the market price. They may have protections for the holders in the event of extraordinary transactions, such as change of control puts. These other provisions are similar to features negotiated in other publicly traded debt and equity instruments.

CVRs also suffer from the same adverse incentive issues discussed above for earn-outs. As is the case with earn-outs, the parties have to carefully design the payout metrics to provide clarity and reduce the risk of litigation. When CVRs are used in public company deals, CVR holders usually appoint a representative to participate in reviewing the triggers and managing any disputes that arise.

CVRs can be used creatively. Their complexity is generally seen as a drawback for deal-makers, but their flexibility can make up for that drawback in specific circumstances.

Litigation Endnotes

1. *See Airborne Health, Inc. v. Squid Soap,* 984 A.2d 126 (Del. Ch. 2009) (buyer was not in breach of contract for failing to sell or market a sufficient amount of target's product to merit an earn-out to the seller; it had not acted arbitrarily or in bad faith, but in response to a corporate crisis that threatened its core business). The earn-out provision in *Airborne* tied the earn-out to sales of the target's main product, but imposed no special requirements on the buyer to market the product.
2. In some cases, a post-closing adjustment in a private deal is also referred to as a contingent value right rather than an earn-out.

CHAPTER 6

Representations and Warranties

Form of Representation

The representations and warranties, which in lawyerly jargon are abbreviated to "representations" or simply "reps," describe in detail the legal facts about the business to be acquired. They state and confirm facts regarding the business and its capital structure, as well as the assumptions that are the basis for the buyer's evaluation of the target. Usually, they do not cover forward-looking information, such as the target's projections.

A representation is typically in the form of an affirmative statement of fact. If the seller represents that fact, it is taking the risk that the fact is not true—depending on the exact function of the representations in the transaction, as discussed below. If the seller does not give a particular representation, then (absent another special provision) the buyer is taking the risk of not having protection on that topic, and must rely solely on its due diligence review.

A representation normally takes the form of a flat statement that confirms the absence of problems. This form governs, even if there are problems. For example, a representation may state that there is no pending litigation against the company, when in fact there is. This conflict between reality and the positive form of representations is resolved by the disclosure schedules. A carve-out to the representations allows exceptions to be identified in a separate disclosure schedule (which is discussed in more detail below). In the preceding example, the seller will make the representation in the purchase agreement that there is no pending litigation subject to disclosure set forth on the disclosure schedules; in order to ensure that the representation is correct, the seller will then identify pending litigation on the disclosure schedule.

There are two main reasons for this positive form combined with exceptions on disclosure schedules. First, the disclosure schedules generally do not have to be filed with the Securities and Exchange Commission (SEC) in public company transactions, and this structure allows details of "negative" facts on these schedules—such as litigation or failures to comply with law—to be kept more confidential by the parties. Second, it allows the lawyers to negotiate the scope of the representations (through revisions to the text of the representations), while business specialists draft and revise the details of the disclosure schedules on a parallel basis. The text of the representations is, therefore, generally comparable across transactions, whereas the disclosure schedules are unique to each transaction.

The difference between a representation and a warranty is generally ignored in practice. They are referred to collectively as the "representations." Technically, representations are statements that confirm facts the parties expect to be true, whereas warranties are guarantees that a fact will be true when the party making the representation is not certain (or does not have control) over whether the fact is or will be true.

Case law historically provided different remedies for an innocent breach of a representation, a fraudulent breach of a representation and breach of warranty.[1] In acquisition agreements, the parties negotiate the contractual remedies that are available in their transaction (e.g., the closing conditions and the indemnity), and everything in the representations and warranties section of the agreement is treated as both a representation and a warranty so that all remedies are available for a breach of any of the provisions in that section. In this way, contract negotiations have eliminated the historical, case-law-driven distinction between representations and warranties.

In some deals, there is no indemnity or other provision that specifically governs the remedies for a breach of representations and warranties. This is rare. When it happens, the parties must rely on case law to define their remedies. Absent contractual terms to the contrary, protections for breach generally survive until the statute of limitations expires, there is no numerical cap on damages, the buyer does not have to bear the first loss under a deductible, and there is no prohibition on claiming punitive and special damages (other than the case law limitations that make such claims difficult to win). On the whole, the buyer would be better off relying on underlying contract law. Modern acquisition agreement contracts, though, contain a number of provisions in the indemnity that limit the buyer's remedies and benefit the seller.[2]

When Representations Are Made

Representations relate to specific points in time, such as the pre-signing period. They look at the present and past, but not the future. If there is a gap in time between signing and closing (as there usually is), then the representations may be repeated as of the closing date as well. By covering events as of the closing, the representations can be prospective to that extent rather than merely historical—that is, provide protection for changes that occur and make the representations false between signing and closing.

When the representations are actually made at closing, the remedies potentially available outside of the contract, such as fraud claims (which some courts believe cannot be waived by the contract, as discussed below) that arise under common law or Rule 10b-5 under the Exchange Act,[3] theoretically could be made for breaches as of closing. Sellers may resist making representations as of closing, particularly for breaches that could arise due to events beyond their control. The lead-in language to the representations will specify when the representations and warranties are actually made under the agreement. It will either state that the representations and warranties are made at signing, or that they are made at signing and at closing.

Sample Provision

Except as set forth in the Disclosure Letter, Sellers [jointly and severally] represent and warrant to the Buyer as of the date hereof [and as of the Closing] as follows: [representations follow]

Representations do not cover post-closing facts. They are not used to divide up the risk that facts will change after the closing date, such as facts related to future performance of the business. Instead, risks related to future performance tend to be placed on the buyer, except to the extent that the seller participates in post-closing performance through an earn-out or CVR.

Scope of Seller's or Targets' Representations

The representations made by a seller or target company will cover a broad range of customary matters. These tend to focus on details of legal rather than business diligence, but include aspects of each. The wording of the representations will be quite detailed, and the subject of technical drafting discussions. The main points covered by the representations include the following:

- *Corporate authority.* The seller or the target, as applicable, has corporate authority to sign the acquisition agreement and close the transaction. The acquisition agreement is binding on the seller or the target.
- *Capitalization.* Details of the corporate structure of the target business (including subsidiaries, debt and joint venture interests).
- *No conflicts.* The transaction does not trigger change of control, anti-assignment or other conflicts under the target's business contracts or charter documents. Engaging in the transaction does not violate law, and no regulatory filings are required for closing.
- *Compliance with law.* The business is currently being, and historically has been, operated in compliance with law.
- *Absence of litigation.* There is no pending or threatened litigation.
- *Financial statements.* Specified historical financial statements fairly present the financial condition of the business.
- *No undisclosed liabilities.* There are no contingent or other liabilities of the business, other than those identified in the financial statements or that arise in the ordinary course of business after the date of the last historical financials.
- *Contracts.* Lists of material contracts are identified and categorized. There are no defaults under those contracts.
- *No material adverse effect.* No material adverse effect has occurred since the date of the last audited financials.[4]
- *Environmental liabilities.* The business is in compliance with environmental laws, and not subject to any environmental liabilities.
- *Intellectual property.* Listing of intellectual property (IP) rights (e.g., patents and trademarks). The IP of the business does not infringe the rights of third parties, and is not being infringed upon by any third parties.
- *Employee matters.* Description of labor and union relations and potential liability under employee benefit plans and applicable regulations.
- *Customers and suppliers.* Specified customers and suppliers have not terminated (or threatened to terminate) their business relations with the target.
- *Industry matters.* Specific to matters arising in the industry that the target is engaged in.

To reduce the risk of liability for unexpected breaches, the buyer will generally seek broad representations; a seller will seek the opposite. The primary way to broaden the representations is to expand their content, such as by adding representations on special topics. If a buyer does not receive a particular representation, the courts may conclude that it assumed that risk that it had adequately diligenced the issue and thus did not need protection through the representations.[5]

The target company usually gives the representations that relate to company matters. In private company deals, the sellers themselves give representations that relate to the sellers and their ownership of the target stock. This bifurcation usually does not change who is responsible for breach under the indemnity. Even where the target gives representations, the seller is still responsible for indemnifying the buyer if the target's representations are breached.

The diligence process often guides which types of representations the buyer should ask for. The topics the buyer is motivated to review as a business matter and the concerns the buyer has uncovered in the due diligence process will often be covered in the representations. Nevertheless, the parties frequently negotiate the representations and warranties on the basis of whether a provision is customary or not—rather than based on whether or not it is appropriate for their deal—so the types and scope of representations given across transactions have substantially converged over time. Even the way in which representations are drafted is fairly consistent across industries, sizes of deal, and across law firms.

There is substantial overlap among individual representations. For example, the representations include a general statement that the target business is operating in compliance with law. They may also include specific statements that there are no violations of environmental regulations, that the company's public disclosures comply with disclosure rules under the federal securities laws, and that the company has complied with specific industry regulations. Any violation of these statements would constitute a breach of both the specific representation and the general compliance-with-law representation.

Often, the parties do not recognize these overlaps. In other cases, overlap is intentional, in order to help support the diligence function of the representations. In any event, meaningful overlap means that the buyer can, to some extent, select the representation under which it wishes to bring a claim for any particular underlying problem. This can result in some drafting mistakes. In particular, if a carve out to one representation is necessary because of a particular situation, the target will need to be careful to qualify all of the relevant representations in the disclosure schedules, not just the most directly related ones.

From a due diligence perspective, problems are more likely to be identified if covered by precise representations. The target's business team usually will not have legal training, and may not understand the structural components of acquisition agreements. By pointing out specific types of legal compliance problems that the buyer cares about through detailed and overlapping representations, the buyer focuses the target's internal team on those matters, leading to more detailed disclosures in the schedules.

Some courts have had difficulty interpreting overlap in representations, in part because there is normally no affirmative statement confirming whether or not the representations are intended to be independent of each other. The court may take the view that, in the event of overlap, only the specific representation governs, and not the general representation. This issue arises if the lawyers for the target qualify the specific representation with disclosure of adverse matters, but do not make the same qualifications to the general representations covering the same topic. Some practitioners believe that courts are likely to try to find a way to avoid letting the buyer have the benefit a breach of representation claim in that type of case, because it appears to be a "gotcha" clause.[6]

When the representations are actually made at closing, the remedies potentially available outside of the contract, such as fraud claims (which some courts believe cannot be waived by the contract, as discussed below) that arise under common law or Exchange Act Rule 10b-5,[7] theoretically could be made for breaches as of closing. Sellers may resist making representations as of closing, particularly for breaches that could arise due to events beyond their control.

The lead-in language to the representations will specify when the representations and warranties are actually made under the agreement. It will either state that the representations and warranties are made at signing, or that they are made at signing and at closing.

Sample Provision

Except as set forth in the Disclosure Letter, Sellers [jointly and severally] represent and warrant to the Buyer as of the date hereof [and as of the Closing] as follows: [representations follow]

Buyer's Representations and Warranties

A seller will want the buyer to also make some representations of its own. Even though the seller is not acquiring a business, it is relying on the buyer to perform its covenants and pay the purchase price, so it does have some interests to be protected through representations. For example, the representation that the deal has been properly authorized and is binding should be made by both the sellers and the buyer.

If the buyer is paying part or all of the purchase price in buyer stock, then the buyer will need to give more extensive representations. How extensive those representations are depends primarily on the percentage of buyer's stock that will be issued and whether the buyer is a public company. The buyer may be required to give representations regarding its capital structure, the accuracy of the buyer's filings with the SEC (assuming it is a public company) and its financial statements to give the seller comfort as to the value of the securities it is receiving.

If the buyer is issuing only a small percentage of its stock as consideration and is a public filer with the SEC, the buyer may give only a few additional representations such as representations as to the accuracy of the buyer's SEC filings. The buyer will argue that the sellers should rely on the buyer's public filings with the SEC (which include its financial statements) and its representation that those filings are accurate. If a very significant percentage of the buyer's stock is being issued as consideration—particularly if the buyer is a private company—then the buyer may end up giving representations that are almost as extensive as the target's representations.

In a cash deal, the seller will ask for representations regarding the buyer's source of capital to fund the purchase price. This may take the form of a representation that the buyer has sufficient cash on hand, or the buyer may instead represent the status and availability of committed financing from third-party sources.

Functions of the Representations

The importance of the representations depends not only on how they are written but also on how they are used in the acquisition agreement. Representations play a role in the indemnity (if there is one), in the closing conditions and in the termination rights. These representations generally function in three ways:

- *Before signing.* The process of negotiating the representations supplements the buyer's diligence review.
- *After signing, but before closing.* The buyer may refuse to close the transaction or may terminate the agreement if the representations by the target/sellers are not sufficiently accurate.

- *After closing.* The buyer may make an indemnity claim against the seller (if the agreement has an indemnity) for breaches of representations by the target/sellers.

Due diligence

The representations support the buyer's due diligence review. By asking a seller to make representations regarding business topics, the buyer can elicit valuable information. The seller may explain that it cannot make a representation due to specific facts about the business that the buyer may not have focused on, or because the seller is not confident that it has all the backup information to confirm the accuracy of the representation. In this way, the seller may be prompted to disclose underlying problems or risks.

Negotiating the representations can provide the buyer with information it cannot spot in a document review. For example, the buyer usually cannot find information about violations of law in the data room, which by their nature are likely to be undocumented. Similarly, a review of diligence documents alone will not normally identify errors or questionable positions taken in the target's financial statements. Well-crafted representations will make the seller feel pressure to "come clean" and disclose information up front to the buyer—rather than looking for loopholes and possibly deciding not to disclose sensitive problems.

The process of negotiating the representations can be used to bring the relevant business experts together to discuss diligence concerns. The seller will usually send specific representations around for review by its internal experts responsible for that specialty. For example, the person responsible for IP will review the IP representation; the environmental specialist will review the environmental representation; and so on. The responses by these specialists invite the buyer to ask for further details and enter into a dialog about the problem spots.

Closing conditions and termination rights

The accuracy of the representations determines whether or not the buyer is required to close the transaction. As discussed in the chapter on closing conditions,[8] an acquisition agreement typically gives the buyer the benefit of a condition under which it is not required to close if the representations are not sufficiently true and correct (subject to materiality qualifiers). The buyer's argument is that it has bargained for a business that meets the description in the representations and therefore should not be required to close and pay the agreed purchase price if it is not receiving the business as bargained for. Of course, the seller also has legitimate interests in having some certainty that it will close the deal, and will want to place limits on the buyer's ability to walk away without closing.

Most acquisition agreements include an early termination right that allows the buyer to terminate the deal if the representations are breached. In most cases, this termination right only applies if the breaches are so material that the buyer would not be required to close in any event. If the representations are not true and correct at the level required for the closing condition to be satisfied, then the buyer may terminate early—without having to wait until the condition is tested.

The target often has the benefit of so-called "cure rights" before the buyer is permitted to terminate for breaches of representations. If the seller has not cured the breaches within the agreed timeframe after receiving notice, the buyer is free to go ahead and terminate.

> **THE MARKET**
>
> On the short end, cure rights give the seller 20 to 30 days to cure breaches of the representations after the buyer delivers notice of the breach. On the longer end, the buyer may not be permitted to terminate the agreement unless the breach is incurable by nature or cannot be cured by the so-called "drop-dead" date.

The buyer cannot start a cure period ticking if it is not aware of the breach. Since the target controls the business, the buyer is unlikely to know of a breach. Many acquisition agreements require each party to notify the other of breaches of the representations, but those provisions are difficult to enforce. The target is very reluctant to self-report a potential issue, as that could be seen as an admission that the representations were in fact breached.

The target typically has the benefit of a reciprocal closing condition and early termination right. If the buyer is not giving substantive representations about its business, those provisions are unlikely to be invoked.

Indemnity

If a representation is made that turns out not to be true, then, after the closing, a claim can be made under the indemnity—if there is an indemnity in the acquisition agreement. An indemnity is structured to require the seller to pay the buyer for losses arising from breaches of the representations (subject to a number of exceptions and nuances).[9] As a result, an indemnity renders every detail of the representations and warranties critical, because it can mean the difference between the seller having, or not having, to make post-closing indemnity payments to the buyer. In public company deals, which have no indemnity anyway, and where the target has public disclosure on file with the SEC for the buyer to rely on, the representations are treated as being less critical.

Qualifications to the Representations

The target will want to limit the assurance it gives through the representations by introducing various qualifiers. Adding qualifiers makes it more likely that the bring-down closing condition will be satisfied (i.e., the buyer will be required to close) and that no payment will be required to be made by the sellers under the indemnity.

Representations can be qualified in several ways. For instance, the representation that the target business is and has been in compliance with all applicable laws could be qualified as follows:

> *Materiality/Material adverse effect.* The Business is and has been in compliance in all material respects with all applicable laws. —OR—

The Business is and has been in compliance with all applicable laws, except where the failure to comply does not have and is not reasonably expected to have a material adverse effect.

> *Knowledge.* To the knowledge of the seller, the Business is and has been in compliance with all applicable laws.
> *Disclosure schedules.* Except as set forth in the disclosure schedules, the Business is and has been in compliance with all applicable laws.
> *Time period.* The Business is and since January 1, [insert year], has been in compliance with all applicable laws. —OR—
> As of the date of this Agreement, the Business is in compliance with all applicable laws.
> *Jurisdiction.* The U.S. operations of the Business are and have been in compliance with all applicable laws.
> *Specialty and scope.* The Business is and has been in compliance with all applicable laws that relate to the marketing of its products.
> *Quantification.* The Business is and has been in compliance with all applicable laws, except where the failure to so comply is not reasonably expected to result in aggregate losses or costs in excess of $1 million to bring the business into compliance.

Materiality qualifiers

Materiality is the most frequently used type of qualifier. These qualifiers use the word "material" or the defined term "material adverse effect." They limit the representations based on the importance of the underlying matter.

Materiality qualifiers have the benefit of limiting the representations in a manner that is unlikely to be viewed as arbitrary. They require the parties to interpret and apply them to the specific facts and circumstances that arise. In the context of any particular dispute, it may be difficult for the parties to determine whether or not the matter is sufficiently important. It may be difficult for the buyer to show that an inaccuracy is material, or for a target to show that it is not.

The use of such qualifiers that are difficult to apply precisely to particular circumstances assumes that when differences in viewpoints arise, the parties are capable of negotiating an agreeable resolution to the conflict. It assumes that the parties can negotiate and settle the ambiguity. During the period between signing and closing of a transaction the parties are required to work closely together on a variety of matters, including the receipt of regulatory approvals and third-party consents under contracts. Thus, it may be reasonable to conclude that the parties should have the right mind-set to negotiate and resolve differences in the interpretation of general qualifiers. Since materiality qualifiers are ubiquitous, over time, practitioners develop a good feeling for what they believe would and would not be considered material by the parties. Whether a court or arbitrator would agree is more difficult to predict.

In some cases, materiality is quantified. For instance, the parties could agree that the target has to list all contracts that provided more than $100,000 in revenue to the target during the last fiscal year. More precise qualifiers, however, can yield results that one party or the other believes are inappropriate (or arbitrary) under the circumstances at hand. For example, the immediate costs of revising a business practice to bring it into compliance may be small, but the reputational harm and long-term effects on expected revenue growth may be quite uncertain yet potentially significant. Looked at from different perspectives, the significance of a problem can appear more or less important. If a quantitative qualifier focuses on one aspect of the costs over another, it can generate results that the parties may not anticipate.

Quantitative qualifiers are also somewhat arbitrary in that they produce cliff determinations. If the measure is one dollar over the threshold, a meaningfully different result may follow than if it is one dollar under.

Knowledge qualifiers

Knowledge qualifiers allocate risk between the buyer and seller based on whether an inaccuracy in the representations was known by the seller. By including a knowledge qualifier, the seller can give a representation that there is no problem or liability, but limit this confirmation to issues it knows about. If the seller knew about an inaccuracy and did not disclose it, then the knowledge-qualified representation would be breached. If the inaccuracy was unknown to the seller, then the representation remains true and buyer bears the consequences of the inaccuracy.

A knowledge qualifier generally means that the buyer is required to close despite and cannot sue for surprise problems. Knowledge-qualified representations tend to be matters that the seller legitimately may not know about.

Sellers are normally inclined to disclose (in the disclosure schedules) all inaccuracies in the representations that they are aware of. Assuming that is the case in a transaction, then a knowledge qualifier does not affect the level of disclosure the seller will include in the disclosure schedules. As a result, adding a knowledge qualifier generally should not impair the buyer's diligence process. If anything, adding a knowledge qualifier could as a practical matter result in the seller feeling obligated to disclose all inaccuracies it has knowledge of, including less material details.

Breaches of representations normally arise from issues that are a surprise to the seller because the seller is usually motivated to disclose all problems in practice. In other words, knowledge qualifiers protect you against "lies" but not "surprises." A knowledge qualifier does not protect the buyer if, in fact, the parties are surprised by an existing problem that comes to light after signing, but it does cover the buyer if the seller knows or strongly suspects that there is a problem and hopes the buyer does not pick up on it in diligence.

A knowledge qualifier is also common in the representation that there is no threatened litigation. The idea of threatened litigation is quite broad—and sellers say too vague. One way to tighten it up is to limit the representation to litigation that has been threatened in writing to the target. However, this formulation would not pick up litigation that was clearly threatened but not in writing (e.g., in a meeting). Another way to tighten up the formulation is to limit the representation to threatened litigation about which the seller has knowledge (whether in writing or not). This solution is commonplace.

If the buyer takes risk by accepting a knowledge qualifier, it typically does so for purposes of both the closing condition and the indemnity. Conceptually, however, those two results need not be tied together. For example, it would be possible for the buyer to take the risk of an unexpected environmental liability arising at a distant time after closing, but preserve the right not to close if that liability arises before closing (in which case, the buyer would have leverage to negotiate an appropriate purchase price reduction)

Testing knowledge qualifiers

The date on which knowledge is tested is important. The test date for the seller's knowledge is determined by a combination of when the representation is made, when the representation is "brought down" in the closing condition (and, possibly, the indemnity), and whether the definition of "knowledge" limits it to knowledge on the signing date.

For instance, a representation may state that, to the knowledge of the seller, the target business is in compliance with all applicable laws. At the date of signing, the seller may know of no violations, in which case the representation is accurate. Between signing and closing, the seller may have learned of historical violations of law. Is the seller responsible for violations it learns about after signing but before closing on the theory that it had knowledge of those violations at closing?

The definition of "knowledge" itself may specify that only knowledge of the seller at signing counts against the seller for purposes of the knowledge qualifier. (Or, more commonly, it may be silent on this issue, which creates some ambiguity.)

Sample Provision

"Knowledge of the Target" means the actual [or constructive] knowledge [as of the date of this Agreement] of any [director or officer of the Target or any other] persons listed on Section __ of the Disclosure Schedules, after [reasonable] [due] inquiry.

If the seller learns of a breach of the representation between signing and closing, it does not change the fact that the seller had no knowledge of the breach at signing. In that case, the seller continues to benefit from the knowledge qualification because only knowledge at signing counts. Thus, the buyer still has the risk, must close over the problem, and cannot sue under the indemnity for the related losses.

Occasionally, knowledge of the seller is tested as of signing and closing. (This may be the result if the knowledge definition does not specify the knowledge date and the representations are made or tested at signing and closing.) The parties may intend this result if they believe the buyer should only take the risk of unknown problems if the seller remains unaware of those problems at closing. If the seller learns of a breach of the representations between signing and closing, then the seller has knowledge of the breach at closing, so the qualification does not help the seller. As a result, the buyer may decline to close, or may close and then sue under the indemnity for that breach if it is sufficiently material.

When knowledge is tested can differ for the closing condition and the indemnity. In many cases, knowledge is tested only at signing for purposes of the indemnity, even if it is tested at both signing and closing for purposes of the closing condition. In this case, problems the seller becomes aware of between signing and closing would allow the buyer not to close (if sufficiently material), but if the buyer decides to close despite those problems, the buyer cannot then immediately sue under the indemnity.

Knowledge persons

The definition of the term "knowledge" clarifies that only the knowledge of specific personnel of the target counts. For instance, the knowledge definition may identify the top five officers of the target, or may generally refer cover the knowledge of all officers.

Whose knowledge should count depends in part on which representations contain knowledge qualifiers. If the financial statement representation uses a knowledge qualifier, then it makes sense for a financial officer of the target to be included as a knowledge person. If the IP representation includes a knowledge qualifier, then the officer responsible for IP should be included.

In many deals, key employees will continue to work for the target after closing. If those key employees are named as the knowledge persons, each party may be concerned about those employees' incentives in the event of a dispute. The buyer will worry that key employees will resist admitting that they had knowledge of a problem, since it could make them appear less than honest to their new owner for not disclosing the problem during the due diligence process. The sellers will worry that the same key employees will cater to their new shareholders by claiming that they had knowledge—in order to support the buyer's indemnity claim—even if their actual knowledge at the time was sketchy.

Actual and constructive knowledge

The knowledge definition may make the seller responsible only for the actual knowledge of specified knowledge persons, or may impute constructive knowledge to individuals who should have known the facts in issue, or would have known those facts if they had looked more closely into the matter.

A common seller-friendly approach is to use an actual knowledge definition, with no duty to investigate. A common buyer-friendly approach is for knowledge to be imputed, so that the definition includes actual knowledge of the specified knowledge persons "after due inquiry." If a proper inquiry were conducted, then actual knowledge is the appropriate standard. If the knowledge person did not conduct a due inquiry into the accuracy of the representation, most practitioners interpret this language to impute knowledge to the target that would have been obtained had a due inquiry been conducted.

THE MARKET

Approximately 70 to 85 percent of deals use an imputed knowledge standard (e.g., requires reasonable or due inquiry). Approximately 15 to 25 percent use an actual knowledge standard. Occasionally, knowledge is not defined.

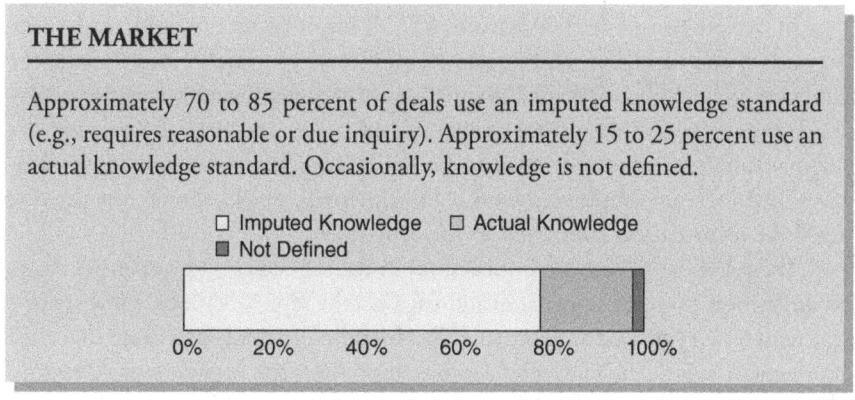

In some cases, the seller wants clarity as to what "due inquiry" requires in practice, so as to avoid ambiguity. A common approach is to stipulate that it requires inquiry of the direct reports to the specified knowledge persons. In buyer-friendly approaches, it may be defined to include inquiry of direct reports but not be limited to direct reports. If inquiry of particular individuals is included, the seller may need to make those individuals aware of the transaction.

In some deals, sellers obtain so-called "backup certificates" from the individuals who are included in the knowledge definition and of whom the seller is required to make inquiry. Those employees would typically sign a simple certificate, in which they confirm that they are not aware of any breaches of the relevant representations. These employees do not usually take on liability to the buyer or the seller, but the act of having to sign a certificate motivates them to study the representations and schedules to ensure that there are no inaccuracies.

Disclosure schedules

The representations are qualified by the disclosure schedules. These are essentially a long list of all of the facts that the seller knows would make its representations untrue if they were not disclosed in a way that qualifies the representations. For example, a representation may state on its face that the seller has no environmental liabilities, other than as set forth in the schedules. The schedule will then identify any of those types of liabilities that it knows about.

Adverse facts are identified in the disclosure schedules, rather than in the text of the representations, in order to help keep them confidential. In transactions with public companies, contracts for material acquisitions have to be publicly filed with the SEC. Those filing requirements, however, have an exception for schedules and exhibits.[10]

In private company transactions, SEC filing rules do not apply unless the buyer is public and the transaction is sufficiently material. Nevertheless, the practice of locating sensitive information in the disclosure schedules is also used in private deals. This is partially out of habit, and partially because the acquisition agreement will need to be made available to various representatives and internal employees whom management would rather not provide sensitive information contained in the schedules.

The seller has to disclose information in the schedules with some specificity in order for it to count as a qualification against the representations. How specific is a matter of negotiation. A broad, seller-friendly provision may state that each representation is qualified by all the information the buyer knows or could reasonably infer from a review of the disclosure schedules. A more typical standard is for disclosure in one section of the schedules to qualify other sections if it is reasonably or readily apparent on its face that it should also qualify the other schedules.

Sample Provision

The disclosure of any matter in any section or subsection of the Disclosure Schedule shall be deemed to be a disclosure for all purposes of this Agreement with respect to any other section or subsection [to which the relevance of such item is [reasonably] [readily] apparent from the text of such disclosure].

In rare cases, the seller will propose that the representations be qualified by all of the information in the electronic data room. A buyer-friendly provision may state that any particular representation is qualified only by information that is readily apparent from the text of the disclosure.

War Story ———

The target was cleaning house following an internal legal investigation that found it to have been operating in violation of law. It fully disclosed the problem to the buyer. The buyer already knew it was acquiring the target as a troubled company on the cheap, and expected to spend money to revive the business before it would turn profitable.

Anticipating further expenses and possibly even a financial restatement in the wake of the legal investigation, the target instructed its lawyers to make sure those events would not present any problems under the representations. The lawyers dutifully made full disclosure of the issue in the schedules that qualified the compliance with law representation.

Shortly before closing, the buyer got cold feet and wanted to walk from the deal. Since the buyer could not reasonably claim a material adverse effect (MAE) had occurred, and did not have the right to pay a fee to simply walk away, it sent its lawyers to look for other exits.

As reasons to walk from the deal, the buyer ended up citing exactly the events that the target meticulously disclosed: namely, the costs of bringing the company back into compliance, and a financial restatement from having improperly recorded revenue it was now required to return to customers.

The target was shocked. From the target's perspective, things were no worse than expected. It had put the buyer on notice and accepted a cheap price for exactly this reason. What had gone wrong?

The target's lawyers had to acknowledge that, while they had qualified the most obvious compliance with law representation, they had not actually qualified other representations that were equally called into question. For instance, the no-undisclosed-liabilities representation and financial statements representation were, on their face, unqualified.

In frustration over the fact that they were dealing with the risk of deal failure despite having tried to protect themselves against it, the target gave the buyer another price reduction, and then closed the deal. The issue was never tested in court.

———

In some cases, courts have weighed in on whether to apply disclosure against one representation to other representations. The buyer is put in a difficult position because, by definition, it had knowledge of the issue at hand. The buyer will usually argue that it bargained for protection despite its knowledge. The seller will often argue the buyer knew about the problem so must have already factored it into the purchase price. As a matter of good practice, if the buyer expects to be protected from problems it knows about, then the buyer should make that explicit, perhaps by using a special indemnity.[11]

If the target company is a public company, it will want to qualify the representations and warranties by all the information included in its public filings with the SEC. SEC filings include "risk factor" disclosure, such as general cautionary statements regarding a wide variety of potential problems that could cause economic harm to the target business. The buyer will want to avoid qualifying the representations and warranties by such broad risk factor disclosure, to prevent the seller from arguing that anything it warned of in the risk factors cannot be the subject of a claim for breach of representations and warranties.

Sample Provision

Except as set forth in the Company's SEC filings (other than any disclosures contained under the captions "Risk Factors" or "Forward-Looking Statements" or any other disclosures included therein to the extent that they are forward-looking in nature) filed with the SEC on or after __ and prior to the date of this Agreement, the Company hereby represents and warrants [...].

The buyer will want to limit the carve-out to historical SEC filings, so that only those that were filed prior to the signing (or a day or two prior to signing), rather than all SEC filings up to closing, count as qualifications to the representations. If SEC filings made after signing qualified the representations, then all adverse disclosures in future filings would count against the buyer—even though the buyer was not aware of those disclosures prior to committing itself to the deal. If post-signing disclosures could qualify the representations, then the target could cure any breach of representations by simply filing an updated disclosure statement with the SEC that described the problem. The buyer may also want to limit their carve-outs to recent SEC filings (e.g., last couple of years), rather than being responsible for all historical disclosure.

Sometimes, sellers will propose to include risk factor language from other contexts in the disclosure schedules. For instance, the seller may propose to incorporate by reference an environmental diligence report confirming that only limited contamination was found at a particular site. The report may nevertheless contain disclaimers, noting that despite the testing that was done, exposure could still lie undetected at the site. The buyer will usually want to exclude this type of qualification, and only take risk on the specifically identified problems. The seller in contrast will want to know that the representations will not be breached, even if potential additional liabilities were to be discovered in the future.

Disclosure schedules are not immune from discovery in unrelated litigation. This can create a conflict between the buyer and seller as to how much disclosure should be provided in relation to potential breaches of contracts or violations of law. Take, for instance, a situation in which the target company is operating in a "grey zone" that is customary in the industry but not free from doubt due to vagueness in the law. To ensure that the sellers cannot be sued under the indemnity, the sellers may want to overdisclose the potential risk that they could be found at a later date to be in violation of law. The buyer, in contrast, will not want a later regulatory probe or litigation to uncover any statements that suggest the target was not in compliance, or that buyer knew that the business practices may not be in compliance. The cover page to the schedules will usually clarify that the target is not making any admissions by virtue of the disclosure.

Timing qualifiers

Timing qualifiers limit the representations by reference to the date that specific events occurred. Most often this qualifier is used in the form of a "look-back" period. The look-back period is the length of time covered by the qualified representation prior to the signing. For example, the target company may give a representation that it has been in compliance with particular laws for the preceding two years, or since January 1 of a particular year.

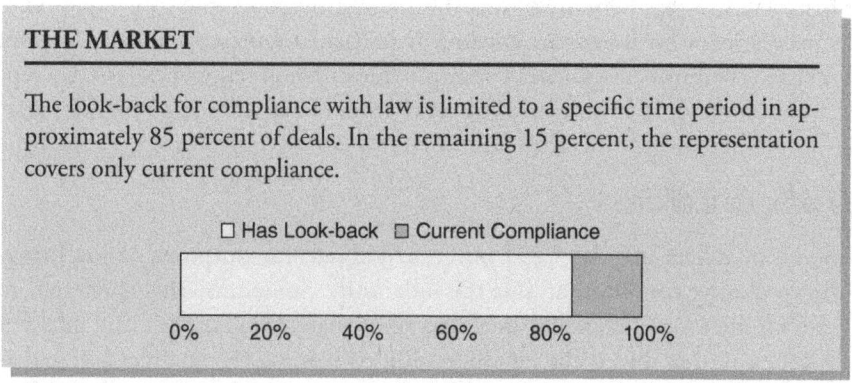

THE MARKET

The look-back for compliance with law is limited to a specific time period in approximately 85 percent of deals. In the remaining 15 percent, the representation covers only current compliance.

☐ Has Look-back ☐ Current Compliance

0%   20%   40%   60%   80%   100%

The buyer may resist inclusion of any look-back period, since it would result in the buyer taking the risk for all adverse matters that occurred prior to the look-back date.

THE MARKET

Look-back periods frequently range from two to five years. In public company deals, the look-back for compliance with law is often between two and three years. Normally in those cases, the look-back goes to the beginning of the fiscal year that started between two and three years prior to the signing date.

Sometimes, a seller will introduce a look-back period simply to limit its liability for potential breaches of representations. Sometimes, the look-back period will be tied to specific events, such as the date that a significant reorganization or acquisition occurred, or a change in management. In some cases, the parties will set the look-back date to be equal to the date that the relevant statute of limitations for previous matters would have expired.

Even if one representation is limited by a look-back period, historical problems may still breach another representation. For instance, if the compliance with law representation has a three-year look-back, a violation that occurred four years earlier could still result in liability to the target that could breach the no-undisclosed-liabilities representation.

Other qualifiers

Others qualifiers are used infrequently, but could be relevant in any particular circumstances. These qualifiers can be in any form that the parties design. For instance, the representations may be limited by geography (i.e., only U.S. subsidiaries or businesses are covered by particular representations). Different divisions within a conglomerate may provide different representations. Or representations could be limited to specific types of activities (e.g., marketing).

Reading out qualifiers

Some qualifiers may be "read out," or ignored, for purposes of the bring-down closing condition and/or the indemnity. Sometimes this is referred to as scraping away materiality qualifiers or a "materiality scrape." If a qualifier is read out, that means the representation containing the qualifier is tested as if it were written without the qualifier. For example, if "materiality" qualifiers are read out, then a representation stating that there are no material undisclosed liabilities would be treated as if it were a statement that there are no undisclosed liabilities at all (whether or not material).

To accomplish this, the reader must basically duplicate the body of the representations, then go through and edit line by line each representation to remove the words "material," "material adverse effect," and similar words.[12] Although it is not explicitly stated in the drafting, in most cases related phrases and grammar must be edited so that the representation makes sense after each deletion. This new (hypothetical) set of representations is treated as the actual representations for special purposes, such as determining whether the closing condition is satisfied.

Qualifiers written into the text of the representations are not ignored when the representations are actually made. However, they may be ignored for purposes of the bring-down closing condition and indemnity.

There are three primary ways in which the representations apply in an acquisition agreement. By selectively reading out materiality qualifiers, the representations can be made to function differently in each of those three contexts. First, the representations are actually made on the signing date (and, sometimes, also the closing date). Second, at closing they are tested as part of the bring-down closing condition as of the signing date (and, usually, on the closing date). Third, after the closing, they are tested as part of the indemnity (if there is one) for their accuracy as of the signing date (and, usually, as of the closing date).

Reading out for bring-down purposes

Materiality qualifiers are frequently read out of the representations for purposes of the bring-down closing condition. The bring-down closing condition may state that the representations must be true and correct "without regard to any qualifications therein as to materiality or material adverse effect." If materiality is read out of the representations for purposes of the bring-down, then a materiality qualifier in the text of a representation will have no effect on whether the closing condition is satisfied.

After removing materiality qualifiers from the text of the representations, the bring-down condition may then apply its own aggregate materiality concept. The bring-down condition may reintroduce the aggregate materiality concept in the text of the bring-down, requiring the representations and warranties to be true and correct, ignoring materiality qualifiers in the representations, "except for such inaccuracies that do not and would not reasonably be expected to have, individually or in the aggregate, a material adverse effect." In that case, while the representations are tested as if they were all made on a flat basis without materiality qualifiers, the breaches of those (hypothetical) representations must, in the aggregate, reasonably be expected to have a material adverse effect before the closing condition would be triggered.

Sample Provision

Each of the representations and warranties of the Sellers contained in this Agreement, other than the Fundamental Representations, shall be true and correct in all respects (without giving effect to any limitation as to "materiality" or any derivative thereof qualification set forth therein) as of the date hereof and as of the Closing Date as though made on the Closing Date [(except for such representations and warranties that are by their terms expressly limited to a specific date, which shall speak only as of such date and without giving effect to such limitations and qualifications)], except for any failures to be so true and correct that, individually or in the aggregate, have not had or would not have a material adverse effect.

Reading out for indemnity purposes

Materiality qualifiers are also frequently ignored for purposes of the indemnity. An indemnity provision may provide that, for purposes of determining whether a representation is true and correct in the context of an indemnity claim, all materiality qualifiers in the text of the representations will be ignored. For instance, the representations may state that the target business has been operated in accordance with law "in all material respects." If materiality is read out of the indemnity, however, the seller will be required to make indemnity payments to the buyer if it turns out that the business was not conducted in accordance with law "in all respects."

Reading out materiality for purposes of the indemnity may initially appear stringent, but the indemnity may have other ways of giving the seller the benefit of other, quantitative materiality qualifiers. These include using de minimis claim exceptions and deductibles. These types of provisions specify fixed dollar amounts that do not have to be paid under the indemnity.[13]

In some deals, materiality qualifiers may be retained for purposes of testing whether a representation was breached under the indemnity. But if breached (in its actual qualified form), the materiality qualifiers are ignored when determining the amount of damage arising from that breach.

It is unusual (though not unheard of) to read out the content of the disclosure schedules and other types of qualifiers from the bring-down closing condition or indemnity. Knowledge qualifiers are occasionally, but rarely, read out of the indemnity, and are not read out of the bring-down closing condition.

Drafting pitfalls

Pitfalls often lie in the way of drafting read-outs. In many acquisition agreements, the materiality qualifiers are read out in a way that, if applied mechanically, could have the opposite result of what was intended.

Consider the following representation: Seller's business has been operated in all material respects in compliance with applicable law. If the parties read out materiality, the representation still makes sense: Seller's business has been operated in all respects in compliance with applicable law. As intended, it has become a statement of absolute compliance.

However, consider a provision that is written in the reverse: Seller's business has been operated in compliance with applicable law, except for breaches by its non-U.S. subsidiaries that are not material. If all references to materiality are ignored, the sentence could be read as: Seller's business has been operated in compliance with applicable law, except for breaches by its non-U.S. subsidiaries. Does that mean all (rather than just immaterial) breaches by foreign subsidiaries are excluded from the representation? The intent, presumably, is to ignore the whole exception for non-U.S. subsidiaries starting with the word "except," but that is not what the read-out mechanic actually says to do.

Another common example shows up in the representation that the financial statements present fairly the financial condition of the target, subject to year-end adjustments that are not material. By reading out the reference to the materiality qualifier, this representation on its face then permits and is subject to any and all year-end adjustments, no matter how material. This would give more flexibility to the target company, even though the intent of the read-out provision is probably the opposite—to make the target company or sellers strictly liable for any adjustments.

Protective provisions

Representations cover only a subset of the information a buyer receives as part of its due diligence process. That diligence process will include oral statements from the sellers as well as projections from the target management of how the business is expected to perform in the future.

Normally, the parties agrees that the representations article in the acquisition agreement contains all the representations to be given in the deal. Additional diligence, oral statements and projections do not constitute representations. The "integration" clause that forms part of the boilerplate in the acquisition agreement confirms that there are no side deals (such as an agreement to provide additional representations) outside the four corners of the contract.

Nevertheless, fraud claims—even for statements that were not part of the representations—are difficult to contract away from. These could arise in the context of the sale of a business if, for instance, the seller were to deliberately make statements about the business that it knows to be false in order to induce the buyer to acquire the business or to acquire it for an inflated price.[14] While actual fraud is quite rare, sellers may worry that actions which fall short of fraud could become the subject of a fraud claim (which may have settlement value, even if not sustainable as a fraud claim). Sellers may be concerned that the buyer could bring a claim that the sellers' projections for the business were fraudulent if circumstances change and the projections proved to be wrong.

Some courts have not permitted the parties to waive fraud claims on the theory that the parties cannot contract around securities law duties, even in private transfers of securities such as an M&A stock sale. Some courts have made it difficult by concluding that specific nonreliance clauses are necessary—otherwise, the integration clause alone would not relieve a party from fraud claims based on extra-contractual statements.[15]

Rather than directly challenging case law by including a waiver of any potential fraud claims, practice has instead developed techniques to cut out one of the basic elements of fraud claims: reliance.[16]

Sample Provision

Except for the representations and warranties contained in this Article __, neither Sellers nor any other Person have made any, and the Buyer has not relied on any, other express or implied representation or warranty by or on behalf of Sellers.

Most protective provisions take the form of a representation or acknowledgement by the other party, confirming that no representations outside of the contract have been given. Some also include a statement that the other party has not relied on any representations outside of the contract. Some courts, however, have taken the position that reliance cannot be disclaimed if the buyer is suing under a fraud claim based on Exchange Act Rule10b-5.[17]

THE MARKET

Approximately one-half of deals include either a statement that there are no other representations or nonreliance language.

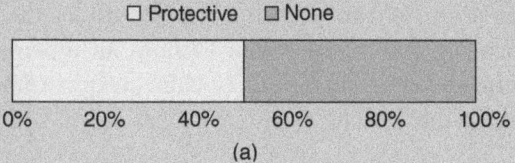

(a)

Of those with protective provisions: roughly three-quarters have a no-other-representations clause; roughly one-quarter have both nonreliance language and a no-other-representations clause. A small handful of deals have only nonreliance language.

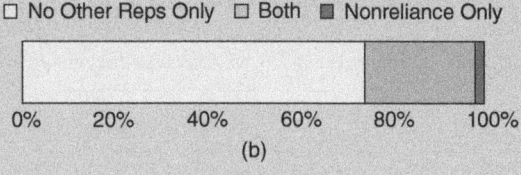

(b)

Obligation to Update Representations

Most acquisition agreements require the target to inform the buyer if it discovers that any have been breached. This obligation covers information required to have been disclosed at signing, and picks up any information that would breach the representations if they were brought down to that date.

THE MARKET

Approximately 90 percent of deals include a covenant to disclose a breach of the representations.

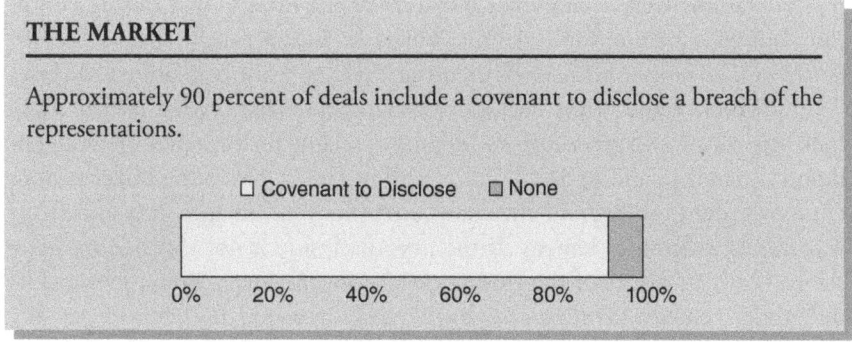

In most cases, disclosure under the covenant to tell the buyer about a breach of representations does not affect the buyer's rights under the indemnity. In the few cases where it does, it normally operates through an update to the disclosure schedules, in which the buyer is basically given the choice of either terminating the acquisition agreement under an existing early termination right (or refusing to close under the related closing condition) or closing over the problem without an indemnity. The buyer does not have the choice in such deals to close and then immediately turn around and sue for the breach.

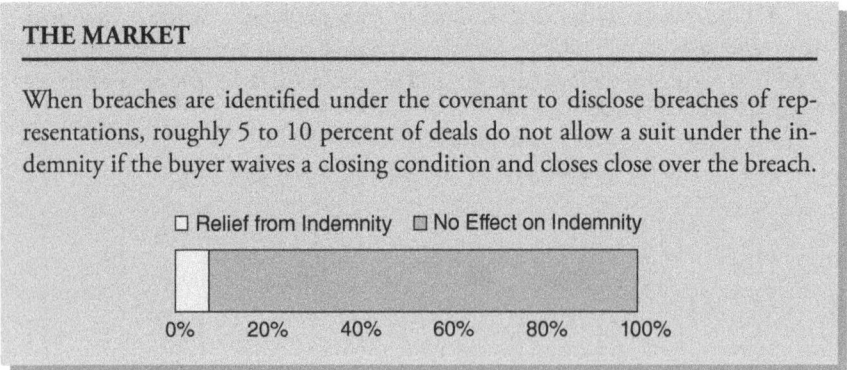

THE MARKET

When breaches are identified under the covenant to disclose breaches of representations, roughly 5 to 10 percent of deals do not allow a suit under the indemnity if the buyer waives a closing condition and closes close over the breach.

☐ Relief from Indemnity   ☐ No Effect on Indemnity

0%   20%   40%   60%   80%   100%

In some transactions, the sellers negotiate the right to update the disclosure schedules between signing and closing. The seller will disclose all known problems in the schedules prior to signing, and any problems that arise or are discovered between signing and closing will be included in updated disclosure schedules.

In most cases in which the seller has the right to update the disclosure schedules, the updated disclosure only counts when determining whether representations were accurate for purposes of the bring-down closing condition, but do not count for indemnity purposes. In those deals, if the seller discloses new adverse information, then the buyer will not be required to close.

However, if the buyer decides to close despite the revised information, then the buyer will have lost its indemnity claim for breaches of representations related to the updated adverse information. Since the buyer cannot close over the problem and then sue to recover for damages, it is effectively waiving its indemnity remedy. If the new disclosure is not sufficiently material to result in failure of the closing condition, the buyer would preserve its indemnity remedy in most cases (otherwise, it would be left without any remedy for the breach).

Litigation Endnotes

1. Claims for a breach of a representation were based on tort law and the remedies were damages calculated to put the parties back to their pre-contract positions and rescission. The remedy for innocent misrepresentations was limited to rescission. Claims for a breach of warranty were based on contract law and the remedies were damages calculated to put the plaintiff it in position it would have been in but for the breach. *See, e.g., Sycamore Bidco Ltd v. Breslin & Anor.,* [2012] EWHC 3443 (Ch) (where buyer in a stock purchase agreement sued for breach of warranty, and in the alternative a claim of misrepresentation, English High Court determined that there was a breach of warranty with damages of £6 million as opposed to a breach of representation, which may have resulted in damages of £16.75 million, which was the purchase price under the stock purchase agreement).

2. *See* Chapter 14, "Indemnities" (discussing relevant indemnity provisions in modern acquisition agreements).

3. 17 C.F.R. § 240.10b-5.

4. *See* Chapter 10, "Material Adverse Effect."

5. *See, e.g., Airborne Health, Inc. v. Squid Soap LP,* No. 4410-VCL, 2010 BL 170208 (Del. Ch. July 20, 2010) (holding that the relevant litigation representation in the acquisition agreement was too narrow to allow for recovery). As part of a dispute over the buyer's failure to achieve sales that would merit an earn-out for the seller, seller claimed that buyer had committed fraud by failing to disclose pending litigation that significantly interfered with the buyer's business. The buyer only promised the seller that there was no litigation that would prevent it from signing the acquisition agreement. The court held that, "[b]y not bargaining for a broader representation, [seller] assumed the risk that its due diligence into litigation might be inadequate. The limited litigation representation did not give rise to an affirmative duty to speak." *Id.* at *10.

6. *See In re IBP, Inc. S'holders Litig. (IBP, Inc. v. Tyson Foods),* 789 A.2d 14 (Del. Ch. 2001) (involving a buyer that sought to terminate a merger agreement, claiming, among other things, that there was a breach of representations and warranties by the target relating to accounting irregularities and restatement of financials at a division of the target). The *IBP* court found that there was no breach of representations and warranties because the buyer learned of the accounting irregularities during the negotiations, the target had included an open-ended exception in the disclosure schedule relating to one of the relevant representations and warranties and the disclosure schedule explicitly stated that an exception to one representation and warranty was deemed to be taken for all relevant representations and warranties. *Id.* at 55–60.

7. 17 C.F.R. § 240.10b-5.

8. *See* Chapter 8, "Closing Conditions."

9. *See* Chapter 14, "Indemnities."

10. Item 601 of Regulation S-K allows for schedules to plans of acquisition, re-organization, arrangement liquidation or succession to be excluded from the filing, unless such schedules "contain information which is material to an investment decision and which is not otherwise disclosed" in the filing. *See* 17 C.F.R. § 229.601(b)(2). While Item 601 typically excuses the filing of the disclosure schedules, the company will of course have to make a determination that the schedules do not contain information material to an investment decision that has not otherwise been disclosed.

11. *See, e.g., In re IBP, Inc. S'holders Litig. (IBP, Inc. v. Tyson Foods)*, 789 A.2d 14, 60 (Del. Ch. 2001). In the *IBP* case, the buyer agreed that any disclosures under the disclosure schedules would apply not only to the representation and warranty under which they were listed on the disclosure schedules, but also to any other representation and warranty that the disclosure was relevant to. When it became clear, between signing and closing, that the target was in significantly more financial trouble than was originally thought, the buyer proposed to terminate the deal, asserting breach of a representation that was not explicitly qualified by the financial trouble disclosures in the schedules. The target sued to force the buyer to complete the acquisition. The court focused on the fact that the matter had been disclosed against a separate representation and agreed with the target. *Id.* at 60 ("Put differently, [buyer] argues that it came out of a hotly contested auction with an option, rather than an obligation, to purchase [target], having silently pocketed an almost sure walk-away right.").

12. *See, generally,* Chapter 10, "Material Adverse Effect."

13. *See* Chapter 14, "Indemnities."

14. *See DCV Holdings, Inc. v. Conagra, Inc.,* 889 A.2d 954, 958 (Del. 2005) (finding that, to prevail on a claim of fraud, the plaintiff would have to show that (1) the defendant falsely represented or omitted facts that the defendant had a duty to disclose; (2) the defendant knew or believed that the representation was false or made the representation with a reckless disregard for the truth; (3) the defendant intended to induce the plaintiff to act or refrain from acting; (4) the plaintiff acted in justifiable reliance on the representation; and (5) the plaintiff was injured by the reliance).

15. *See ABRY Partners V, LP v. F&W Acquisition LLC,* 891 A.2d 1032 (Del. Ch. 2006). The buyer entered into a nonreliance agreement stating that it was not relying on any representations and warranties not included in the purchase agreement, such as information obtained in pre-signing discussions, the data room and management presentations. Nevertheless, the Delaware Supreme Court held that if the buyer could prove that the seller lied during the course of negotiations, it could collect damages in excess of an indemnification cap, or even unwind the transaction. The court explained that—this court consistently has respected the law's traditional abhorrence of fraud in implementing this reasoning. Because of that policy concern, we have not given effect to so-called merger or integration clauses that do not clearly state that the

parties disclaim reliance upon extra-contractual statements. Instead, we have held … that murky integration clauses, or standard integration clauses without explicit anti-reliance representations, will not relieve a party of its oral and extra-contractual fraudulent representations. The integration clause must contain "language that … can be said to add up to a clear anti-reliance clause by which the plaintiff has contractually promised that it did not rely upon statements outside the contract's four corners in deciding to sign the contract." *Id.* at 1058–59 (internal citations omitted).

16. *See, e.g., RAA Mgmt., LLC v. Savage Sports Holdings, Inc.,* 45 A.3d 107 (Del. 2012). The would-be buyer signed a confidentiality agreement, expressly disclaiming reliance on extra-contractual representations and any warranty as to the accuracy or completeness of such representations. After spending $1.2 million on due diligence, the potential buyer discovered a series of material liabilities pending against the target, and sued to recover the costs, alleging that had target disclosed the material liabilities at the outset, potential buyer would not have incurred such costs. The court held that the reliance disclaimer in the confidentiality agreement was valid, and barred recovery. *But see TransDigm Inc. v. Alcoa Global Fasteners, Inc.,* No. 7135-VCP, 2013 BL 141248 (Del. Ch. May 29, 2013). In *TransDigm,* a seller omitted to inform the buyer of a major customer potentially dropping 50 percent of its business with the target and the target's having offered that customer a 5 percent discount, effective after consummation of the acquisition agreement. The court acknowledged that the acquisition agreement had an effective provision barring the buyer from relying on extra-contractual representations, but it found that the agreement had no provision disclaiming reliance on extra-contractual omissions, and as a result, the seller was potentially liable for its omissions. *Id.* at *9–10.

17. *See AES Corp. v. Dow Chem. Co.,* 325 F.3d 174 (3d Cir. 2003), *cert. denied,* 540 U.S. 1068 (2003). Following the acquisition of a company, the buyer in the *AES* case discovered that the extra-contractual information made available by the seller relating to the value of the target company (including a confidential offering memorandum) was false and led buyer to believe the target was more valuable than it actually was. Buyer had previously signed a confidentiality agreement and later signed an acquisition agreement disclaiming reliance on information outside of such acquisition agreement. Buyer sued seller under Rule 10b-5 of the Exchange Act, alleging that seller had misrepresented the value of the target company in the financial projections made available. *See* 17 C.F.R. § 240.10b-5. The Third Circuit agreed that reliance could not be disclaimed, and that reliance is an essential element of a Rule 10b-5 claim. It necessarily follows that, if a party commits itself never to claim that it relied on representations of the other party to its contract, it purports anticipatorily to waive any future claim based on the fraudulent misrepresentations of that party. The same is true if the commitment is more limited, for example, a promise not to claim

reliance on any representation not set forth in the agreement. The scope of the anticipatory waiver is more limited, but it is nevertheless an anticipatory waiver of potential future claims under Rule 10b-5. 325 F.3d at 180. Thus, although the court was unwilling to allow the parties to contract a blanket immunity from Rule 10b-5 fraud liability, the court *was* willing to allow such a contract to shift the burden of proof further onto the buyer than would otherwise have been the case.

CHAPTER 7

Covenants

Covenants in M&A Negotiations

Covenants are a collection of agreements between the parties to take or refrain from taking specific actions during—and in some cases after—the acquisition process.

The operating covenants govern the operation of the target's business between signing and closing. The so-called "get the deal done" covenant, which is also referred to as the efforts covenant, obligates the parties to use their efforts to satisfy the closing conditions and to take actions designed to support bringing the deal to closing. An acquisition agreement may also include any number of other specific covenants relevant to the transaction, such as a noncompete obligation by the seller, post-closing confidentiality arrangements, a restriction on the seller hiring or soliciting employees of the target business, or procedures to regulate the process for antitrust and other regulatory approvals.

Some covenants apply only between signing and closing, such as the operating covenants and the covenant to use efforts to satisfy the closing conditions. Other covenants are designed to apply only after closing, such as a restriction on the seller competing with the business it just sold in the transaction.

Operating Covenants

The operating covenants balance the interests of the buyer and the seller in controlling how the business is run during the period between signing and closing. On the one hand, the buyer has committed itself to acquire the target,

117

as long as the closing conditions are satisfied. The buyer wants to ensure that the business is appropriately managed until the buyer obtains control. On the other hand, the seller still owns the business and has an interest in managing it to ensure that the closing conditions are satisfied. The buyer has not yet paid the purchase price, so the seller does not want to cede control to the buyer without certainty that the closing will actually occur.

The operating covenants require the seller to operate the business in the ordinary course between signing and closing. This prevents the seller from taking unusual actions, such as trying out an untested new business strategy. Since the buyer would also bear the burden of a mistaken strategy, this covenant allows the buyer to have a say over any such non-ordinary-course activities. A related covenant specifically requires the seller to use an agreed level of efforts to preserve the existing business and the commercial relationships of the target.

Sample Provision

During the period from the date of this Agreement to the Closing, except as otherwise [contemplated by] [permitted by] this Agreement or as the Buyer otherwise consents in writing [(such consent not to be unreasonably withheld)], the Target shall, and shall cause its Subsidiaries to, (x) conduct the Business in the ordinary course and (y) use their [reasonable best] [commercially reasonable] efforts to preserve intact the Business and their relationships with their customers, suppliers, creditors, and employees.

So-called negative operating covenants prohibit the seller from taking a number of specific actions. These often include restrictions on settling major litigation, making capital expenditures, acquiring or selling assets, incurring or guaranteeing new debt, paying dividends, increasing the compensation of employees, making changes to tax and accounting practices, and many other items.

Sample Provision

During the period from the date hereof to the Closing, except as otherwise [explicitly] [contemplated by] [permitted by] this Agreement or as the Buyer otherwise consents in writing [(such consent not to be unreasonably withheld)], the target shall not, and shall cause its Subsidiaries not to: [litany follows]

Three key types of qualifications are used in negative covenants. First, negative covenants are subject to an exception for permitted actions that are set forth on a schedule. The business teams of the seller will try to include in that schedule all the activities they want to conduct that may otherwise violate the negative covenants.

Second, the text of each covenant itself will include negotiated exceptions. This has the same effect as putting the exceptions into the schedule. If the exceptions are of a general type and are acceptable for the public to see (if the acquisition agreement will be filed with the Securities and Exchange Commission), then they may be written into the agreement itself rather than put into a schedule. For example, a covenant may prohibit capital expenditures other than those described in an agreed operating budget.

Third, the negative covenants normally permit any actions to which the buyer consents. This allows exceptions to be made for specific operational matters during the period from signing to closing with simple consents from the buyer, rather than a more cumbersome amendment to the acquisition agreement. In some cases, the buyer's consent to an exception can be withheld for any reason. In others, it cannot be withheld unreasonably. And, in some cases, a combination of standards is used: for example, in some cases the buyer's consent to deviate from the general requirement to operate in the ordinary course cannot be withheld unreasonably, but consent to deviate from the specific negative covenants can be withheld for any reason.

More often than not, the negative covenants operate independently from each other and are independent of the covenant to operate in the ordinary course. In other words, an exception to one specific negative covenant will not necessarily constitute an exception to others, because the qualifications used in specific negative covenants only qualify that particular covenant. This complexity can often create interpretive difficulties in practice.

For example, a negative covenant may restrict the target company from incurring debt, with an exception for debt up to $5 million. If all covenants operate independently, then to close the debt deal the target company must not only satisfy the specific negative covenant on debt, but must also satisfy the general ordinary course requirement—which would only be met if the debt is being incurred in the ordinary course.

Capital expenditures are another good example. Capital expenditures in excess of budgeted amounts may be restricted, for instance, with a $10 million general exception for unanticipated capex needs. Another covenant may restrict acquisitions, without a $10 million general exception. In that case, despite the $10 million capex exception, the target company may nevertheless be prohibited from acquiring a $10 million capital asset because of the tighter prohibition on acquisitions.

The $800 million deal to acquire a manufacturer prohibited the target from buying assets or businesses between signing and closing, but contained a negotiated exception for up to $50 million in small acquisitions. The target's business team and lawyers were happy with the $50 million figure, and thought this exception allowed the company to buy up to that amount in assets.

However, neither the requirement to operate the business in the ordinary course nor the covenant restricting capital expenditures included a similar exception.

The deal process with the buyer was a rocky road. The buyer had even started suggesting that one of its closing conditions might not be satisfied. Given that uncertain situation, the target did not want to sit still as a lame duck in the meantime.

Midway through the process, the target proposed a small roll-up acquisition of a struggling start-up competitor. The target thought it was a great opportunity. The target noted that it was spending its own money and that it had a $50 million exception to do just this.

But the buyer disagreed as to the strategic wisdom of that small roll-up acquisition. The buyer pointed to the ordinary course and capex covenants. It argued that those equally restricted the small roll-up acquisition, and did not have any exceptions.

The target's lawyers had to acknowledge that the buyer was right and the buyer prevailed. The target did not go forward with the proposed roll-up acquisition.

━━

In some (rare) transactions, the exceptions are turned into affirmative rules. In those deals, if an action is specifically permitted by any covenant, then it is considered to be permitted by all covenants, including the covenant to act in the ordinary course. In other transactions, a hybrid approach is used: if an action is specifically permitted by an exception to a negative covenant, then it need not meet the ordinary course requirement, but it may still be restricted by other negative covenants.

"Get the Deal Done" Covenants

The so-called "get the deal done" covenant requires the parties to use an agreed level of efforts to cause the closing conditions to be satisfied. This includes obtaining antitrust and other required regulatory approvals,[1] as well as successfully holding any shareholder vote upon which the transaction is conditioned.[2]

The parties may agree to different levels of efforts in this covenant. If they agree to use "best efforts," then they are potentially agreeing to a high level of commitment, as those words have sometimes been interpreted by courts.[3] A lesser and much more common level of commitment is described in contracts as "reasonable efforts."

The hybrid of "reasonable best efforts" contains a damper on the potentially unreasonable efforts that could be required by the "best efforts" standard. Particularly where routine commercial decisions are involved, the parties may also choose "commercially reasonable efforts" as the standard, which implies that commercial logic under the circumstances should prevail in interpreting which actions a party is required to take.

Sample Provision

The Sellers and the Buyer shall cooperate and use their [commercially reasonable] [reasonable best] [best] efforts to fulfill as promptly as practicable the conditions precedent to the Buyer's and the Sellers' respective obligations hereunder, and to secure as promptly as practicable all governmental and third-party consents that are required or advisable in connection with the transactions contemplated by this Agreement.

Rarely do parties specifically define what the efforts standard means, leaving the matter to the interpretation by the parties (and, potentially, courts) in the event a dispute arises. This can be especially problematic given that courts often apply varying standards when interpreting efforts clauses.[4]

The actions required by the parties under the efforts covenant are broader than the closing conditions. For instance, the efforts covenant often requires efforts to obtain any third-party consents that are not necessarily closing conditions, but which are called for by the terms of the target's commercial contracts.

Likewise, the parties' obligation to close may be conditioned only on receipt of U.S. antitrust approval, even if antitrust filings need to be made in several jurisdictions around the world. This covenant typically requires the parties to seek those additional approvals, whether or not receipt of such approvals rises to the level of a negotiated condition to closing.

Antitrust and Regulatory Approval Covenants

Most business acquisitions require antitrust approval unless they are small enough to fall under an antitrust filing size threshold. The parties can actually request antitrust approval before signing the acquisition agreement on the basis of a term sheet agreement between them, but they usually wait to seek approval until the full acquisition agreement has been signed. Depending on the type of business operated by the target company, there may also be a range of other regulatory approvals needed to complete the transaction (e.g., for a defense contractor, asset management firm, a player in the gaming industry, telecommunications companies, etc.).

These covenants address antitrust and other governmental approvals in four primary ways, by:

- Often including process requirements to ensure a timetable and cooperation to make antitrust filings on time;
- Requiring the buyer and seller to use a certain level of efforts to obtain approval[5];
- Specifying that the buyer is (or is not) required to accept divestitures or business restrictions (if those prove necessary for obtaining antitrust approval); and
- Providing that the buyer must (or need not) engage in litigation with the government (if required to prevent the transaction from being blocked).

Process requirements for obtaining antitrust approval may specify a deadline for making initial filings (e.g., 10 business days after signing the acquisition agreement). They will often state that the parties must cooperate in obtaining approvals, and may prevent either party from meeting with the government without giving the other party an opportunity to participate in such meetings. They may give each party the opportunity to review and comment on all communications with the government. In some cases, a party is only entitled to a copy of communications rather than having a right to comment.

Sample Provision

Each party hereto shall, as promptly as possible, (i) make, or cause or be made, all filings and submissions (including those under the HSR Act) required under any Law applicable to such party or any of its Affiliates, and (ii) use [reasonable best] efforts to obtain, or cause to be obtained, all consents, authorizations, orders and approvals from all Governmental Authorities that may be or become necessary or advisable for its execution and delivery of this Agreement and the performance of its obligations pursuant to this Agreement. Each party shall cooperate fully with the other party and its Affiliates in promptly seeking to obtain all such consents, authorizations, orders and approvals. The parties hereto shall not willfully take any action that will have the effect of delaying, impairing or impeding the receipt of any required consents, authorizations, orders, and approvals.

If the antitrust authorities seek to condition their approval of the deal on specific divestitures or business restrictions, or deny approval, the buyer and the seller will need to interpret what the general efforts language requires in terms of specific actions. If the authorities inform the parties that approval would be granted, but only if the buyer agrees to divest a particular product line or agrees to restrict its business practices in the future (in a way the antitrust authorities believe would limit the impact of the transaction on competition), then the buyer must decide whether it will accept those conditions.

Likewise, if the government proposes to block the transaction, the buyer must determine whether it will pursue litigation against the government in an attempt to force the antitrust authorities to grant approval. In these circumstances, the buyer will then often turn to its counsel to help determine what it is contractually required to do. If the acquisition agreement does not contain specific provisions with respect to divestitures or business restrictions, the answer will depend on the interpretation of the general efforts standard, which leads to uncertainty. Efforts levels are usually left undefined in agreements. Case law interpreting the various efforts standards is equally unclear, as discussed above.

Many buyers are comfortable with relying on the interpretation of the general efforts covenant under the circumstances. Government contractors in particular may wish to avoid litigation with any arm of the government at all costs, and may wish to clarify that the buyer is not required to engage in any lawsuit with the government.

Sample Provision

Notwithstanding anything in this Agreement to the contrary, neither the Buyer nor the Sellers shall be required to litigate (or defend against) any Action challenging any of the transactions contemplated hereby as violative of any competition, antitrust, foreign investment or similar Law.

In some acquisition agreements, the parties are more specific as to whether divestitures or business restrictions must be accepted by the buyer in order to obtain regulatory approvals. These specifications come in a positive or a negative form, and may be based on general materiality levels or on deal-specific thresholds. In the negative form, an exception to the efforts covenant will state that, notwithstanding the efforts covenant, the buyer is not required to accept specified divestitures or business restrictions.

Sample Provision

Notwithstanding anything in this Agreement to the contrary, [neither] the Buyer [nor] Sellers shall be required to agree to sell, divest, dispose of or hold separate [any] [material] assets or businesses, or otherwise take or commit to take [any] [material] action that could reasonably limit their freedom of action with respect to, or their ability to retain, one or more businesses, product lines or assets.

In the positive form, an exception to the efforts covenant will specify that the efforts covenant does require the buyer to accept specified divestitures or business restrictions.

Sample Provision

The Buyer and the Target shall cooperate with each other and do all things necessary, proper or advisable on its part under this Agreement and applicable Laws to consummate the Transaction, including negotiating, proposing and/or agreeing to the sale, transfer or other divestiture of [any] assets or any operating restriction required by, or agreed to with, any Government Entity in connection with obtaining Government Consent.

The limits on what the buyer is or is not required to accept are often formulated based on general materiality standards. For instance, the buyer may be required (or not) to accept divestitures or business restrictions that are "material," or that would rise to the level of a "material adverse effect" (MAE).[6]

If there is no materiality qualifier,[7] the buyer may be required to simply accept any and all required divestitures and business restrictions. This is referred to as a "hell or high water" standard.

THE MARKET

In private equity transactions, roughly one third of deals have a "hell or high water" provision.

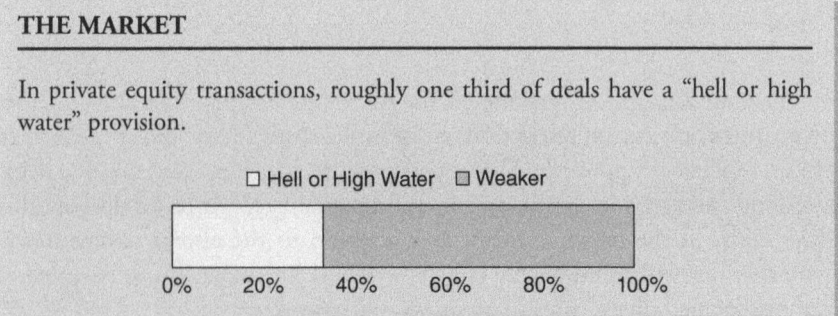

The materiality and MAE qualifiers can be applied relative to the target business or, to create a higher standard, the combined businesses of the target and the buyer in a strategic transaction (e.g., divestitures must be made unless material to the combined businesses taken as a whole).

Materiality standards can be applied in different ways for each party's business. For instance, the acquisition agreement could specify that the buyer is not required to accept any divestitures for its existing business, whether or not material, but must accept material divestitures of the target's businesses.

Although commonly used in these circumstances, MAE and, depending on the formulation, materiality qualifiers can create interpretive difficulties.[8] A seller could take the position that almost no divestitures, even sizeable ones, would have an MAE as long as the assets are sold for fair value. In theory, the target's business is not harmed if it receives equivalent value for the divested assets.

The buyer may be concerned about the loss of estimated synergies from the transaction, which would be foregone if a key asset or business is divested. A standard MAE qualifier in the antitrust divestiture standard would not protect the buyer in this respect. The definition of "material adverse effect" asks whether there has been an adverse effect on the target business itself. A loss of synergies is measured relative to future projections, rather than today's business. As a result, in its customary configuration, the MAE qualifier rarely addresses the loss of such future prospects.

Instead of relying on materiality and MAE qualifiers, the antitrust covenant can be tailored to the specifics of the buyer's and the target's businesses. For instance, if the parties recognize that one of the target's product lines is likely to cause a problem for obtaining antitrust approval, the acquisition agreement could specify that the buyer must (or that the buyer need not) divest that particular product line if necessary to receive regulatory approval.

The parties may be concerned that concrete provisions tailored too closely to the real antitrust issues could create a "road map" for regulatory authorities, leading them directly to any problems. Some buyers believe that tailored provisions invite authorities to view the product line in question as an issue, when they may not have otherwise done so. Others feel that the underlying issue will be obvious to the regulator in any event, so specifically identifying and allocating the risk between the parties should not have any adverse impact.

Private equity buyers usually establish special purpose entities to act as the acquiring vehicle and to be party to the acquisition agreement. Since the private equity fund itself and its management company are not party to the agreement, they are not bound by the covenants, including the efforts covenant. In some cases, the target needs to consider whether having the acquiring entity alone be subject to the covenants is sufficient, especially if undertakings could be required of the fund or management company as a regulatory matter.

War Story

In negotiating purchase of a company in the nuclear energy industry, a private equity buyer and the target agreed to a customary purchase agreement. There were no bells or whistles; it was a middle-of-the-road deal. The deal teams patted themselves on the back for dispensing with a complicated agreement in short strokes.

As usual, the actual buyer vehicle was not the private equity fund, but a new special purpose entity set up to be the buyer for that transaction.

Since the target was in a regulated industry and carried a heavy debt load, the authorities concerned themselves with the target's financial stability—and were even somewhat concerned about the potential for its bankruptcy an account of the heavy debt load the target was taking on as part of the buyer's financing.

Figuring that a private equity fund would not be willing to guarantee the target's debt, the regulators did not ask it to. They did, however, ask the private equity fund to take on a modest, procedural commitment within narrow circumstances to make sure the regulators were informed and had enough time to intervene to deal with a problem if there should be financial distress at the target.

Little did they know that the buyer was already having second thoughts about the deal. The private equity buyer resisted the simple request. It noted, correctly, that only its special purpose entity was party to the acquisition agreement; the fund and its management company were under no obligation to provide any assurances to the government. The government dug in its heels and the buyer refused to yield. The target's lawyers had not required the fund itself to agree to take any actions to get regulatory approval, so the fund was not going to do so.

On that technicality, the deal was not approved; the buyer took the easy way out. The regulatory approval condition was not satisfied, so the buyer had a right not to close.

Failed regulatory approvals can trigger a reverse breakup fee. A "reverse" breakup fee is any breakup fee paid by the buyer to the target. (Since public company merger agreements require the target to pay the buyer a breakup fee if it exercises its "fiduciary out," fees payable in the opposite direction—by the buyer to the target—are termed "reverse" breakup fees.)

If the target is concerned that regulatory approval will not be obtained, a reverse breakup fee can provide a financial incentive to motivate the buyer.

The reverse breakup fee is structured as a contingent financial payment that is usually payable only if all the conditions to the buyer's obligations (other than regulatory approval) have been satisfied.

If the deal would not have closed for other reasons, then the fee is not payable. For the most part, reverse breakup fees are not used outside of the reverse financing breakup fee context,[9] but, where needed, they can be critical to bridging the gap between the buyer and the target over the antitrust covenant. The size of the fee varies widely across transactions.

War Story

The number one and number three players in their field were proposing to merge. While the target elicited a great price from the buyer in the deal, the target could not convince it to improve the antitrust covenant. The buyer insisted that it would use "best efforts" to obtain approvals, but refused to commit to accepting even immaterial divestitures or business restrictions if those were required by antitrust authorities.

After some negotiations, the buyer sweetened the package with a substantial antitrust reverse breakup fee. A 9 percent fee would be payable if the deal failed to close on account of the strategic buyer's refusal to accept divestitures or business restrictions imposed by antitrust authorities. With that reverse breakup fee commitment, the target signed up the deal.

Some members of target management were convinced that the strategic deal would fall apart, because it would surely never be able to close without any antitrust adjustments. After all, the combined business would control such a large share of the market, and many felt that divestitures would inevitably be required.

After a long process of working with the regulators, the strategic deal did close. No restrictions or divestitures were even requested by the antitrust authorities. The strategic buyer had somehow convinced the government that stronger competition from foreign upstarts was just around the corner, and the United States needed a strong national champion to compete effectively.

Access Covenants

In most deals, an access covenant allows the buyer reasonable access to the target business it just agreed to acquire. That access right is usually drafted quite broadly. It often covers access to books and records, including financial data. In addition, it frequently covers access to the target's employees, as well as physical access to the target's premises.

Sample Provision

___

From the date hereof until the Closing, Sellers shall, and shall cause their Subsidiaries and their Representatives, to provide, [and to the extent not yet existing, prepare and furnish] as reasonably requested by Buyer or its Representatives full access to the offices, employees, properties, books and records of Sellers and their Subsidiaries, [including access to Sellers' and their Subsidiaries' customers, suppliers and others with whom they have material commercial dealings (provided that Sellers and their Subsidiaries shall have the right to participate]. Buyer shall reimburse Sellers promptly for reasonable expenses they incur in complying with any of the foregoing requests by or on behalf of Buyer.

These provisions generally came into being in the public company target context, and have not changed much, in terms of drafting, since most data became electronic. The provision in its original context would have allowed a few representatives of the buyer to stop by the target's headquarters to talk to employees, inspect the premises and, perhaps, inspect some financial records. Today, these provisions may be read much more broadly than many target companies expect. It is only the "reasonableness" qualifier and custom that prevent the buyer from obtaining, for instance, direct access to the target's information technology network, or direct access to the target's research and development personnel and their latest findings.

Even after signing, some deals fail to close for a variety of reasons. While the target should be much more open with the level of data it is willing to share between signing and closing than it was before signing, there should still be some limits given the uncertainty of closing. Often, those limits are understood by the parties, but do not get expressed in detail in the drafting of this covenant. To some extent, similar limits are also imposed by the requirements of antitrust law.

Limits on Covenants

Antitrust laws prevent the buyer from obtaining too much operating control over the target between signing and closing. Until antitrust approval is obtained (and, to some extent, after obtaining approval until the closing actually occurs), the target and buyer are two separate enterprises; they must continue to observe the substantive antitrust laws and avoid collusion in any way that would run afoul of those rules. Generally speaking, the operating covenants do not normally give the buyer sufficient influence to violate the antitrust rules. However, if the negative covenants were so restrictive as to require the target to ask the buyer's permission to continue with ordinary course operations, or if the buyer and target decided to cooperate closely for other reasons, antitrust issues could be raised.

Similarly, if the target is in the zone of insolvency, the buyer will want to be careful that it is not seen as directing the activities of the target. In extreme cases, a third party, such as a buyer, can be held responsible for liabilities of the target if that third party is effectively making operational business decisions on behalf of the target.

Other Covenants

Transactions include various other covenants tailored to the specific deal. For instance, public company deals will contain covenants governing the proxy statement and shareholder voting process. Public deals using stock consideration will have covenants governing the SEC registration process. Private deals may have a noncompete obligation that binds the sellers. The target in a private deal may also agree to a no-shop covenant (typically, without a fiduciary out).[10]

Litigation Endnotes

1. *See* Chapter 8-C, Antitrust and Other Regulatory Approvals.
2. *See* Chapter 8-B, Shareholder Approval.
3. *See, e.g., Kroboth v. Brent,* 625 N.Y.S.2d 748, 749–50 (N.Y. App. Div. 1995); *Pfizer Inc. v. PCS Health Sys.,* 650 N.Y.S.2d 164, 165 (N.Y. App. Div. 1996); *Showtime Networks Inc. v. Comsat Video Enters., Inc.,* No. 600849/95 (N.Y. Sup. Ct. June 29, 1998) ("difficulty of performance occasioned only by financial difficulties, even to the extent of insolvency, does not excuse performance of the contract"). *See also Cal. Pines Property Owners Ass'n v. Pedotti,* 206 Cal. App. 4th 384, 394–95 (Cal. Ct. App. 2012) (stating that the "best efforts" standard is more exacting than the "reasonable best efforts standard"). *But see Crum & Crum Enters., Inc. v. NDC of Cal., LP,* No. 1:09-CV-00145, 2010 BL 260191 (D. Del. Nov. 3, 2010) (finding that the "best efforts" standard requires only that the promisor undertake "contractual obligations diligently and with reasonable effort").
4. *See Crum & Crum Enters.,* 2010 BL 260191, at *4 ("Delaware courts do not define the precise contours of the duty of best efforts"). *See also Triple-A Baseball Club Assocs. v. Ne. Baseball, Inc.,* 832 F.2d 214, 225 (1st Cir. 1987) (noting that the "best efforts" standard has been found to be equivalent to "good faith," and that "[t]he standard, whether it is expressed in terms of good faith or best efforts, cannot be defined in terms of a fixed formula; it varies with the facts and the field of law involved").
5. *See* Chapter 7-C, "Get the Deal Done" Covenants.
6. *See, generally,* Chapter 10, Material Adverse Effect.
7. *See* Chapter 6-F1, Materiality qualifiers; Chapter 14-F1a, Materiality qualifiers.
8. *See* Chapter 10-B, Interpreting Material Adverse Effect Provisions.
9. *See, generally,* Chapter 12-B3, Reverse financing failure breakup fee; Chapter 14, Indemnities.
10. *See* Chapter 9-C2, Fiduciary out; Chapter 6, Representations and Warranties.

CHAPTER 8

Closing Conditions

Overview of Closing Conditions

Closing conditions define the circumstances that must exist before the parties are obligated to close the transaction. Many of the key closing conditions are discussed in this chapter. In most transactions, the closing cannot occur immediately upon signing because corporate or regulatory approvals necessitate a delay before closing. For example, U.S. antitrust law requires the parties to submit documentation and await approval before consummating a transaction.

In some deals, public shareholders of the target must approve the transaction before a merger can close, and the target must prepare and distribute a proxy statement in advance of the shareholder vote. Such restraints on immediately closing a transaction result in a gap between signing and closing, which can range from a matter of weeks to more than a year. This gap generates or shapes a large portion of the intricacies governed by an acquisition agreement. If there were no gap between signing and closing, the parties would normally close the transaction at the same time it is signed. Given the gap between signing and closing, however, the parties must agree on the circumstances under which they will have to close and under which either party can avoid closing.

Sample Provision

The obligations of each party to effect the Closing are subject to the satisfaction or waiver at or prior to the Closing of each of the following conditions: [litany follows]

Some closing conditions govern both parties' obligation to close the transaction. For example, in a transaction requiring antitrust approval, either party may refuse to close if approval is not obtained. Other closing conditions govern only one party's obligation to close. For instance, the requirement that the buyer has complied with its covenants is a condition only to the target's obligation to close. These examples are fairly clear as to which party should benefit from the condition, but in other situations the parties will have to negotiate who has the benefit of a condition.

A condition can be waived by the party who is entitled to the benefit of that condition. For instance, the buyer is normally not required to close if the target has suffered a "material adverse effect (MAE)."[1] If the buyer decides to close over a potential MAE (and waives its right not to close), the target would still be required to close.

Shareholder Approval

If the target is a publicly owned corporation, approval by its shareholders is required as a matter of law. In that case, receipt of shareholder approval is customarily listed as a condition for the benefit of both parties. In a private transaction, the shareholders are usually involved in the transaction itself, so shareholder approval is typically not a condition at all—in order to avoid giving those shareholders a "free option" to cause the transaction to fail after signing.

Sample Provision

The Company Stockholder Approval shall have been obtained in accordance with applicable Law, the certificate of incorporation and bylaws of the Company and applicable stock exchange rules.

Under corporate law, both parties to a merger need shareholder approval to merge. If the target is publicly held, it must obtain approval from its shareholders, and obtaining that approval will be a closing condition. If the target is a closely held corporation and its shareholders are actively involved in the transaction, shareholder approval will still be required but there is no risk of failed approval because they will grant approval promptly upon signing the merger agreement.

Mergers are normally structured as triangular rather than direct mergers. This means that the target will merge with a newly formed subsidiary of the buyer, rather than the buyer's parent company. As a result, on the buyer's side the newly formed buyer entity needs shareholder approval, which is given by its direct shareholder (the buyer). There is no risk of not obtaining that approval; the buyer is, after all, the party proposing the deal. As a result, the ultimate shareholders of the buyer need not approve the deal, and no condition is included for buyer shareholder approval.

Antitrust and Other Regulatory Approvals

Generally speaking, receipt of antitrust approval or termination of the related waiting period in the United States must be received before either party is required to close the transaction.

Sample Provision

Any waiting period (and any extension thereof) applicable to the consummation of the transactions contemplated by this Agreement prescribed by the HSR Act shall have expired or shall have been terminated [(without the imposition of [any] [material] restrictions or conditions)].

If approval under European Union (EU) competition law is required, receipt of such approval is usually a condition favoring both parties. For other jurisdictions, antitrust approvals may take various forms, and may be more or less material to the transaction.

Sample Provision

Any other [material] Governmental Approvals necessary or advisable in connection with any competition, antitrust, [foreign investment] or similar Law of [any] jurisdiction shall have been obtained or filed or shall have occurred [(without the imposition of [any] [material] restrictions or conditions)].

For antitrust approvals outside of U.S. and EU law, the parties may decide that receipt of any of a particular approval should be a condition in favor of the buyer, in favor of the seller, or in favor of both parties. Often, it will only be a condition in favor of the buyer (unless the seller has actual risk if these approvals are not obtained, e.g., risk of criminal liability), since future divestitures or business restrictions would only be a burden to the buyer. As such, the seller may not benefit from a similar condition. Instead, the seller may be required to close despite the absence of those approvals if the buyer is willing to take the risk associated with not obtaining such approvals or obtaining only conditional approval.

In some deals, specific regulatory approvals may not even be a condition for the buyer—in which case the closing cannot be held up pending approval of those authorities.

Accuracy of Representations and Warranties

The acquisition agreement will contain representations by the target company and/or the sellers, as well as the buyer.[2] Most agreements have a closing condition relating to accuracy of representations. Although representations may be made only at signing, closing conditions will require them to be sufficiently accurate at closing, as if they were made again on the closing date. This is known as the "rep bring-down." Rep bring-down conditions differ from each other in four key ways.

Level of accuracy

Different levels of accuracy of the representations can be required for the bring-down condition to be satisfied. In order to satisfy the closing condition, the representations need not be strictly true in most cases. Sometimes, the parties have to close over inaccuracies that are not material. Sometimes, they have to close over inaccuracies unless they rise to the level of an MAE.[3]

Sample Provision

Each of the Fundamental Representations and Warranties of the Target contained in this Agreement shall be true and correct in all respects [...].

Some "fundamental" representations need to be strictly true, such as the representation that the seller has authority to enter into the acquisition agreement, and the representation which confirms that the transaction does not conflict with the target's or seller's charter. The representation that a seller owns the stock it is selling is also viewed as fundamental. (The accuracy of that representation determines the buyer's ability to acquire 100 percent of the equity at the aggregate price per share the buyer expects to pay.)

Sometimes, an exception allows that representation to be inaccurate in insignificant ways, or inaccurate as long as the breach does not increase the purchase price by more than a small dollar amount—which is frequently in the range of 5 to 50 basis points as a percentage of the aggregate deal consideration (i.e., 5 to 50 percent of 1 percent; or 0.05 to 0.50 percent).

Sample Provision

[...] except, in the case of the representations and warranties in Section __, where failure to be true and correct would not result in an increase in the aggregate amount of consideration required to be paid by Buyer under Article II of this Agreement by more than $__.

In private deals, the basic representations (i.e., nonfundamental) need to be true in all material respects. Others may only need to be true to the extent that inaccuracies do not rise to the level of an MAE.

THE MARKET

Roughly one-half to two-thirds of private deals require the representations to be true in all material respects. Most of the remainder require accuracy at the aggregate MAE level. A small number of deals require accuracy in all respects for all reps.

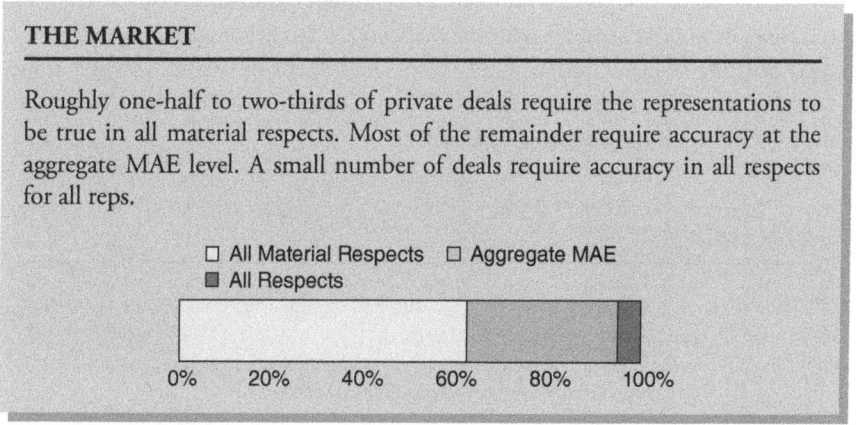

When the target is a public company, the target's need for closing certainty usually results in the use of the MAE qualification in the bring-down condition.

Under that standard, the representations and warranties must be true except to the extent that breaches would not, in the aggregate, result in an MAE.

Ignoring materiality qualifiers in representations

Accuracy of the representations can be tested based on representations as written, or materiality qualifiers in the text of representations can be "read out" (or ignored, or disregarded) for purposes of testing the accuracy of the representations in the bring-down condition.[4] In other words, in some cases, materiality qualifiers in the representations are "blue penciled" out of the representations, and the accuracy of a hypothetical set of representations (without materiality qualifiers) is tested to determine whether the closing condition is satisfied.

Sample Provision

[...] shall be true and correct (without regard to any qualifications therein to materiality or Material Adverse Effect) [...].

The primary purpose of reading out materiality qualifiers in the representations is to avoid so-called "double materiality." This can occur in circumstances where the closing condition introduces its own concept of materiality. For instance, a representation may state that a party is in compliance with law in all material respects, then the bring-down condition requires that representation to be true in all material respects. In that case, absent a materiality read-out, the seller would arguably have the benefit of two materiality qualifiers for the same issue: a materiality qualifier in the condition on top of a materiality qualifier in the representation.

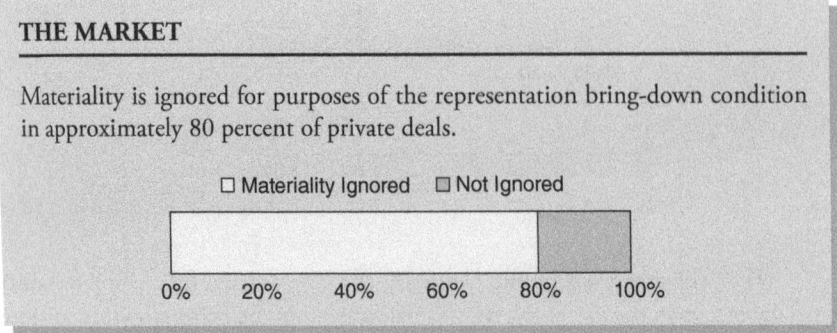

THE MARKET

Materiality is ignored for purposes of the representation bring-down condition in approximately 80 percent of private deals.

☐ Materiality Ignored   ☐ Not Ignored

0%   20%   40%   60%   80%   100%

If, for illustrative purposes, $5 million is "material," then a $6 million problem would breach the representation. In that instance, a seller could argue that the representation is breached by only $1 million—because of the built-in $5 million materiality buffer in the text of the representation. Since the condition requires breaches (rather than underlying problems) to separately be material ($5 million), and, arguably, the representation was only breached by $1 million, the seller would argue that the closing condition is still satisfied.

Aggregate materiality

Materiality qualifiers in the bring-down closing condition can be applied on a representation-by-representation basis or on an aggregate basis. If materiality qualifiers are read out of the representations for purposes of the condition, the condition itself will normally include its own materiality qualifier, as noted above. The materiality qualifier that is built into the condition can require that each representation be accurate at the specified level of materiality, or it can require that inaccuracies across representations in the aggregate not exceed the specified level of materiality.

Sample Provision

[...] except for such inaccuracies that do not and would not reasonably be expected to have, individually or in the aggregate, a Material Adverse Effect.

Using an aggregate test is generally better for the buyer. When it comes to measuring the accuracy of representations on an aggregate MAE basis, any breach that individually rises to the level of an MAE is, of course, going to cause the aggregate of all breaches to rise to the level of an MAE. The aggregate test allows a buyer to add up multiple breaches that, individually, would not amount to an MAE, but which, as a whole, do so. In practice, almost all MAE tests are at the aggregate level (which is the same as referring to breaches that "individually or in the aggregate" rise to the level of an MAE).

The same distinction arises for breaches at the "all material respects" level. An aggregate test will allow the buyer to add up less significant breaches, while testing the accuracy of each individual representation means that several separate breaches cannot be added together. In contrast to the practice for MAE standards (which are tested on an aggregate basis), materiality standards are usually tested on an individual basis.

Sample Provision

Each of the representations and warranties of the Target contained in this Agreement shall be true and correct in all material respects [...].

The term "material" is hardly ever defined in acquisition agreements. It may be the case that courts would interpret the word material in the context of aggregate materiality to require a higher level of materiality (better for the seller), because the court may see materiality relative to the deal as a whole.

On an individual representation basis, the level of materiality may be interpreted to require only a low level of materiality (meaning only a small error makes the condition not satisfied, which is better for the buyer), because a court may assume that the level of materiality is measured relative to the importance of the particular representation at hand. As with much of merger and acquisition (M&A) drafting, this issue is left to the interpretation of key words and concepts (such as the term "materiality") after a dispute arises.

Putting together the level of accuracy required, whether to ignore materiality qualifiers in the representations and whether to aggregate breaches across representations, four dominant patterns emerge in practice:

- *All respects/individual rep basis.* After reading out materiality qualifiers, each of the representations must be true and correct in all respects.
- *As written/individual rep basis.* Each of the representations must be true and correct as written (giving effect to materiality qualifiers in the representations).
- *All material respects/individual or aggregate.* After reading out materiality qualifiers, the representations must be true and correct in all material respects.
- *Aggregate MAE.* After reading out materiality qualifiers, the representations must be true and correct, except to the extent that breaches of representations individually or in the aggregate do not rise to the level of an MAE.

These four patterns can also be combined. For instance, fundamental representations can be required to be true in all respects, while the remainder of the representations are required to be true in all material respects or at the aggregate MAE level.

When representations are tested

Accuracy of the representations is tested on two different dates. In order to satisfy the closing condition, representations may have to be true and correct at the agreed level of accuracy at signing, at closing, or at both signing and closing.

Sample Provision

[…] shall be true and correct as of the date hereof and as of the Closing, as if made at and as of such time (or, if made as of a specific date, at and as of such specified date) […].

The buyer will want the representations to be true at closing. That is the date that the buyer takes ownership of the target business and pays the purchase price. A closing condition determines whether the buyer may walk away from the deal or is required to close, so the buyer wants to know that as of closing the target looks like what was promised in the representations.

Facts may have changed for the worse between signing and closing. For instance, the ownership of the stock the buyer is acquiring could have changed, and the sellers' representations that they own the stock free and clear of liens may no longer be true. This fact is most relevant at the instant of closing, and the buyer will want the representations to protect it from any change that arises before closing.

On the other hand, facts may have changed for the better between signing and closing. For instance, the business may not have been fully in compliance with law at signing, but could have brought itself into compliance before closing by obtaining a missing permit. The target company may have been the subject of threatened litigation, but may have settled the case without any significant expense in the meantime. These types of circumstances raise the question of whether the representations need to be true as of signing as well.

THE MARKET

Virtually all deals (public and private) have a bring-down condition that requires the target's reps to be true at closing. In approximately two-thirds of deals, the condition also requires the reps to be true as of signing.

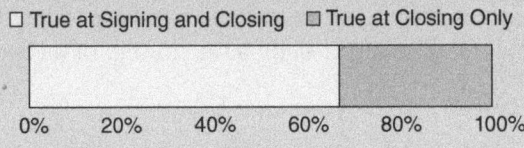

☐ True at Signing and Closing   ☐ True at Closing Only

0%   20%   40%   60%   80%   100%

Many buyers will also insist that the closing condition require accuracy as of signing. Signing is the point at which the buyer agrees on the purchase price. The buyer may have negotiated a different price had it known about the problems underlying the breach of representations on that date. Even if the representations are required to be true as of signing, if the breaches have been corrected prior to closing a court may not view those breaches as material.

Some representations are not intended to be true at closing. They are made only as of signing (or some other specific date). For instance, the target may represent that it has provided an accurate list of all material contracts. Usually, it will only represent that the list is accurate as of signing, because such a list would naturally evolve between signing and closing. In addition, changes that make this representation untrue are not necessarily harmful to the buyer.

Compliance with Covenants

Each party's obligation to close is conditioned on the other party complying with its various obligations under the acquisition agreement, such as the covenants that govern the operation of the business between signing and closing.

Sample Provision

[...] The Target shall have performed in all material respects all obligations required to be performed by it under this Agreement at or prior to the Closing.

In most cases, the wording of this condition includes a materiality qualifier. Most covenants do not contain their own materiality qualifiers, so the "double materiality" concern for representations does not usually arise for covenants.[5]

Covenants do contain different types of general limitations and qualifications. Covenants are more likely to be qualified by reference to reasonableness (which is thought of as defining the scope of the obligation) rather than materiality (which is thought of as defining the scope of acceptable or nonproblematic breaches). For instance, the parties are frequently required to do only what is commercially reasonable under the circumstances, or to use reasonable best efforts to accomplish a goal. Combining those types of limitations in the covenants with the materiality qualifier in the text of the condition is usually not viewed as giving rise to a double materiality concern.

Receipt of Third-Party Approvals

In some transactions, third-party approvals are required. Some contracts, for instance, require consent of the counterparty under change-of-control clauses.

Most deal structures—merger, stock purchase, asset purchase, asset sale—result in a change of control. Depending on the wording of the change of control clause, sometimes a structure can be used to avoid a change of control. Anti-assignment provisions, which prevent one party from assigning its side of the contract to a third party, can sometimes be written so broadly that the acquisition is treated like an assignment by the target to the buyer even in a stock deal or a merger.

If the acquisition agreement will be made public, such as through a filing with the Securities and Exchange Commission, the third parties whose approval are required could become aware that each of their consents is a condition to the transaction and believe they have hold-up value. In that case, including such a condition can create problems that otherwise would be less significant. To reduce the risk, the conditions could be structured so that they do not name the specific approvals, but, instead, refer to the approvals listed in the schedules or disclosure letter.

Sample Provision

[…] All [material] Consents required to be obtained from third parties (other than Governmental Entities) in connection with the transactions contemplated by this Agreement [that are set forth on Schedule __] shall have been obtained.

Absence of Injunctions and Litigation

No injunctions

Absence of a court order or injunction prohibiting the transaction is a common joint closing condition. Parties are not required to close over the objections of a court or in violation of a newly enacted law that makes the transaction illegal.

Sample Provision

There shall not be enacted, issued, promulgated, enforced or entered by any court or other Governmental Authority of competent jurisdiction any Law or Order (whether temporary, preliminary or permanent) that is in effect and that enjoins or otherwise prohibits the consummation of the transactions contemplated by this Agreement.

The court order or injunction does not need to be permanent or beyond appeal. If it is permanent and nonappealable, the acquisition agreement may contain a separate termination trigger that would entitle either party to terminate the transaction right away (in advance of the so-called drop-dead date) on the theory that continuing to work toward closing the transaction would be futile.[6]

No litigation

In some deals, the parties agree that neither party will be required to close as long as there is any pending government litigation that challenges the deal.

Sample Provision

[…] There shall not be pending or threatened [by any Governmental Authority] any Action challenging or seeking to enjoin or otherwise prohibit any of the transactions contemplated by this Agreement or seeking to obtain from the Buyer in connection with the transactions contemplated by this Agreement any damages or to impose any [material] restrictions or conditions.

In some cases, this condition covers threatened as well as actual litigation. A "no-threatened-litigation" condition can protect the parties from, for example, being required to close after the antitrust waiting period has lapsed, yet in the face of threatened legal action if the parties do actually close.

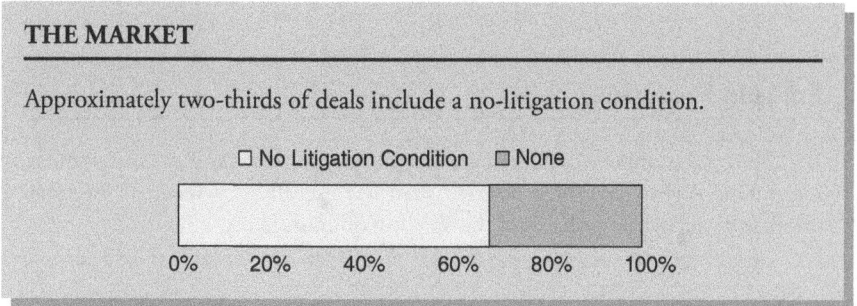

THE MARKET

Approximately two-thirds of deals include a no-litigation condition.

☐ No Litigation Condition ☐ None

0%   20%   40%   60%   80%   100%

In some deals, the no-litigation condition is expanded to cover the absence of litigation by third parties (not just governmental entities) challenging the deal. This could arise, for instance, in the case of a shareholder "strike suit." In other cases, third-party litigation is ignored, and only litigation by a governmental authority would count—such as a suit by the antitrust authorities to block the deal.

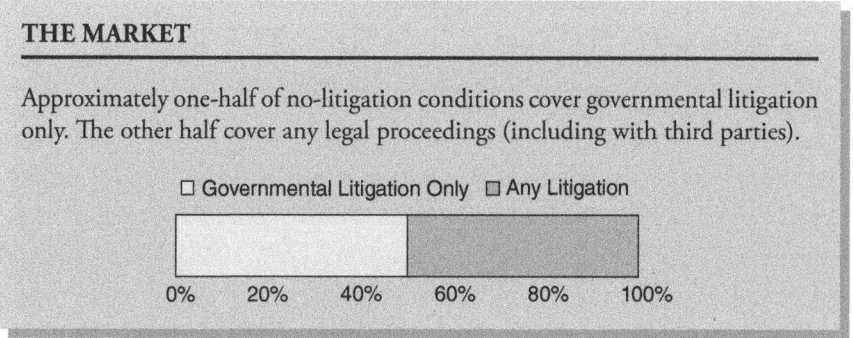

THE MARKET

Approximately one-half of no-litigation conditions cover governmental litigation only. The other half cover any legal proceedings (including with third parties).

☐ Governmental Litigation Only ☐ Any Litigation

0%   20%   40%   60%   80%   100%

Appraisal Rights

If a shareholder exercises appraisal rights, then instead of the deal consideration, it will receive fair value as determined by a court. That fair value may end up being more or less than the deal consideration. As a result, the exercise of appraisal rights puts the buyer at risk of potentially having to pay more than the agreed deal price.

An appraisal condition ensures that the buyer does not have to close if more than a limited number of shareholders exercise appraisal. It is tied to shareholders staking the appraisal claim, not to the actual results of the eventual appraisal valuation proceedings.

Sample Provision

[...] The total number of shares of the Target Common Stock, if any, as to which Dissenters' Rights have been asserted shall not exceed __ percent of the total number of outstanding shares of the Target Common Stock.

In public deals, appraisal rights conditions have become rare. Targets are concerned that arbitrage investors betting on deal failure could exercise appraisal rights solely in order to give the buyer a walk right.

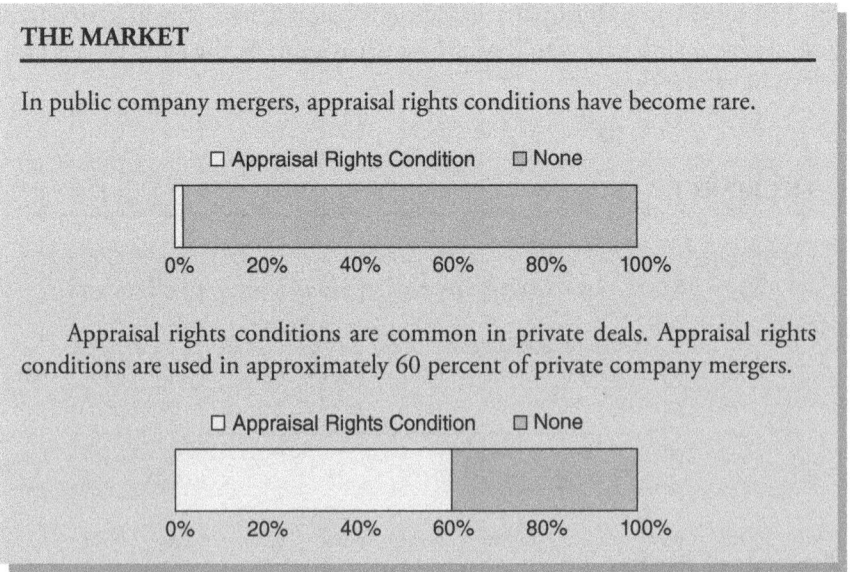

THE MARKET

In public company mergers, appraisal rights conditions have become rare.

☐ Appraisal Rights Condition   ☐ None

0%   20%   40%   60%   80%   100%

Appraisal rights conditions are common in private deals. Appraisal rights conditions are used in approximately 60 percent of private company mergers.

☐ Appraisal Rights Condition   ☐ None

0%   20%   40%   60%   80%   100%

When an appraisal rights condition is used, the parties have to negotiate the percentage of shareholders exercising appraisal rights that would trigger the failure of that condition.

THE MARKET

When appraisal rights conditions are used in public deals, they are often triggered by 10 to 20 percent of the shareholders exercising appraisal rights.

In private deals, the triggers are lower. Ninety percent of private deals with appraisal rights conditions have triggers at or below 10 percent of shareholders exercising appraisal rights. The percentage triggers are roughly evenly distributed below 10 percent, with approximately one-half of deals falling within a couple of percentage points of 5 percent.

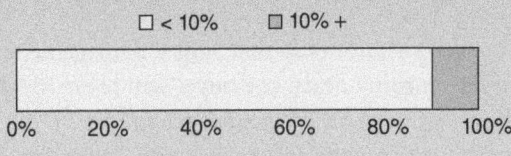

The primary reason for using a merger agreement in a private transaction is to address the risk that one or more of the shareholders may try to hold the process up by refusing to sell in a private stock sale. The parties may expect a particular shareholder to try to disrupt the deal. In that context, the appraisal percentage that triggers the buyer's walk-away right may be set in excess of the amount held by the potentially dissenting faction of shareholders, to ensure that it does not give them additional leverage. The buyer can also add an indemnity in a private merger to protect itself from excess payments through the appraisal process.

Legal Opinions

In many private deals, each party requires the law firm on the other side to give a legal opinion as part of the closing conditions.

THE MARKET

Approximately one-third to one-half of private deals have legal opinion conditions.

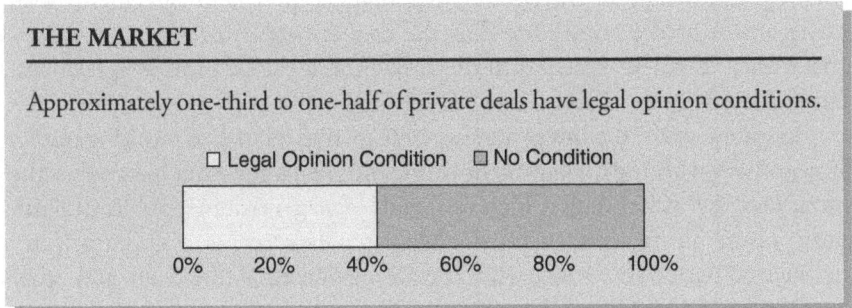

It is rare for a law firm to be sued on the basis of opinions they have provided. Law firm opinions also tend to be highly qualified, which shields the firm from risk. Nevertheless, a legal opinion may give the counterparty comfort that the law firm is acting as a so-called "gatekeeper." Since law firms rely heavily on their reputation in the market, they would presumably refuse to give an opinion that was questionable even if they were not concerned about liability, which would alert the counterparty to the existence of an issue.

Employment Agreements

The buyer may want to assure itself that target management intends to remain with the target. In some deals, the buyer will bring in its own management team and does not need existing management.

The simplest way to provide the buyer with assurance that important team members will remain in place is a condition that management has signed up new, long-term employment agreements. However, buyers may worry that such a condition gives the management team hold-up power. If they do not sign, the deal may not close. Hold-up value could result in higher salary and bonus packages than necessary in the buyer's view.

Sample Provision

[…] [The Employment Agreements with each [member of Key Management] shall be in full force and effect.]
  —OR—
[Each [member of Key Management] shall have executed and delivered to the Buyer new employment agreements [reasonably acceptable] to the Buyer.]

In private deals, the buyer often negotiates employment agreements with management at the same time that the deal is negotiated with the sellers. Sometimes, it will be signed up at the same time as the acquisition agreement, but will not become effective until the closing.

In public deals, the buyer often prefers to take the risk of working out an arrangement with the management team, and the target often insists that the buyer take that risk. Negotiating a deal with management in a public deal can put pressure on the analysis of whether the transaction is a "going private" transaction under SEC rules, which creates incremental disclosure and other burdens for the buyer and the target.[7]

Due Diligence

Occasionally in private deals, the parties sign the transaction agreement before the buyer has completed its due diligence review. In those deals, the buyer may propose a condition that the buyer is reasonably satisfied with its due diligence review. Sellers are usually concerned that such broad and subjective conditions give the buyer an option to walk (with no reverse breakup fee).

Sample Provision

[...] The Buyer shall have received from the Sellers all material information reasonably requested in connection with the Buyer's due diligence review of the Target, and all such information shall be [reasonably satisfactory] to the Buyer.

A diligence condition can be limited in time. For instance, the buyer may be required to declare that its due diligence review was not satisfactorily completed prior to a specified date, such as 30 days after signing. The period can sometimes be extended if the sellers have not provided all of the requested diligence information.

Litigation Endnotes

1. Most deals are conditioned upon the absence of a "material adverse effect" on the business of the target. *See, generally,* Chapter 10, "Material Adverse Effect."
2. *See, generally,* Chapter 6, "Representations and Warranties."
3. *See, generally,* Chapter 10, "Material Adverse Effect."
4. *See* Chapter 6-F, Qualifications to the Representations.
5. *See* Chapter 8-D2, Ignoring materiality qualifiers in representations.
6. *See* Chapter 9, "Termination Rights."
7. *See* 17 C.F.R. §§ 240.13e-3 (Exchange Act Rule 13e-3), 240.13e-100 (Schedule 13E-3). *See also Going Private,* SEC.gov (providing an in-depth explanation of the SEC's "going private" rules).

Termination Rights

Overview of Termination Rights

Termination rights permit a party to terminate a transaction agreement upon notice. Usually termination rights are provided for a subset of the matters that would give rise to a failure of a closing condition. Termination rights operate differently from closing conditions because they can cut short the deal process without requiring the parties to wait to determine whether or not the conditions will be satisfied.

Termination rights operate in the gap between signing and closing. In the rare deals that sign and close at the same time, there would be no need for termination rights.

Almost all acquisition agreements include a termination right that is generally referred to as the "drop-dead date" or "outside date." Either party can terminate after that agreed date has passed. All other termination rights can be thought of as "early" termination rights, allowing the parties to terminate in advance of the drop-dead date.

Termination rights can permit termination by the buyer, the seller or both, depending on the particular right and the circumstances. The parties can also terminate by mutual agreement.

Drop-Dead Date

As noted above, acquisition agreements typically have a termination right in favor of each party as of the drop-dead date. That is the point at which the parties are no longer, in effect, required to keep using their efforts to satisfy the closing conditions and close the transaction. Of course, until they actually exercise their termination right, they would be required to use those efforts. The drop-dead date does not normally trigger payment of a fee. It is a "free" walk right.

If the drop-dead date is, for instance, six months after the signing date, the parties will typically be required to use a specified level of efforts to close the deal during that period. If significant issues arise during the course of trying to satisfy the conditions, one party can force the other to continue trying to solve those problems and "wait it out." At the end of that period, though, either party can terminate.

Sample Provision

[…] by either the Buyer, on the one hand, or the Company, on the other hand, by giving written notice of such termination to the other party, if the Closing shall not have occurred on or prior to [drop-dead date].

The duration of the drop-dead date depends on the reason for the gap between signing and closing. If the need for antitrust approval drives the delay in closing, and only a short antitrust process in the United States is required (and no shareholder vote or filings with the Securities and Exchange Commission [SEC] are required), then the parties could reasonably decide that the drop-dead date should be available as early as three or four months from the signing date. If an SEC review of any filings is required prior to closing, such as review of a proxy statement for a shareholder vote, then six to nine months would be more reasonable. If there are significant antitrust processes that must be completed in multiple jurisdictions, or the parties expect to need to negotiate with regulatory authorities, then a year or longer could be appropriate under the circumstances.

After the parties estimate the period of time they expect to need to achieve the closing conditions, they usually add a buffer period to it. This prevents either side from opportunistically terminating the deal just before an expected closing. If the parties anticipate potential litigation with antitrust authorities in order to obtain antitrust approval, and the buyer would be required to engage in litigation to achieve approval, then it would be appropriate to add a lengthy buffer zone for the legal process to play out in its normal course.

In some deals, the drop-dead termination right cannot be exercised by the party at fault for the deal not closing when expected. This concept can manifest itself in a clause that prevents a party in material breach of its covenants from exercising the termination right. A party in material breach of its representations can also be prevented from exercising its termination right.

Sample Provision

[...] so long as the terminating party is not in material breach of its covenants [or representations] under this Agreement.

This provision could have somewhat unfair results. For instance, if a party has breached unrelated representations (or covenants) but is not actually the cause for the delay in closing, it could be trapped indefinitely in the deal without an ability to terminate.

Another common solution is for the termination right to prevent a party from terminating under the drop-dead date provision if it is primarily or proximately responsible for the failure to close the transaction. That standard means, though, that the innocent party would have to show not only breach but also causality.

Sample Provision

[...] so long as the failure of the terminating party to comply with its covenants under this Agreement is not the [proximate] [primary] cause of the failure of the Closing to have occurred on or prior to such date.

If a private equity buyer has obtained commitment letters from its financing sources for debt financing needed to fund the purchase price, those financing commitments will contain their own drop-dead date. The buyer will want to make sure to coordinate the expiration of those commitment papers with the drop-dead date in the acquisition agreement; otherwise, the buyer could be required to close the acquisition after its banks are no longer obligated to fund the debt.

The drop-dead date may allow extensions, for one or either party to push out the drop-dead date. This is mostly used when a condition outside of a party's control could take longer than expected. For example, either party can extend the drop-dead date if particular regulatory approvals are not obtained by the initial drop-dead date. If those regulatory approvals are holding up the closing, then the parties have to continue to work through the governmental process for the duration of the extension period. Extension rights often run from one to three months.

Several critical provisions of an acquisition agreement rely on inherently vague terms, including the range of materiality qualifiers and the range of efforts standards. The drop-dead date, in contrast, is a critical provision which takes the opposite approach. It sets forth an unmistakable deadline, which provides certainty, but which can also be arbitrary when applied to a particular deal. For example, regulatory approval may be expected the day after the drop-dead date.

War Story

The deal was supposed to be quick and simple. The buyer was a multinational construction firm, which operated some outsourced military base operations. The target was a small company operating in a niche advisory business, in which the buyer was not involved. Regulatory approval was expected to be easy to obtain.

The deal teams thought they needed around three months to get to closing, but gave themselves ample room—or so they thought—by setting a drop-dead date six months out.

Four months after signing, they realized they had a problem. A small technical overlap in services presented a conflict: the target was advising the government on services at one of the bases operated by an affiliate of the buyer.

The issue was small, so everyone still expected regulatory approval. However, while the problem could easily be fixed, it was going to take longer than anticipated.

Six months from signing, the drop-dead date passed. Each party held its breath, not knowing for sure whether the other side actually wanted to terminate or voluntarily extend. All the lawyers on each side wished they had built in a regulatory extension right, but it was too late for those thoughts now.

In the end, neither side terminated, and the deal closed three days after the drop-dead date.

Change in Recommendation and Fiduciary Out

In a public company merger, the target agrees that its board will recommend the deal to the target's shareholders and that it will include the recommendation in the voting disclosure (proxy) statement sent to shareholders. The target's board also adopts resolutions approving the transactions.

The target board has a "fiduciary out" right that allows it—despite the covenant to recommend the deal—to recommend against the deal if that recommendation would violate the fiduciary duties of the target's board of directors.[1] However, exercising that fiduciary out right comes at a cost to the target company. If the board changes its recommendation, the buyer can immediately terminate. If the buyer exercises its termination right, it is entitled to collect a "breakup fee."

> ## Sample Provision
>
> This Agreement may be terminated and the Merger may be abandoned at any time prior to the Effective Time by the Buyer by action of the board of directors of Buyer if [...] (i) the Company Board shall have made a Change of Recommendation.

This termination right is often broadly drafted. It can be triggered by a wide range of actions beyond a straightforward change in recommendation. It covers other actions that make the deal impossible or detracts from the board's support, such as: retracting the board's approval, refusing to put its approval in the proxy statement that is being sent to the target's shareholders or altering the board's resolutions in support of the transaction.

> ## Sample Provision
>
> Except as set forth in this Section, the Company Board (or any committee thereof) shall not (i) withhold, withdraw, qualify or modify (or publicly propose or resolve to withhold, withdraw, qualify or modify), in a manner adverse to Parent, the Company Recommendation, (ii) fail to include the Company Recommendation in the Proxy Statement, or (iii) authorize, adopt, approve, recommend or declare advisable, or propose to authorize, adopt, approve, recommend or declare advisable (publicly or otherwise), an Acquisition Proposal, or cause or permit the Company to enter into any Alternative Acquisition Agreement (any of the foregoing, a "Change of Recommendation").

The buyer may choose not to exercise its termination right in hopes of turning the deal around. But it usually has the continuing option to terminate while the board's adverse change in its recommendation remains in place.

In a handful of cases, the buyer is subject to a "use it or lose it" window. If the buyer does not exercise this termination right within, for example, 10 business days after the change in recommendation, then its termination right expires. This forces the buyer to decide, up front, whether it wishes to wait it out and see whether the shareholder vote can be obtained despite the change in recommendation (and despite circumstances that led to the change in recommendation).

Sample Provision

[...] provided that Parent's right to terminate this Agreement pursuant to this clause __ [change in recommendation] shall expire at 5:00 p.m. on the tenth Business Day following the date on which such right to terminate first arose; [...].

In many cases, the merger agreement treats the failure of the target's board to reaffirm its recommendation in the face of a competing bid the same as the board affirmatively changing its recommendation. Silence is treated as acquiescence to the competing offer. The buyer would argue that the target board cannot remain ambivalent because the failure to take a stand in favor of the existing deal will likely be viewed as support for the new bid.

Usually, this provision works by giving the buyer a termination right if the target board does not reaffirm its recommendation within 10 business days. If the competing bid is announced shortly before the stockholder vote, however, the target board may need to give its reaffirmation a couple of days before the vote.

Sample Provision

[...] if [...] (iii) the Company Board shall have failed to recommend against any publicly announced Acquisition Proposal and reaffirm the Company Recommendation, in each case, within 10 Business Days following the public announcement of such Acquisition Proposal and in any event at least two Business Days prior to the Stockholders Meeting; [...].

While a change in recommendation gives the buyer a right to terminate, it does not give additional rights to the target. The target must continue to hold the shareholder vote on the original deal even if its board recommends against. Usually, a provision in the merger agreement clarifies as much.

Sample Provision

Unless this Agreement has been terminated pursuant to Article __, if, after the date of this Agreement, the Company Board shall have made a Change of Recommendation, the Company shall nevertheless convene the Stockholders Meeting and solicit the Company Stockholder Approval at such Stockholders Meeting.

This provision confirms that a mere change in recommendation does not give the target a right to stop pursuing the deal and a shareholder vote. This is different from a "force the vote" provision.[2] A "force the vote" situation arises when the target cannot terminate even to take a better deal that is currently being offered.

Failure of Representations and Covenant Compliance

If a party's representations have been breached or its covenants have not been complied with to such an extent that the related closing condition would not be satisfied, then the other party can usually terminate the deal. The materiality trigger normally matches the closing condition. In other words, if the closing condition tied to accuracy of the representations calls for them to be true and correct except for breaches that in the aggregate do not rise to the level of a material adverse effect (MAE), then the trigger for the termination right will also require MAE-level breaches.

Sample Provision

[…] if the Seller shall have breached any of its representations or warranties or failed to perform any of its covenants or agreements set forth in this Agreement, which breach or failure to perform would give rise to the failure of a condition set forth in [related closing condition under] Sections __ […];

The termination right requires formal notice of breach to be sent and provides the other party with a cure period.

Sample Provision

[…] and such breach or failure to perform is incapable of being cured prior to the Outside Date or has not been cured within [30] days following written notice from the Buyer;

It is not always clear in practice whether a breach is curable.[3] If a breach is curable, the termination right can be exercised only if the breaching party fails to sufficiently cure those breaches within an agreed window of time (such as 30 days) after receiving notice. If the breach is not curable, no cure period or advance notice is required.

In some cases, the seller may not want to permit early termination of the acquisition agreement on account of breaches. In order to increase closing certainty, the seller may require the buyer to wait it out until the closing date in order to know for sure whether a problem can be cured prior to closing. The seller may worry that a problem could unnecessarily trigger an early termination right on the part of the buyer, especially when the problem may work itself out prior to closing if the parties had more time.

Forward-Looking Aspects of Termination Rights

Termination rights can be used to address specific problems that arise in a deal. A termination right allows the parties to terminate early when an event arises whereas a condition can be used to prevent closing until the drop-dead date passes. Exercising a condition simply causes the deal to be delayed until the drop-dead date occurs. Exercising a termination right cuts off the deal process permanently. Of course, a termination right and a condition can be used in tandem to address different aspects of the same problem.

It is more common for a closing condition to be triggered by forward-looking wording (e.g., an adverse event being "reasonably likely" to occur) than a termination right. Termination rights usually do not have a forward-looking element; they are triggered by an adverse event having actually occurred.

War Story ───

In a public company transaction, the target mining company was dealing with whether it was required to restate its mineral reserves. If it did, the target could be subject to substantial liability from shareholder suits.

The buyer's lawyers immediately proposed a solution. Thinking that post-closing recourse against a public company target was not feasible, the buyer proposed a closing condition in its favor. The buyer did not propose—and possibly did not even consider—an early termination right as well.

The target's counsel readily accepted the proposed closing condition. It was drafted to state that the buyer could walk away if the adverse event (a restatement of mineral reserves) occurred. The draft did not include a requirement that material liability actually arise from the adverse event (which was expected by all) and did not have any forward-looking element to it (the restatement had to actually occur).

Shortly after the acquisition agreement was signed, the target's business collapsed due to a major slump in commodity prices. The buyer immediately examined the no-MAE condition, but it was not triggered because of a broad exception for adverse events affecting the industry. So the buyer went looking for another way to get out of the deal.

Three months after signing, and very shortly before the target's shareholders voted on the transaction, the target's auditors required an unexpected restatement due to an unrelated technical calculation issue they stumbled upon when looking at the mineral issues. The restatement came as a surprise and had nothing to do with the issues everyone was aware of.

Both sides had to face the shortcomings of their contract drafting. The buyer immediately sought to terminate the deal. From the buyer's perspective, the closing condition (that there had been no restatement) could not be satisfied, so pursuing the transaction was futile.

Yet to the buyer's dismay, it realized that it did not have the option to terminate. The target could force the buyer to continue pursuing the deal, and using its reasonable best efforts to do so, knowing that it was never actually going to close. Fortunately for the buyer, after a short period of negotiation, the target agreed to part ways amicably. In exchange for the early release, the buyer paid the target's deal expenses.

For the target, the adverse event was technical in nature and never did result in any liability. In fact, an insurance carrier ended up covering what few expenses there were related to the event. But that did not matter, since as drafted the condition was triggered whether or not the restatement resulted in any real harm. The target's shareholders lost a substantial cash premium for what, arguably, was no good reason.

Damages Following Termination

Terminating an acquisition agreement may or may not terminate claims for breaches. In most deals, the parties are permitted to seek damages for fraud from the other party after termination. The extent to which other damages can be pursued is negotiated.

Sample Provision

In the event of the termination of this Agreement, this Agreement shall thereafter become void and have no effect, and no party hereto shall have any liability to the other party hereto or their respective Affiliates, or their respective directors, officers or employees, except that nothing in this Section __ shall relieve any party from liability for [fraud or] [any] [intentional] [willful] breach of this Agreement [that is material and] that arose prior to such termination.

A handful of deals allow all damage claims to survive termination; some allow all "material" claims to survive. Most deals, however, allow a party to seek damages only for willful or intentional breach.

THE MARKET

Approximately 95 percent of deals restrict damage claims to willful or intentional breaches.

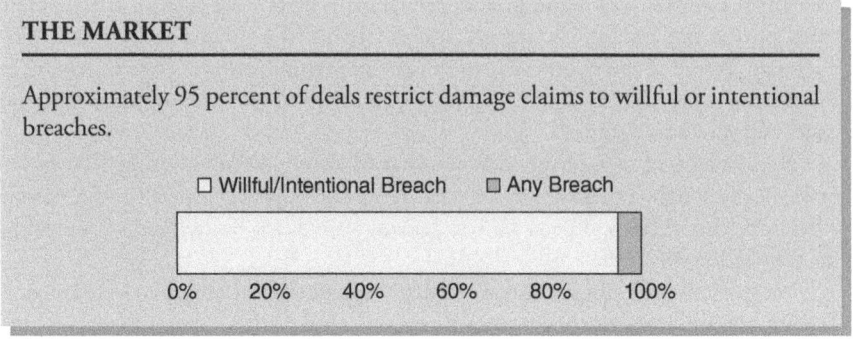

What constitutes a "willful" or an "intentional" breach is not always obvious. Common drafting does not distinguish what is meant by these phrases.[4]

If a merger agreement is breached, the target company (as the counterparty) has standing to enforce the contract. In many deals, the agreement clarifies that the target's shareholders do not have the right to directly sue the buyer as a third-party beneficiary. Only the target can sue. However, the target itself is not necessarily the party being harmed—instead, it is the shareholders who stand to lose the premium offered in the deal.

After a particular case called into question the ability of the target to include the lost deal premium in its damages claim, many deals began to clarify that the target's damages are deemed to include either the shareholders' lost deal premium or the amount that the shareholders would be entitled to claim if they were third-party beneficiaries (even though they are not).[5] Absent clarification, the target may not be able to pursue a damage claim for the lost deal premium; the shareholders may not be able to pursue the claim either because they are not third-party beneficiaries.

THE MARKET

Roughly one-fourth of public company deals clarify that lost shareholder premium counts as target company damages.

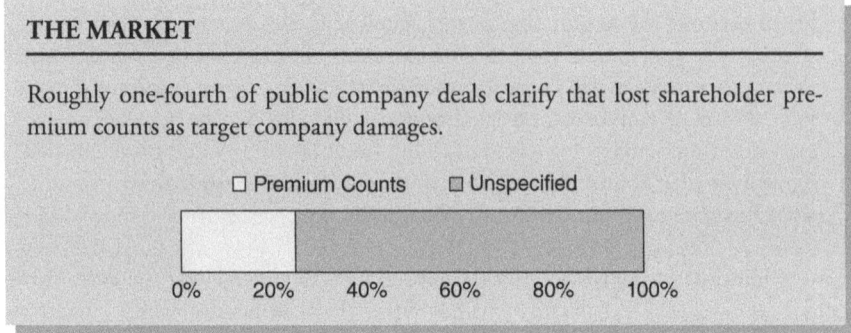

Limitations on damages have to be coordinated with the reverse breakup fee and related walk right provisions. For instance, if a reverse breakup fee is intended to be the sole remedy, then no damage claims should survive termination in circumstances in which that fee is payable. Deals with so-called "walk rights" should not permit any damage claims after termination.[6]

In deals with indemnity provisions, the types of damages that may be recovered and quantitative limitations on those damages are negotiated.[7] For instance, an indemnity may not permit claims based on punitive or speculative damages,[8] and may provide for a cap on the amount of damages that may be recovered.[9] Those limitations normally apply by their terms to the indemnity (which applies from and after closing), but they do not apply if the parties terminate the agreement.[10]

As a result, these pre-closing breaches are governed by underlying contract law without the negotiated indemnity limitations. For instance, the prohibition on recovery of punitive and special damages would not apply (meaning those types of damages could be claimed), and thus there would be no caps, deductibles, or de minimis thresholds. In a small handful of deals, indemnity-like limitations apply to the damages that can be recovered by post-termination claims.

Litigation Endnotes

1. For detailed discussion of the fiduciary out and the right of a target to terminate a deal in order to accept a better offer from a competing bidder, *see* Chapter 13, "Topping a Public Merger."
2. *See* Chapter 13-B4, Restriction on signing competing deals.
3. *See, e.g., Manpower v. Mason,* 377 F. Supp. 2d 672, 677 (E.D. Wis. 2005) (defining "incurable breaches" as a "breach [that] is either one that the contract provides no opportunity to cure or one that cannot logically be cured," instead of, as suggested by the plaintiffs, breach that went "to the very essence" of a contract or evidenced a lack of trustworthiness in the counterparty).
4. For further discussion of these terms and their meanings, *see* Chapter 12-B3, Reverse financing failure breakup fee; Chapter 12-B4, Walk right; no further liability; Chapter 12-D2, Sole and exclusive remedy.
5. *See Consol. Edison, Inc. v. Ne. Utils.,* 318 F. Supp. 2d 181, 195 (S.D.N.Y. 2004), *rev'd in part,* 426 F.3d 524 (2d Cir. 2005) (finding that the right to pursue damages based on the merger premium lay with the shareholders and not the corporation).
6. *See* Chapter 12-B4, Walk right; no further liability.
7. *See* Chapter 14-D, Indemnity Amounts, Limitations and Calculations. *See, generally,* Chapter 14-A, Indemnities in M&A Negotiations.
8. *See* Chapter 14-D4, Measuring Loss; Chapter 14-F2, Exclusive remedy.
9. *See* Chapter 14-D3, Caps on recovery.
10. *See* Chapter 14-C, Survival Periods. *See also* Chapter 14-F, Claims, Remedies, and Related Issues.

CHAPTER 10

Material Adverse Effect

Material Adverse Effect Provisions in M&A Negotiations

What are "material adverse effect" provisions?

"Material adverse effect" (MAE) provisions primarily function in an acquisition agreement to give the buyer an "out" if the target's business has suffered unique, significant, and extended deterioration.[1] When the buyer enters into a transaction, it expects in most cases that the target business at the closing will be worth the value it placed on the business at signing (when the buyer commits to pay the full purchase price). If an MAE on the target business has occurred, the buyer is not required to close the transaction. In some transactions, the MAE provision also allows the buyer to terminate the transaction early if an MAE has occurred.

In many cases, if the value of the target business increases between signing and closing, the buyer benefits from that increase in value. The seller is not permitted to terminate the transaction or refuse to close simply because it is not receiving as good a deal as it may have wanted under those circumstances. However, if the value of the target business declines between signing and closing, the buyer takes the risk of the decline in value—but only to some extent. MAE provisions put a lower limit on the decline (and types of declines) that the buyer must accept and still be required to close the transaction. The defined term "material adverse effect" is primarily negotiated and drafted for its function as a condition.

Separate from its function as a closing condition, the term "material adverse effect" is also used as a measure of materiality, the primary function of which is to qualify representations. The concept of materiality can be thought of as a scale: strict accuracy or compliance, material accuracy or compliance, and accuracy or compliance failures that would result in an MAE. Its use as a high materiality qualifier is based on the widely held view that the MAE term requires a higher level of significance than a mere "materiality" qualifier.

Types of material adverse effect provisions

There are two types of MAE provisions: qualitative and quantitative. Qualitative MAE provisions are most common and are based on concepts of materiality, which are inherently vague and require review in light of all facts and circumstances. Quantitative MAE provisions tend to be based on objective, readily determinable factors, such as accounting measures of cash, earnings or other business metrics. Quantitative MAE provisions are in part a response to the trend for qualitative MAE provisions to be increasingly favorable to targets.

Interpreting Material Adverse Effect Provisions

Judicial interpretations

Most deal provisions are simply interpreted as drafted. MAE provisions are somewhat different. In this area, courts have significantly imposed themselves into the picture. Generally, when it comes to deal certainty, there appears to be a greater risk of case law overriding the parties' intentions in the name of interpreting the wording of the contract, and courts have tended to favor the target's arguments for deal certainty (certainty that closing will occur).

It is often noted that no Delaware court has ever found an MAE on a target to have occurred in the acquisition context.[2] Courts tend to place the burden of proof on the buyer[3] and have frequently come to a narrow interpretation of the traditional MAE wording. Nevertheless, other courts have on occasion found MAEs to have occurred.[4]

Contractual definitions

No definition

Occasionally, the parties will decide not to define the term "material adverse effect." When it is defined, it usually includes a litany of carve-outs for effects that do not count toward an MAE determination. Without defining MAE, the target would not (on the face of the drafting) necessarily receive the benefit of customary carve-outs.

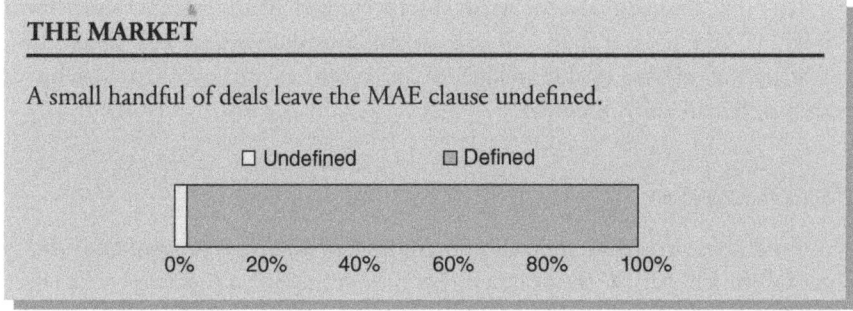

THE MARKET

A small handful of deals leave the MAE clause undefined.

☐ Undefined   ☐ Defined

0%   20%   40%   60%   80%   100%

Adverse and material

The MAE definition has two main components:

- First, there must have been an adverse effect on the target business that is material to the target and its subsidiaries, taken as a whole. Although the definition uses the term "material," it is interpreted by courts and practitioners to refer to a relatively high standard of materiality. The phrase "taken as a whole" helps ensure that the level of adverse effects must be significant before the test is met.
- Second, the definition will specify a litany of business matters that may be adversely affected, such as the financial condition, assets and liabilities of the target business.

Sample Provision

"Material Adverse Effect" shall mean any change, event, violation, inaccuracy, effect or circumstance (each, an "Effect") that, individually or taken together with all other Effects that have occurred prior to the date of determination of the occurrence of the Material Adverse Effect, is or would reasonably be expected to be materially adverse to the business, financial condition or results of operations of the Target and its Subsidiaries, taken as a whole; provided, however, that [...].

Courts have generally interpreted the MAE definition to require adverse effects that are longer term in nature—such as adverse effects that "substantially threaten the overall earnings potential of the target in a durationally significant" manner.[5] An acquirer is presumed by courts to have a long-term strategy that should guide the MAE interpretation. In any event, a short-term "blip" in earnings is usually not sufficient. Some courts have also focused on whether the adverse change relates to an "essential purpose" that the buyer wanted to achieve in the deal.[6]

Prospective components

In some cases, the MAE definition includes a prospective component. This is helpful for a buyer. Without it, a target may argue that a future adverse effect that has not yet impacted the target should not count toward an MAE.[7] The absence of a prospective component would make it harder for a buyer to treat a contingent liability or event as an adverse effect on the target that should count toward an MAE.[8]

A prospective component is achieved in two primary ways in practice. First, the MAE definition may clarify that it covers adverse effects on not only the target's business, but also on the target's "prospects." In this way, if there is an adverse effect on the prospective value or business opportunities of the target, those adverse effects would clearly count toward an MAE determination.

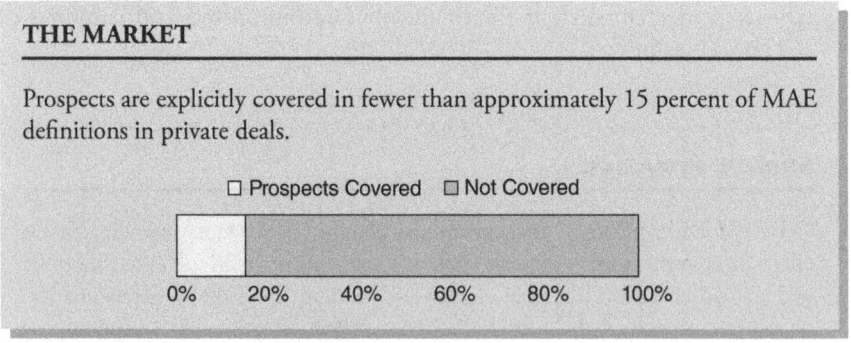

THE MARKET

Prospects are explicitly covered in fewer than approximately 15 percent of MAE definitions in private deals.

☐ Prospects Covered   ☐ Not Covered

0%   20%   40%   60%   80%   100%

The second way to include a prospective component in the MAE provision is to include some form of forward-looking language. By doing so, the MAE definition will cover not only adverse effects that have actually occurred prior to closing, but also, for instance, adverse effects that are reasonably likely to occur after closing in the future.[9] In that way, an adverse effect that has not yet impacted—but that is expected to impact—the target business can trigger an MAE.

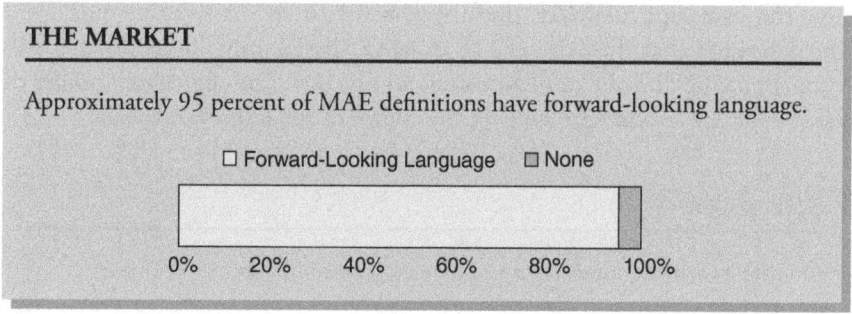

THE MARKET

Approximately 95 percent of MAE definitions have forward-looking language.

☐ Forward-Looking Language   ☐ None

0%   20%   40%   60%   80%   100%

Carve-outs

The MAE definition usually contains many carve-outs for types of adverse effects on the target business that do not count toward an MAE determination. No-MAE provisions started out (long ago) as a condition in favor of the buyer that generally allowed the buyer to refuse to close if the value of the target had materially deteriorated between the signing and closing. Buyers would argue that if the buyer agrees to pay full price, why should it not have the right to walk away if the target is no longer worth full price.

Over time, the leverage in these negotiations has shifted from the buyer to the sellers, in favor of the sellers being able to force a closing even in the face of a drop in value to the buyer. This shift has primarily manifested itself in the form of an ever-growing list of carve-outs for adverse effects which may have a real impact on the target business but which do not count toward an MAE. These carve-outs represent types of adverse effects for which the buyer takes the business risk. This shift has also been supported by court rulings and interpretations that make it difficult for a buyer to show and enforce a no-MAE closing condition.

Sample Provision

[…]; provided, however, that no Effect (by itself or when aggregated or taken together with any and all other Effects) directly or indirectly resulting from, arising out of, attributable to, or related to any of the following shall be deemed to be or constitute a "Material Adverse Effect," and no Effect (by itself or when aggregated or taken together with any and all other such Effects) directly or indirectly resulting from, arising out of, attributable to, or related to any of the following shall be taken into account when determining whether a "Material Adverse Effect" has occurred or may, would, or could occur: [litany of carve-outs]

The evolution of MAE drafting has led to so many carve-outs from the definition that the existence of an MAE (based only on factors that still count) may be difficult to demonstrate in practice. The aggregate number of carve-outs has steadily grown over the course of the last several years.

> **THE MARKET**
>
> On average, current deals have approximately nine different carve-outs.

Actually teasing apart the impact of factors that count and those that do not can be challenging in practice. For instance, assume that a business decline can be clearly traced (which is rarely the case in reality) to two factors, each contributing to roughly one half of the decline (e.g., loss of a major customer and a general slow-down in the economy (excluded)). If as usual adverse effects on the general economy are covered by the carve-outs to the MAE definition, then those adverse effects do not count toward an MAE. The effect of the nonexcluded factor alone would have to be separately determined on a hypothetical basis. That hypothetical, stand-alone effect of nonexcluded factors would have to be analyzed to determine whether it is significant enough to constitute an MAE.

How to perform this factor analysis leaves much to the imagination. What if the customer left due to quality concerns but in a growing economy may have held out longer if it had lots of money to burn? Excluded and non-excluded factors can interact with each other. Factors that count toward an MAE determination may be more or less significant depending on whether they occur during a booming or collapsing industry and economy (which are usually excluded factors). The drafting of MAE clauses does not usually address this issue.

The most important carve-outs are for changes that generally affect the economy or that generally affect the industry in which the target operates. General changes in the economy following (or causing) a disruption in the financial markets may impact many industries and businesses. With these carve-outs, the adverse effects arising from those changes in the economy do not count toward an MAE determination, which means that such changes are at the risk of the buyer.

As a result, the buyer would not be able to avoid closing or terminate the transaction under the MAE clause because of adverse effects on the target business from those sources, no matter how bad those effects were. Similarly, changes that generally affect a particular industry, such as the banking industry or the pharmaceutical industry, are commonly excluded from the scope of the MAE definition.

Sample Provision

[…] (i) changes in general economic conditions in the United States or any other country or region in the world, or changes in conditions in the global economy generally; (ii) changes in conditions in the industries in which the Company and its Subsidiaries conduct business;

These two carve-outs can be quite significant in practice. For example, following the recent financial crisis, financial institutions were challenged both by changes in the industry and changes in the overall economy. Under a customary MAE provision, those changes would presumably not count toward an MAE determination, despite how dramatic they were for many businesses in the financial industry.

Of course, each bank's story was a little different, so a refined analysis would be required to know the extent to which a particular institution's troubles were caused by general changes in the industry and economy or by its own particular circumstances and investments.

War Story

The target was a small, privately owned airline, with a cyclical business tied to the travel industry. The deal documents, of course, included a no-MAE condition, but, for whatever reason, the seller never asked for traditional carve-outs from the MAE definition.

The buyer recognized that adverse effects on the securities markets would not necessarily let it avoid closing unless they resulted in an adverse effect on the target itself. So the buyer proposed a special condition that would have allowed the buyer to refuse to close if the securities markets became unstable. This special condition is different from a general MAE condition. Whereas the special condition deals with disruption in the markets, the MAE condition deals with adverse effects on the target business.

This time the seller objected strongly. Already happy with the general MAE definition, the buyer let the seller win that point, so that special condition—sometimes referred to as a "market material adverse change (MAC)"—was deleted from the acquisition agreement. However, since market conditions can affect the target, the seller's lawyers could have taken the next step to specifically carve out changes in securities markets from the general MAE definition.

While the parties were waiting for regulatory approval, markets destabilized and the target's business slumped. The buyer claimed that the target's business was severely damaged. The seller exclaimed that it had fought hard to get rid of the separate condition tied to the stability of the securities markets. The buyer noted that the MAE definition still covered adverse effects on the target business caused by changes in the securities markets.

When the buyer threatened to walk, the seller sued. Eventually, the parties settled. The deal went forward, but at a reduced purchase price. The weak MAE definition had given the buyer leverage to re-price its deal.

Another key exception covers changes in law or regulation. Where this carve-out is included, regulatory changes that reduce the profitability of the target business cannot form the basis for an MAE. Changes in law would presumably affect the entire industry, so they may already be covered by the general industry carve-out. As with changes in the industry, this carve-out can excuse events that turn out to be significant.

War Story ───

The target provided a long-standing service. It was a lucrative enterprise, even though the environmental soundness of its practices had been called into question. Happy with the target's profitability and growth prospects, the buyer offered a significant premium.

Unexpectedly, some environmentalists had gotten the ear of the state legislature in the target's most active state. After signing up the M&A deal, the buyer learned through some of its contacts that the legislature was soon to propose a new bill designed to stop the core business of the target and others in the same industry.

The buyer balked. It was not going to take the risk of paying a premium for a business that might not be able to survive in a few months. The CEO of the buyer immediately told his legal team that they needed to find and exercise a termination right. With the target's business potentially vanishing into thin air, there was certainly an "out" somewhere in the documents he thought.

Unfortunately for the buyer, the MAE definition included a carve-out for general effects on the industry as well as a carve-out for changes in law. The buyer could not find a condition to rely on and had to close the deal in the face of substantial legal uncertainty.

Adverse effects related to the announcement of the transaction are frequently excluded from the MAE definition. In this way, the buyer takes the risk of changes in the customer and employee base once they learn that the buyer is acquiring the target business. If the target's customers take issue with the buyer's identity—for example, if the buyer is a foreign corporation in a sensitive industry, has a questionable reputation, or is a competitor of some of the key customers—those facts will not give the buyer leverage to terminate or refuse to close the transaction under the no-MAE condition.

War Story

The target was a popular, iconic American brand. When reports of a foreign buyer's agreement to purchase it surfaced, the reaction was quick and strong, especially in the American manufacturer's home state.

Some vocal consumers appeared uneasy with the foreign ownership of what they thought of as a patriotic brand. Several opposition websites were launched, urging both the rejection of the deal and the boycott of target's products if the hostile takeover were to succeed.

Moreover, since the buyer had acquired a reputation for aggressive cost-cutting, fears over U.S. job losses were raised in the media. Joining the bandwagon, politicians took issue with the deal, several vowing to do what they could to block it (which was very little, since the target was not in a regulated industry).

The target's lawyers had carefully excluded from the MAE definition any negative fallout due to the announcement of the transaction. So any risk that consumers would reject the new company was on the buyer. Fortunately, the reaction soon began to die down. If it hadn't, the buyer would have been stuck with the deal and its fallout.

Other common carve-outs include changes in the securities markets, changes in generally accepted accounting principles (GAAP), and failure by the target to meet its own projections. With numerous carve-outs, it becomes more likely that declines in the target's business performance can arguably be attributed to one or more of the excluded factors.

Many of the carve-outs contain exceptions of their own (i.e., exceptions to the carve-outs), so that the carve-out does not cover effects that disproportionately impact the target business. For instance, an adverse effect on the industry will not be excluded from counting against an MAE to the extent it disproportionately affects the target, relative to the target's peers.

Sample Provision

[…], except, in the cases of clauses __, to the extent such Effect has not had a disproportionate impact on the Company relative to other companies in the industries in which the Company and its Subsidiaries conduct business.

The exception for disproportionate effects is, in most cases, a way of restating that only the "general" portion of adverse effects are excluded. If a change in the industry disproportionately impacts a particular company, then that impact was arguably not, in fact, the consequence of a change in the industry. Instead, it must be due to something particular about the target company. In such cases, to the extent there is a disproportionate impact on the target company, it will count toward an MAE.

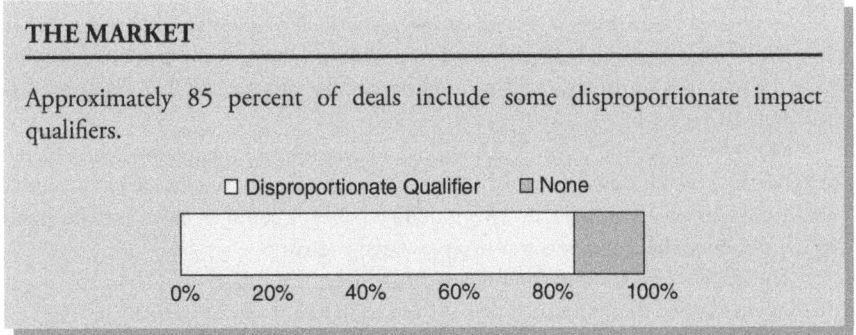

THE MARKET

Approximately 85 percent of deals include some disproportionate impact qualifiers.

☐ Disproportionate Qualifier   ☐ None

0%   20%   40%   60%   80%   100%

Implementing MAE Rights

Closing condition vs. representation bring-down condition

A buyer can achieve a no-MAE closing condition in two primary ways. The first is to include a stand-alone closing condition in the conditions section. The condition would state that an MAE has not occurred since a particular date, frequently since the signing date.

The other method is to rely on the representation bring-down condition, which would require the no-MAE representation to be accurate. The representations normally include a confirmation that there has not been an MAE on the target business since the date of the target's last audited financial statements. The closing conditions normally include a requirement that the representations of the target business be accurate at closing. When the no-MAE representation and the bring-down condition are put together, the result is that the buyer has the benefit of a closing condition that requires the no-MAE representation to be accurate.

The effect of these two methods of achieving a no-MAE condition differ based primarily on the time periods covered and whether disclosure in the schedules counts against the buyer for the no-MAE clause.

Qualified by disclosure in schedules

The bring-down of the no-MAE representation is normally qualified by matters described in the disclosure schedules while a stand-alone no-MAE condition is not qualified by disclosure in the schedules. As a result, adverse effects that were disclosed in the schedules count against the buyer in the bring-down of the no-MAE representation, but typically do not do so in the stand-alone condition.

More specifically, representations generally have an exception for matters described in the schedules. The disclosure schedules may include a wide variety of adverse statements related to the target business, designed to counteract the affirmative statements made in the representations.[10] Some of those adverse disclosures may qualify the no-MAE representation. In contrast, a closing condition which states that there has not been an MAE is not usually qualified by the disclosure schedules. Accordingly, if the buyer has the benefit of a stand-alone closing condition, the adverse information in the schedules would not usually count against the buyer.

The buyer may disclose in the schedules that there has been a significant change in the target's business, describing particular adverse consequences expected to occur on account of those facts. If that disclosure qualifies the no-MAE representation, then those adverse effects would not result in a breach of the no-MAE representation. However, such adverse effects—even if disclosed—would count toward and could constitute an MAE in the case of a stand-alone no-MAE closing condition, allowing the buyer to refuse to close.

Different time periods covered

Different time periods tend to be covered by a stand-alone no-MAE condition and a bring-down of the no-MAE representation. Buyers are generally concerned about material adverse effects that occur during two periods:

* *Financials to signing* (pre-signing period from target's last audited financial statements to signing date); and
* *Signing to closing* (from signing date to closing date).

The period covered by a no-MAE representation, as a statement of historical fact, normally begins at a pre-signing date, such as the date of the last audited financial statements of the targeted business. The buyer may start with the last unaudited financials because it relies on those to provide snapshot of the business. A stand-alone closing condition, in contrast, may start at either a pre-signing date or the signing date itself. The period covered by either can end at signing or end at closing.

Acquisition agreements are not clear as to how to combine or keep separate these two time periods in determining the extent of an adverse effect. If each of the two periods are covered by a separate provision, then presumably adverse effects in each time period would not be aggregated with each other. If, in contrast, one provision covers both time periods, then adverse effects over the whole period would be measured.

Aggregation (or lack thereof) across those two periods could work for the benefit of either party. For instance, assume that a target business has experienced significant growth since the date of the last financial statements through the signing, but all of that growth is lost due to adverse effects occurring between signing and closing. Over the aggregate period there may have been no change, but during the period between signing and closing the change may have been significant.

The analysis above assumes that adverse changes are measured relative to the beginning of a period. The MAE provision does not specify how it is measured, however. Another reading would be that any adverse effects are measured relative to the point of which they occur.

Implementation

No-MAE representation only

There are three main options for providing no-MAE coverage to the buyer. In the first option, no-MAE coverage is provided through a no-MAE representation that spans both periods: from the last audited financial statements of the target, through the signing, and up to the date of closing.

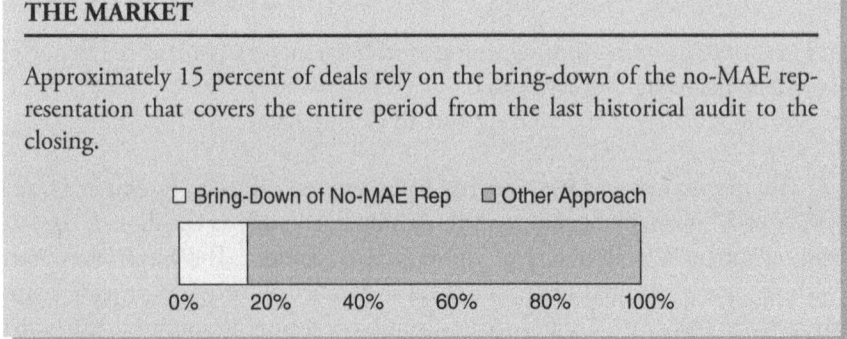

THE MARKET

Approximately 15 percent of deals rely on the bring-down of the no-MAE representation that covers the entire period from the last historical audit to the closing.

☐ Bring-Down of No-MAE Rep   ☐ Other Approach

0%   20%   40%   60%   80%   100%

As a result of using a representation to provide no-MAE coverage, under this option the no-MAE closing condition is qualified by disclosure contained in the disclosure schedules. Adverse events or risks disclosed against the no-MAE representation in the disclosure schedules will not count toward whether the buyer can refuse to close on the basis of an MAE.

Sample Provision

Representation: From the [insert date of the last audited financial statements of the Target business] to the Closing Date, there has not been any Material Adverse Effect.

Since the time period covered by the no-MAE representation spans both periods in this case, this method aggregates the impact of adverse events across both periods. If a partial MAE were to occur during the first period, and another partial MAE were to occur during the second, these two partial MAEs could theoretically be aggregated and, together, could cross the MAE threshold. Aggregation is not specifically addressed in MAE provisions, but on its face would be the consequence of how these terms are normally drafted.

War Story

In the early stages of running an auction to sell a division, a large consumer products company changed the manufacturing method for its flagship product. To its surprise, the product got worse, not better. Consumers reacted negatively, leading to a significant decline in sales. The company quickly reversed course, made improvements, and hoped to win back its lost market share.

The buyer was well aware of this issue, and presumably took that into account in the price it offered. The seller believed that it would be unfair for the buyer to take that discount for the risk yet still be protected from that risk.

The seller structured the no-MAE protection as a rep bring-down condition (i.e., a closing condition that the no-MAE representation remained accurate as of closing). The disclosure schedules (which qualify the representations) clearly laid out the facts and risks.

By the time of closing, the consumer turn-around effort had stalled and the auction winner started talking about the possibility that an MAE had occurred. Because the no-MAE provisions were all in the form of a bring-down of the no-MAE representation, the winner could not claim that loss of sales constituted an MAE, and had to close.

Because no-MAE coverage is provided by a representation that includes the period between signing and closing, in a private deal the buyer could sue under the indemnity for breaches during that period (if allowed by the indemnity).

Stand-alone no-MAE condition only

No-MAE protection can also be provided by a stand-alone no-MAE condition that spans both periods (from the last audited financials to closing).

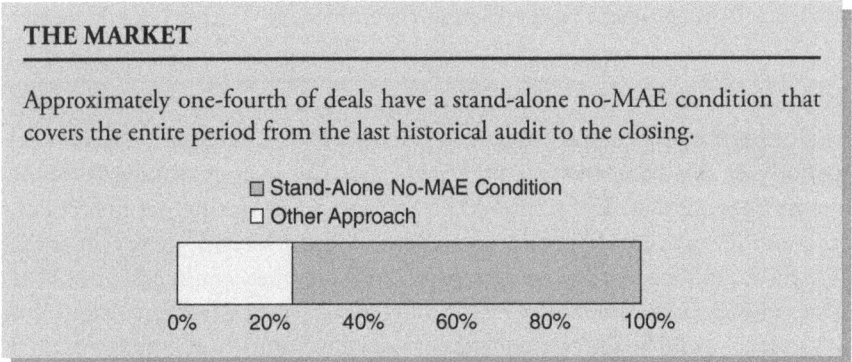

THE MARKET

Approximately one-fourth of deals have a stand-alone no-MAE condition that covers the entire period from the last historical audit to the closing.

☐ Stand-Alone No-MAE Condition
☐ Other Approach

0%   20%   40%   60%   80%   100%

In contrast to a no-MAE representation, such a stand-alone condition is not by its terms qualified by the disclosure in the schedules. Adverse statements in the schedules will not count against the buyer's ability to refuse to close or terminate the transaction on the basis of an MAE having occurred.

Sample Provision

Closing Condition: From the [insert date of the last audited financial statements of the Target business] to the Closing Date, no Material Adverse Effect shall have occurred [and be continuing].

Similar to relying on the bring-down of the no-MAE representation, both periods are spanned under one condition, which means that adverse events are aggregated across those periods. The no-MAE representation is normally not extended to cover the period between signing and closing under this option. The buyer, as a result, cannot sue under an indemnity if an MAE were to occur during that period.

Combined no-MAE representation and stand-alone condition

The stand-alone no-MAE condition, on the one hand, can be combined with the no-MAE representation and its bring-down condition, on the other. Under this hybrid construct, a no-MAE representation covers the period from the date of the last audited financial statements through the signing date. The stand-alone closing condition then picks up the no-MAE coverage from signing through the closing.

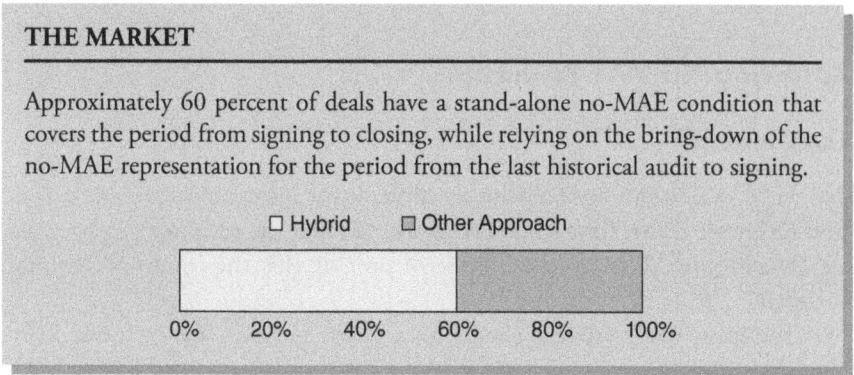

THE MARKET

Approximately 60 percent of deals have a stand-alone no-MAE condition that covers the period from signing to closing, while relying on the bring-down of the no-MAE representation for the period from the last historical audit to signing.

☐ Hybrid   ☐ Other Approach

0%   20%   40%   60%   80%   100%

Disclosure schedules only qualify the historical aspects of the no-MAE condition. That is, the disclosure only qualifies the representations which cover the period from the last financial statements through the date of signing. Disclosure in the schedules does not qualify the stand-alone no-MAE condition. As a result, that disclosure does not qualify the period from the signing through the closing date.

Sample Provision

Representation: From the [insert date of the last audited financial statements of the Target business] to the date of this Agreement, there has not been any Material Adverse Effect.

Closing Condition: From the date of this Agreement to the Closing Date, no Material Adverse Effect shall have occurred [and be continuing].

In this case, the buyer would not be able to assert that the no-MAE condition fails on the basis of adverse facts included in the disclosure schedules that existed at signing. But the buyer would not be required to take the "forward-looking" risk of adverse effects of risks described in the schedules that occur after the date of signing—even if it had notice of those potential effects through the disclosure schedules.

The no-MAE representation and the stand-alone no-MAE condition are each independent provisions. As a result, if a partial MAE occurs in each of these two time periods, the acquisition agreement would not appear to aggregate them. The buyer could only sue under an indemnity (in a private deal) for breaches arising in the period before closing.

Enforcing No-MAE Protection

Closing condition

No-MAE conditions are notoriously difficult for buyers to prove. New York and Delaware courts have generally concluded that the party seeking to avoid its obligation to close has the burden of proving that the condition was not satisfied.

The most likely adverse effects on a target business are excluded from the MAE determination as a result of the carve-outs contained in the MAE definition.[11] This includes general adverse effects on the economy and industry. Even if the buyer can show specific effects on the target business that are not generalized to the industry or economy, the buyer still has the challenge of demonstrating that those effects are sufficiently significant and long term to qualify as an MAE.

Asserting that a closing condition has not been met is a risky proposition. It will almost always be uncertain whether an MAE has occurred. If the buyer refuses to close or purports to terminate the acquisition agreement on that basis, the buyer is taking legal risk. If the target later is able to show that the adverse effects did not rise to the level of an MAE, the buyer is in breach for failing to close the transaction when it was required to do so.

Damages for breach in such cases could be large relative to the size of the deal. The buyer in most cases has agreed to a price that represents a premium for the target business. Not only is the deal premium gone, but if substantial adverse effects have occurred, the target is also worth significantly less than its base value at the time the deal was negotiated. Further, the post-breach value of the business may be impacted by the very fact that the buyer is refusing to close, due to the so-called "damaged goods" perception in the marketplace. The difference between the premium deal price and post-breach value would arguably represent the target's damages.

This measure of damages could, in fact, exceed the total amount of equity financing that the buyer had intended to invest in the target business for a private equity deal. Also, note that a private equity buyer would presumably have to fund the entire damages claim out of equity financing from its fund (to the extent guaranteed by the fund)—thus subjecting the fund to the maximum exposure it expected to incur in the deal, without offering any potential upside if the target does recover.[12]

Due to the riskiness of refusing to close over a claimed MAE, the buyer may informally assert that an MAE has occurred as part of a negotiating strategy to encourage the target company or seller to negotiate a lower price, without actually affirmatively refusing to close or terminate the transaction.

Representation bring-down condition

In private deals, a breach of representation triggers a claim under the indemnity.[13] (In public deals there is normally no indemnity.) A breach of the no-MAE representation would, accordingly, also result in an indemnity claim. The failure of a stand-alone no-MAE condition, in contrast, gives the buyer the right not to close the deal, but does not give it the right to close over an MAE and then sue under the indemnity.

How relevant the indemnity is depends on whether materiality is read out of the representation. More often than not, materiality qualifiers are read out of the representations for purposes of the indemnity.[14] Some deals limit the read-out provisions so that materiality qualifiers are not read out of the no-MAE representation. Others do not. It is not exactly clear what happens to the no-MAE representation if materiality (including MAE) qualifiers were read out of it. On one theory, the entire representation is ignored. On another, the word "material" is deleted, such that it covers all adverse effects on the business (subject to the carve-outs), whether or not material.

Quantitative MAEs

Over time, MAE provisions have become more difficult for the buyers and more favorable to sellers and target companies. The number of carve-outs to what may count toward an MAE determination has increased, and courts have handed down interpretations supporting sellers and the target companies. In part as a response to that trend by buyers, a handful of transactions include so-called "quantitative" MAE provisions as deal conditions.

Quantitative MAE conditions typically take the form of stand-alone conditions. The condition requires that a particular minimum financial metric has been achieved. Minimum earnings before interest, taxes, depreciation, and amortization (EBITDA) during specified periods and maximum leverage (EBITDA compared to debt) are the most common measures used in quantitative MAE conditions.

Sample Provision

The Company's [insert financial metric] for the __ period ending __ (or, if the Closing Date shall occur on or after __, for the __ period ending __) shall not be less than $__.

Quantitative MAE conditions can be tailored to the deal as well. For instance, a quantitative MAE may require a minimum amount of cash in the target company at closing, or could be tied to customer retention metrics.

The second major difference is that quantitative MAE provisions are not subject to the litany of carve-outs that have eroded qualitative MAE provisions. A quantitative MAE provision would not, for example, normally contain exceptions to allow the target's financial metrics to fall below specified amounts as long as the shortfall is due to general adverse changes in the industry or the economy. Instead, if the target fails to achieve those metrics for any reason, including changes that are beyond its control, the buyer will be allowed to refuse to close the transaction.

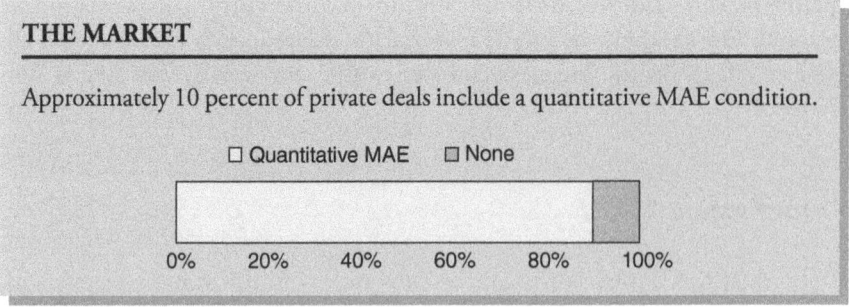

THE MARKET

Approximately 10 percent of private deals include a quantitative MAE condition.

☐ Quantitative MAE   ☐ None

0%   20%   40%   60%   80%   100%

There is no conceptual reason why quantitative MAE conditions could not be subject to the same variety of carve-outs as qualitative MAEs, but the provision would then lose the benefit of certainty as to whether it has been satisfied or not.

Litigation Endnotes

1. The term "material adverse change" (MAC) is used interchangeably with MAE. Although "material adverse effect" has become more common in recent years, the acronym "MAC" is more commonly used than MAE.
2. *See Hexion Specialty Chems., Inc. v. Huntsman Corp.,* 965 A.2d 715, 738 (Del. Ch. 2008) ("commentators have noted that Delaware courts have never found a material adverse effect to have occurred in the context of a merger agreement"). During the 2008 credit crisis, the buyer in *Hexion* attempted to back out of its obligations under a merger agreement it signed before the crisis (without a financing out), on the grounds that the target had suffered an MAE and the combined company would be insolvent after the deal closed. While the parties were obtaining necessary regulatory approvals, the target reported disappointing quarterly results that missed projections it had made when the deal was signed. The court declined to rule on whether the combined entity would be solvent or insolvent at closing, and rejected the buyer's argument that it can be excused from performing its freely undertaken contractual obligations because performance of those obligations would risk insolvency. *Id.* at 722. The court reasoned that it was the duty of the buyer's board of directors to explore the many available options for mitigating the risk of insolvency while causing the buyer to perform its contractual obligations in good faith and concluded that the target had not suffered an MAE. *Id.*
3. The *Hexion* court placed the burden of proof on the buyer, the party attempting to avoid obligations under the merger agreement by claiming the target had suffered an MAE. 965 A.2d at 736–739.
4. *See, e.g., Pan Am Corp. v. Delta Airlines, Inc.,* 175 B.R. 438 (Bankr. S.D.N.Y. 1994) (20 percent drop in bookings and 15 percent decline in monthly revenue); *Katz v. NVF Co.,* 473 N.Y.S.2d 786 (1984) (drop from $2 million profit to $6 million loss); *Allegheny Energy, Inc. v. DQE, Inc.,* 74 F. Supp. 2d 482, 491 (W.D. Pa. 1999) (42 percent reduction in net income); *KLRA, Inc. v. Long,* 639 S.W.2d 60 (Ark. Ct. App. 1982) (48 percent decline in profits). *But see IBP, Inc. v. Tyson Foods, Inc.,* 789 A.2d 14 (Del. Ch. 2001) (65 percent reduction in earnings not an MAE under New York law).
5. *See id.* at 68 (citation omitted). The court noted that a short-term hiccup in earnings should not be sufficient to constitute an MAE, and concluded that an MAE should be material when viewed from the longer-term perspective of a reasonable acquirer.
6. *See Shore Invs., Inc. v. Bhole, Inc.,* No. S09-C-09-013, 2011 BL 303169, at *6 (Del. Super. Ct. Nov. 28, 2011) (holding that a "material breach" was a failure to do something that is so fundamental to a contract that the failure to perform that obligation defeats the *essential purpose* of the contract or makes it impossible for the other party to perform under the contract). In other words, for a breach of contract to be material, it must "go to the root" or "essence" of the agreement

between the parties, or be "one which touches the fundamental purpose of the contract and defeats the object of the parties in entering into the contract." *Id.*

7. Some buyers have argued that an adverse effect on prospects is an adverse effect on the "business" has occurred, such that a separate reference to prospects is not required. *See, e.g., Pacheco v. Cambridge Tech. Partners (Mass.), Inc.,* 85 F. Supp. 2d 69, 73, 77 (D. Mass. 2001); Memorandum and Order at 29–32, *Goodman Mfg. Co. v. Raytheon Co.,* No. 1:98-CV-02774 (S.D.N.Y. Aug. 31, 1999).

8. *See, e.g., S.C. Johnson & Son, Inc. v. DowBrands, Inc.,* 167 F. Supp. 2d 657 (D. Del. 2001) (reasoning that a patent infringement claim against the target could not constitute a material adverse change unless and until the plaintiff raising the patent infringement claim actually wins its case).

9. *See Cendant Corp. v. Commonwealth Gen. Corp.,* No. 98C-10-034 (Del. Ch. Aug. 28, 2002) (where parties argued both sides of whether the phrase "could reasonably be expected to have a material adverse effect" was actually meant to cover prospects of the target).

10. *See* Chapter 6-F3, Disclosure schedules.

11. *See* Chapter 10-B2d, Carve-outs.

12. For discussion of limits on remedies against private equity buyers, *see* Chapter 12-E, No Recourse against Private Equity Buyer.

13. *See* Chapter 6-E3, Indemnity.

14. *See* Chapter 6-F6, Reading out qualifiers.

CHAPTER 11

Equity and Debt Commitment Letters

Private Equity Deal Structures

Private equity deals require two sources of financing: equity financing from the private equity fund, often referred to as the sponsor, and debt financing from third-party lenders. Each source of financing is supported by a commitment letter that is signed at the same time the acquisition agreement is entered into.

A private equity fund is a pool of money. A range of third-party investors will deposit money into the fund and/or commit to deposit money into the fund as needed. This fund entity is the holder of value and those funding commitments.

The fund has no operations or employees; it just holds investments. The investment activity of the fund is usually managed by a management company (or general partner of the fund). The management company acts for the fund under an investment management agreement. The deal team that the target interacts with in negotiating the transaction is usually made up of employees or partners of the management company.

None of these entities—neither the fund nor the management company (nor any general partner of the fund, if there is one)—sign up as parties to the acquisition agreement. Instead, on the buyer side two special purpose vehicles (SPVs) with no assets of their own enter into the purchase agreement.

This structure alone would present a significant problem for the target. If the target needed to sue, it would have no one to sue with any assets. Two documents address this concern: an equity commitment letter and a fund guarantee; both are discussed in this chapter.

One of the buyer's two SPVs is referred to as the "parent." The other is referred to as the "merger subsidiary." The private equity fund owns the parent. The parent, in turn, owns the merger subsidiary.

Structuring is discussed in more detail in 343 SPS § XVI. In short, the merger subsidiary is party to the actual merger. It is usually merged into the target in what is referred to as a reverse triangular merger. The parent SPV is party to the merger agreement, but not the actual merger. Instead, once the merger subsidiary and the target merge, the parent SPV ends up owning the stock of the target (the combined entity).

Equity Commitment Letter

Under the equity commitment letter, the private equity fund makes a commitment to the parent SPV. It commits to provide funds to the parent in the form of equity financing, to enable the parent to fund a portion of the purchase price.

The equity commitment letter has several conditions that must be satisfied before the private equity fund is required to fund the equity financing to the parent SPV. In particular, it is conditioned on the simultaneous closing of the merger. This means that the equity financing cannot ever be funded to the parent SPV unless the deal closes, in which case the financing will be used as intended to pay the purchase price. As such, this financing cannot provide a resource for a target to recover against if the target tries to sue the parent SPV for damages.

The target is not a party to the equity financing letter from the private equity fund to the parent SPV. As a result, the target needs a way to ensure that the parent SPV will actually draw down the equity financing from the private equity fund. Without an enforcement right, theoretically the fund could decline to pay under the equity commitment letter without any risk that the parent SPV (which is owned by the fund) would sue the fund.

These enforcement rights by the target under the equity commitment letter come in two forms. In some deals, the target is named as an express third-party beneficiary under the equity commitment letter. Third-party beneficiaries are not a signatory to the agreement themselves, but have standing to sue to enforce the agreement. That way the target does not have a right to collect the proceeds of the equity financing because it is not party to the equity commitment letter, but has the right to force the private equity fund to pay over the proceeds to the parent SPV. If the proceeds are paid over to the parent SPV, the target can use its remedies under the merger agreement to require the parent SPV to close the deal.

The other way for the target to ensure that the equity financing is funded is to use the target's specific enforcement rights under the merger agreement. Under the merger agreement, the parent SPV will commit to using its efforts to cause the private equity fund to pay over the equity financing once the equity commitment letter conditions are met. The target can use its specific enforcement right against the parent SPV, making the parent SPV in turn pursue parent's remedies against the private equity fund. Through this daisy chain, the target can indirectly force the private equity fund to pay the equity financing to the parent and from there to the target.

Limited Fund Guarantee

If the private equity fund only signed an equity commitment letter, then the target would be left with no ability to sue for damages. As noted above, the equity financing by its terms is only paid when and if the deal closes. Absent a closing, the parent SPV has no money to pay damages to the target. In particular, the private equity buyer may have to pay the target a reverse breakup fee in some cases.[1] By definition, the deal is broken up and the closing never happens when the fee is payable. The target wants to know it can collect on that fee.

To solve this problem, the private equity fund typically enters into a guarantee. The guarantee normally reflects the commitment of the private equity fund to pay the reverse breakup fee if the parent SPV is ever obligated to pay it. In many cases, the fund will also guarantee to pay a damages claim that the target may have against the parent SPV, usually subject to a cap on damages. The cap on damages is often limited to the same amount as the reverse breakup fee, although in some structures the damages cap can be higher.

Debt Commitment Letter

Private equity buyers also obtain commitment letters from lenders prior to signing an acquisition agreement. The target will normally insist that the buyer obtain as strong a commitment from its lenders as possible. In fact, the target will play a significant role in negotiating the debt commitment letter with the buyer's lenders.

The lenders want conditions in their commitment letter to the buyer so that the lenders cannot be required to close in the face of specified adverse events, such as disruption in the capital markets in which the lead banks intend to syndicate the loan to various other lenders.

Matching up the conditions in the bank financing to the conditions in the acquisition agreement is an important part of negotiating the commitment letters, from the perspective of both sides. Matching means that any condition in the bank's commitment letter should conform to the equivalent condition in the buyer's acquisition agreement.

For instance, the buyer may refuse to close the acquisition if the target has suffered a material adverse effect (MAE); the lenders may refuse to lend if the target has suffered an MAE. By ensuring that the MAE-out is identical between the commitment letter and the acquisition agreement, the buyer can ensure that there is no case in which it is required to close the deal when its banks are not required to fund.

The target will usually have back-to-back specific enforcement rights for the debt financing. The target will be able to force the buyer, in turn, to force the lenders to fund. This specific enforcement right is highly conditioned, as discussed in 343 SPS § XII.

Litigation Endnotes

1. *See* Chapter 4-A, Elements of the Acquisition Agreement.

CHAPTER 12

Financing Risk

History of Financing Provisions

Many buyers need some form of debt financing to pay the purchase price in a cash deal, and possibly to refinance debt of the target and pay deal expenses. At signing, the buyer's ability to obtain debt financing at closing is never certain. The financing provisions of an acquisition agreement address what happens if debt financing is not actually available to the buyer at closing. The number of deals using debt to finance some or all of the purchase price, and the amount of leverage used, fluctuates depending on market conditions and credit availability.

An overview of the history of financing provisions will help describe their current status. Private equity firms started out in the 1980s frequently having the benefit of a clean "financing out" condition, with no guarantee of performance or financing by the private equity fund. If debt financing was not available, the private equity fund could refuse to close, without owing any fees or damages. Private equity firms at the time frequently offered substantial premiums over the price that a strategic buyer could pay. This generally gave private equity firms meaningful leverage in negotiating with targets.

Over time, private equity firms began agreeing to pay fund-guaranteed reverse breakup fees to the target in the event that the deal could not close because the buyer could not obtain debt financing. In some cases, private equity firms also began providing limited fund guarantees for nonfinancing breaches by the acquisition vehicle—sometimes with and sometimes without those payments counting as a cap on damages or liquidated damages.

Even though the initially very buyer-friendly provisions in private equity deals have been chipped away at over time, financing provisions still remain more buyer-friendly for private equity firms than they are for strategic acquirers. Historically, strategic buyers have not benefited from any type of similar financing conditions or caps on damages, although recently a small percentage of strategic deals have included such features.

Instead, strategic buyers are simply required to close and would be in breach if they could not come up with the purchase price. Because they sign and are liable under the purchase agreement directly, strategic buyers are subject to specific performance provisions under which they could be forced by a court to close. In contrast, private equity funds still only sign limited guarantees and equity commitments and have the acquisition agreement signed by a special purpose vehicle.[1]

Overview of Financing Contingency Provisions

Financing contingency provisions are complicated. There are several variations on what could occur, and several elements of the transaction agreement that have to work in tandem in order to achieve the desired result. Because these elements show up in different places in the document, interact with each other, and vary significantly from deal to deal, this area of practice is rife with drafting issues.

If the buyer cannot pay the purchase price, it cannot close. The acquisition could be structured so that, if the buyer's debt financing is not available, the buyer could have the right to terminate or refuse to close, or the buyer could be required to close nevertheless (which it cannot do) and simply be held in breach and liable for damages when it does not do so.

If the buyer does not have the money to close, it could be subject to specific performance (i.e., the court can make it close), or the target's remedy could be limited to a damages claim. If the buyer is able to walk away and limit its exposure to a damages claim (rather than performance), those damages can be capped or not capped.

The buyer may or may not have to pay a breakup fee if it cannot close, which if so can have multiple tiers and fee levels for different causes of the deal failure. The buyer's fee may be the sole and exclusive remedy, or the target may be able to choose its remedies (take the fee only, sue for damages generally, or do both). The fee may represent the measure of liquidated damages, or the target may have to prove its damages, which may or may not be subject to a cap.

For a private equity fund buyer, the agreement may limit the target's legal recourse so that it cannot sue the private equity fund or employees of the fund manager, or it may leave open a potential claim by the target to pierce the corporate veil.

These differences are commonly packaged into four primary configurations, which are described as options below. There are variations on each of these in practice:

- *No financing provision.* The buyer must close whether or not it receives financing (because there are no financing-related termination rights or closing conditions) and is subject to specific performance as a remedy. There is no cap on damages. This is typical for strategic deals.
- *Financing condition.* The buyer is not required to close unless it receives the debt financing. This was used historically in private equity deals. It is occasionally discussed, but is rare in current transactions.
- *Reverse financing failure break-up fee.* If the buyer does not receive debt financing despite using appropriate efforts to obtain it, the agreement can be terminated and the reverse financing breakup fee will be due from the buyer. Assuming the buyer was not otherwise in breach, it will have no further liability beyond paying that breakup fee. This is the most common financing provision used currently in private equity deals.
- *Walk right.* The buyer can terminate upon payment of a reverse breakup fee for any reason, whether or not the debt financing was available. Once it pays the fee, it has no further liability. This gives the buyer the option to walk away from the deal for any reason. The reverse breakup fee in walk right deals is higher than reverse financing breakup fees. Walk rights have become much less common since the 2008 financial crisis, but are still used on occasion in private equity deals.

Each of these options is discussed in more detail below.

No financing provision

Under this option, there are simply no financing contingency provisions included in the acquisition agreement. The same rules apply in the deal as do for a transaction in which the buyer does not require financing. If the closing cannot occur because the buyer does not receive its debt financing, then the buyer is in breach. Damages can be substantial, including the lost share premium that would have been paid to the shareholders of the target in some cases. There are no limitations or caps on those damages, and there are no reverse breakup fees. The buyer may also be subject to a specific performance remedy under which it can be required by a court to actually close and perform under the contract.

The distinction between strategic and private equity deals is not that sharp in some situations. Strategic buyers may finance as much or more of the purchase price with debt as a private equity buyer. Both strategic and private equity buyers may or may not have synergies in mind when pricing the deal (e.g., private equity firms do synergistic roll-ups of companies in the same industry, while strategic buyers do opportunistic deals in businesses they are not already in).

Recently, a small handful of strategic deals have begun to introduce some of the options discussed below—financing conditions, reverse financing breakup fees and walk rights—that historically were used only in private equity deals.

Financing condition

Under this option, the buyer has the benefit of a closing condition which states that the buyer's debt financing has been funded or is ready to fund. If the buyer does not receive its debt financing, then the financing condition will not be satisfied. The buyer would not be required to close, and would not be required to pay any breakup fees or damages. Specific performance is not applicable, because the buyer is not obligated to close.

Sample Provision

The lenders who are parties to the Commitment Letter (or, in the event that Alternative Financing has been arranged, the lenders or other financing sources who have committed to such Alternative Financing) shall not have declined on the date that would otherwise have been the Closing Date to make the Financing (or such Alternative Financing) available to the Buyer [on terms that are not [materially] less favorable to the Buyer than the terms of the Commitment Letter] (the foregoing, a "Financing Failure").

A financing condition can be narrowed to only protect the buyer from specific risks that are identified as triggers for the financing failure. If those specified triggers cause the buyer's debt financing to fail, the buyer has an out. If other triggers cause the financing failure, the buyer does not have an out.

Sample Provision

[…] provided that such Financing Failure shall only be a condition if it was [primarily] caused by a [ratings downgrade of the Target] [or a material adverse effect on the lending market having occurred].

For instance, the financing out can be triggered by the failure of the banks to fund due to a condition in the bank's commitment letter that itself is tied to the target's credit quality, such as its credit rating. If the banks do not fund because the target was downgraded, then the target shares part of the financing risk, on the theory that this type of failure is to some extent the target's "fault."

Such a condition could also be conceptualized as a type of hybrid between a financing condition and quantitative material adverse effect (MAE)/walk right. In other words, the buyer can walk (subject to possibly paying a reverse breakup fee) in the case of adverse changes in circumstances at the target, but only if such changes manifest themselves in the form of a ratings downgrade.

Reverse financing failure breakup fee

Under this structure, the target has the right to terminate the deal and require the buyer to pay a flat fee if the buyer cannot close because its debt financing is not available. If the buyer's financing is available, the target can force the buyer to obtain debt financing and close the deal.

The reverse breakup fee has become the dominant structure since the financial crisis to address the risk of a private equity buyer's debt financing falling through. It has grown in prominence, and is now the market norm.

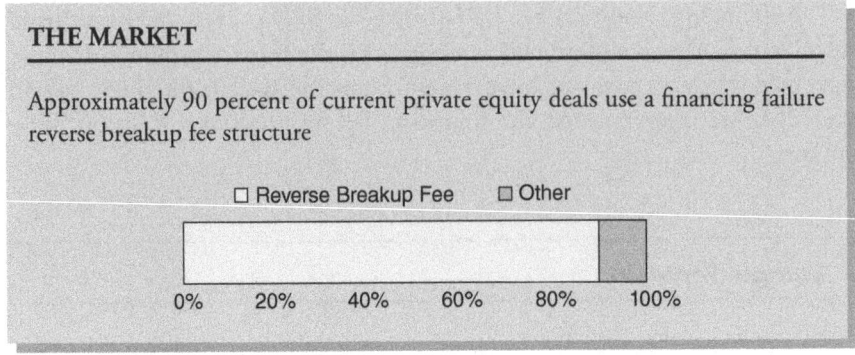

THE MARKET

Approximately 90 percent of current private equity deals use a financing failure reverse breakup fee structure

Under this structure, a general termination right can be exercised by the target, which triggers the reverse breakup fee obligation. The termination right is only available if the target is fully ready to close and the buyer is otherwise obligated to close but fails to do so by the drop-dead date. Usually, the target cannot exercise this right until just before the drop-dead date, to ensure that the buyer has been given the full amount of time to obtain alternative financing.

Sample Provision

This Agreement may be terminated and the Merger may be abandoned by the Company by action of the Company Board [...] at any time on or subsequent to the first Business Day immediately preceding the Termination Date, if (i) all of the conditions to the buyer's obligations to close (other than those conditions that by their terms are to be satisfied at the Closing) are satisfied or waived in accordance with this Agreement, (ii) the Company has indicated in writing to Parent and Merger Sub that all certificates to be delivered by the Company at Closing will be so delivered and that the Company is ready, willing and able to consummate the Closing, and (iii) Parent and Merger Sub shall have failed to consummate the Closing on the day Closing is required to occur.

This is usually the target's termination right, not the buyer's. (If it were the buyer's, the buyer could opportunistically terminate, pay the reverse breakup fee and avoid the target suing for specific performance to seek alternative financing.) Along the same lines, if the target does exercise the termination right, it will become entitled to the reverse breakup fee payment, but will lose the ability to pursue specific performance—the target cannot ask the buyer to perform a contract that has been terminated.

These are variations on exactly how the termination trigger works. For instance, if the target is not meant to have specific performance rights, then the buyer could also be given the right to trigger this termination provision and stop any specific performance action.

At the point of enforcement, the target is usually required to choose between the reverse breakup fee remedy and ordinary damages for breach. Of course, a buyer does not want to pay the fee and then be sued on top of it. Because the buyer will want the benefit of certainty provided by the reverse breakup fee, it will not want the contract to allow the target to additionally sue for breach. If the buyer gets its way, the agreement will provide that, upon termination, the buyer has no other liabilities than the obligation to pay the reverse breakup fee.

Some strategic deals also use a reverse breakup fee structure. This is particularly true when the strategic buyer needs substantial debt financing to fund the purchase price, and the size of the target is large relative to the size of the buyer.

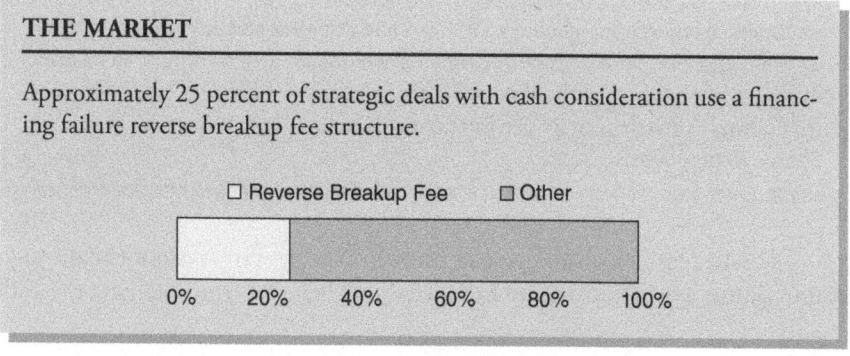

THE MARKET

Approximately 25 percent of strategic deals with cash consideration use a financing failure reverse breakup fee structure.

In order to achieve the reverse breakup fee structure, several somewhat duplicative concepts are employed. Each of these is discussed separately in more detail in this chapter.

Implementing a reverse breakup fee

The merger agreement will provide that, upon termination (which is what triggers the reverse breakup fee), the parties shall have no further liability to each other. The reverse breakup fee is set up as liquidated damages. That means it represents the parties' pre-signing view of actual damages and, when paid, will represent payment in full.

Along the same lines, collecting the reverse breakup fee is the sole and exclusive remedy of the target company. If the reverse breakup fee is triggered, specific enforcement will not be available to force the buyer to close. Beyond that, the merger agreement will provide for a cap on damages equal to the amount of the reverse termination fee. To ensure that the target company does not circumvent all of these provisions by suing individuals—such as employees of the buyer entities or its private equity fund manager—rather than the buyer entities that are party to the agreement, the agreement clarifies that there are no remedies at all against any such persons.

Sample Provision

[…] and in no event shall the Company or any Company Party seek any other loss or damage or any other recovery, judgment or damages of any kind, including consequential, indirect, or punitive damages against Parent, Merger Sub, the Guarantor, the Financing Sources and each of their respective former, current and future directors, officers, employees, agents, general and limited partners, managers, members, shareholders, Affiliates and assignees and each former, current or future director, officer, employee, agent, shareholder, general or limited partner, manager, member, shareholder, Affiliate or assignee of any of the foregoing (including, with respect to the Financing Sources, their respective Financing Source Representatives) […].

Likewise, this provision usually clarifies that the target cannot make any claim against the private equity fund itself (for instance, on a piercing the veil theory).

Sample Provision

[…] whether by or through attempted piercing of the corporate, limited partnership or limited liability company veil, by or through a claim by or on behalf of Parent against the Guarantor or any other Parent Party, by the enforcement of any assessment or by any legal or equitable proceeding, by virtue of any statute, regulation or applicable Law, whether in contract, in tort or otherwise […].

The financing failure breakup fee is sometimes available if the target terminates the deal due to the buyer's breach of its covenants or representations (rather than being limited to termination under the financing failure trigger). This gives the target an option to terminate and take the reverse breakup fee in the event that the buyer fails to pursue its financing (or breaches other covenants), without the target having to pursue a damages claim and actually prove up its damages.

Sample Provision

In the event that this Agreement is terminated by the Company pursuant to Section __ [breach of reps or covenants] or Section __ [failure of buyer to close when required], then Parent shall promptly, but in no event later than three Business Days after the date of such termination, pay or cause to be paid to the Company an amount equal to $_____ by wire transfer of same-day funds.

Two-tiered reverse breakup fees

Occasionally, the amount of the reverse breakup fee is split into a two-tiered structure. In that case, a private equity buyer has to pay a lower reverse breakup fee for a pure financing failure, but a higher reverse breakup fee if the buyer willfully (or knowingly and intentionally, or other variations on such phrases) breaches its obligations.

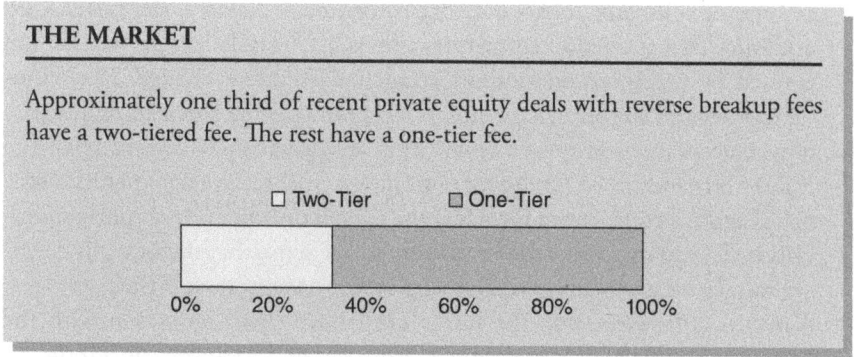

THE MARKET

Approximately one third of recent private equity deals with reverse breakup fees have a two-tiered fee. The rest have a one-tier fee.

The higher level of a two-tier structure can act as the equivalent of a walk right.[2] In those cases, the higher reverse breakup fee applies if the buyer has committed a knowing, intentional or willful (or some combination of those terms) breach. For those types of breaches, a higher fee is triggered but the target may be prevented from pursuing specific performance (or other damage remedies in excess of the fee).

If specific performance is not permitted, the buyer may simply refuse to close if it is willing to pay that fee. If specific performance is permitted, then the provision acts as an option on the part of the target to either take the higher fee or sue to force the closing to occur.

War Story

A recent transaction had a two-tier reverse breakup fee with a twist. The parties had negotiated a customary financing breakup fee. In addition to the normal financing breakup fee, a smaller breakup fee applied if the target's financial performance suffered between signing and closing.

If the target's financial performance suffered to the extent that the quantitative terms in the financing bank's commitment letter was not met, then the buyer could walk away after paying a special reduced fee. This provision acted as a hybrid concept between a quantitative MAE condition and a reverse breakup fee.

Terms like "knowing," "intentional" and "willful," which tend to trigger higher-tier fees, are often used in practice without definition.[3] Different interpretations are possible, and some deals define them to remove some of the ambiguity.

- *Broadest interpretation.* The buyer need only know that it is taking an action, or intentionally take an action, that constitutes a breach. The buyer need not know that the action constitutes a breach. The only actions that are not covered by this interpretation are accidental events or changes in circumstances beyond the buyer's control (which, for instance, make its representations inaccurate or prevent it from being able to satisfy its covenants).
- *Hybrid interpretation.* The buyer must have actual knowledge that its intentional actions constitute a breach at the time it decides to take such actions. This is close to the concept of bad faith, in the sense that the buyer is deciding to take an action despite knowing that it constitutes a breach.
- *Narrowest interpretation.* The buyer must have taken an action with the purpose of breaching the contract. This stands in contrast to taking an action that also had another predominantly commercial purpose.

Under all of the above interpretations, the action in question may need to have constituted a breach in and of itself, or it may be sufficient for that action to have resulted (perhaps indirectly) in a breach.

Sample Provision

["Willful Breach" shall mean a breach that is a consequence of an act [or failure to act] by the breaching party with the [actual] [or constructive] knowledge that the taking of such act [or failure to act] would [or would reasonably be expected to] result in a breach of this Agreement.]

—OR—

["Willful Breach" shall mean a breach of this Agreement that is a [direct] consequence of a deliberate act undertaken by the breaching party, regardless of whether a breach of this Agreement was the object or the act and regardless of whether the breaching party had knowledge that such act would result in a breach of this Agreement.]

Size of reverse financing breakup fees

Despite their different origins and legal underpinnings, the size of the reverse financing breakup fee tends to proportionately track the amount of the fiduciary out breakup fee.

There is no legal—and, some say, no logical—connection between the size of the fiduciary out breakup fee and the size of the reverse breakup fee. Fiduciary out breakup fees are governed by the law of the target's state of incorporation. Their size is guided by corporate law governing the fiduciary duties of boards in the context of merger and acquisition (M&A) deals. If the fee is too high, it could run afoul of case law that prohibits a public company target from locking a deal up too tightly.

THE MARKET

In roughly one-third of deals, the reverse financing breakup fee is 1× the fiduciary out breakup fee. In roughly one half of deals, the reverse financing breakup fee is 2× the fiduciary out breakup fee. In most of the remainder, the reverse financing breakup fees are higher than 2× the fiduciary out breakup fees. In a few cases, the reverse financing breakup fees are between 1× and 2× the amount of the fiduciary out breakup fees.

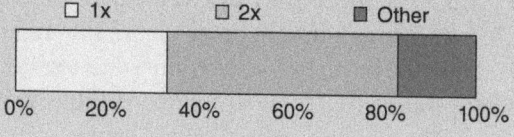

In contrast, reverse financing breakup fees are not subject to any legal limitations. They arise purely from business negotiations designed to balance the buyer's risk that its financing fails despite its efforts to secure the financing, and the public company target's desire to ensure that a meaningful financial obligation backs up the buyer's efforts to secure the funds. Nevertheless, reverse financing breakup fees tend to be proportionate to breakup fees.

The number of deals in which the reverse breakup fee is two times the fiduciary out breakup fee is growing. For two-tier fees that apply the reverse breakup fee to willful breaches, the range in fee size is quite wide in practice—in fact, on the upper end, fees can reach 30 percent or more of the deal value.

THE MARKET

Single-tier reverse financing breakup fees average around 5 to 6 percent of deal value, and typically range from around 2 percent to around 8 percent.

Two-tier reverse financing breakup fees are more complicated. In those cases, the first tier—the lower fee—has a median percentage of a little more than a fiduciary out breakup fee, or just over 3 percent. (This is due primarily to some being 1× the fiduciary out breakup fee and some being 2×.) The higher-tier breakup fee tends to be around twice the lower-tier fee, or 6 to 7 percent. If the higher reverse termination fee acts as a walk right, it will often be much more substantial.

Walk right; no further liability

Walk right

Under a so-called "walk right," the buyer may terminate the transaction for any reason, upon payment of a reverse breakup fee. The target does not have specific enforcement rights and cannot force the buyer entity to close. It cannot cause the private equity fund to invest the equity financing needed to close the deal, even if the debt financing is available.

The reverse breakup fee once paid acts as the sole remedy and a cap on damages. As long as various other aspects of the documents are drafted accordingly, this allows the buyer to "walk" from a deal for any reason, as long as it pays the reverse breakup fee. These structures continue to be less common since the financial crisis.

THE MARKET

Approximately 20 percent of current private equity deals have a walk right structure.

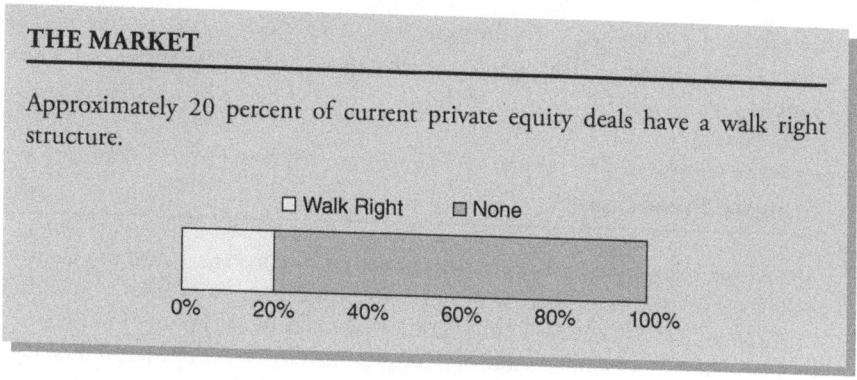

No further liability

The termination provisions of the acquisition agreement can cut off liability after termination. This means that electing to terminate is an election to not pursue damages except those claims that survive termination.

In a reverse termination fee structure, the fee will survive termination in the circumstances in which it is (by its terms) payable. In those circumstances, no other claims would survive termination. If the reverse breakup fee has not been triggered, then all claims, or at least all claims for intentional or willful breaches, would normally survive termination.

Sample Provision

In the event of termination of this Agreement and the abandonment of the Merger pursuant to this Article VII, this Agreement shall become void and of no effect with no liability to any party hereto (or any of its Representatives or Affiliates); provided that, except as otherwise provided herein, no such termination shall relieve any party of any liability to pay the fees, expenses and other amounts due pursuant to this Section [breakup and reverse breakup fees] [...].

Specific Enforcement

Practitioners focus on two primary remedies: the right to sue for damages and the right to sue for specific performance. In the M&A context, specific performance refers to the right to ask the court to force the buyer to close the deal and fund and pay the purchase price. If only a monetary remedy is intended to be available, then the agreement will specify that specific performance is not available. This would, for instance, be the case if the buyer had a walk right.

Sample Provision

The parties acknowledge and agree that under no circumstances shall the Company have any right to initiate or pursue, either directly or indirectly, or by, with or through any other Person, any Action that seeks to obtain any injunction or injunctions to prevent breaches of this Agreement by Parent or Merger Sub, to enforce specifically the terms and provisions of this Agreement against Parent or Merger Sub or to obtain any other equitable relief or equitable remedy against Parent or Merger Sub.

In private equity deals using a reverse breakup fee structure, specific performance is available to force the buyer to close, but only if its debt financing is available. If the buyer's debt financing is not available, the reverse breakup fee is normally the target's only remedy.

THE MARKET

In roughly three-quarters of deals with a financing failure reverse breakup fee structure, the target may only seek specific performance if the buyer's debt financing is available. In the remainder, the target has full specific performance rights, but the buyer can cut that right off by exercising a termination right.

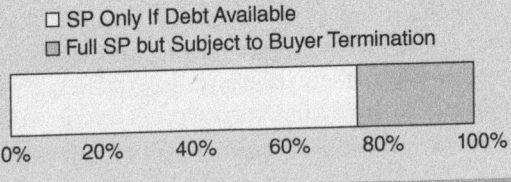

☐ SP Only If Debt Available
☐ Full SP but Subject to Buyer Termination

0%   20%   40%   60%   80%   100%

Equity financing

As a matter of drafting, the specific performance provision will generally confirm the general right to specific performance, but then limit and condition its application when it comes to forcing the buyer to pursue the funding of the debt financing or cause the funding of the equity financing.

In the case of equity financing, in order to be able to force the buyer to close, the target would have to be able to force the buyer vehicle to, in turn, force the equity financing to be provided by the private equity fund under the terms of its equity commitment letter. This specific performance remedy lets the target force the buyer to exercise the buyer's own back-to-back specific enforcement rights under the equity commitment letter with the private equity fund.

The circumstances under which the target can use this right, however, are highly conditioned. It can only be used if, among other things:

The closing is required to occur under the terms of the acquisition agreement. The buyer must first breach its obligation to close. Everything else must have first fallen into place so that the agreement requires (at that time) the parties to close.

Sample Provision

At any time subsequent to the date upon which the Closing is required to occur pursuant to Section __: (A) the Company shall be entitled to seek specific performance to cause Parent to cause the Equity Financing to be funded to fund the Total Common Stock Merger Consideration, including by demanding that Parent enforce the terms of the Equity Commitment Letter, but only in the event that Parent and Merger Sub fail to consummate the Closing by the date the Closing is required to have occurred.

The buyer's conditions to closing are satisfied. The private equity fund does not want to provide the equity capital to the buyer vehicle when it does not intend (or have an obligation) to close in any event.

Sample Provision

(i) all of the conditions set forth in Sections __ and __ [conditions for buyer's benefit] (other than those conditions that by their terms are to be satisfied at Closing, but subject to the satisfaction or waiver of those conditions at the Closing) have been satisfied or waived in accordance with this Agreement;

The target has confirmed that its conditions to closing are satisfied. This avoids the buyer funding only to learn that the target does not intend (or have an obligation) to close.

Sample Provision

(ii) the Company has irrevocably confirmed in writing to Parent that all conditions set forth in Section ___ [conditions for the target's benefit] have been satisfied or waived and if specific performance is granted and the Equity Financing and Debt Financing are funded, then the Closing will occur[...];

The debt financing has funded or is ready to fund. This ensures that the target cannot try to force the buyer to close when it does not actually have the funds to do so.

Sample Provision

and (iii) either (x) the Debt Financing has been funded or (y) all of the conditions to the consummation of the financing provided for by the Debt Commitment Letter (or, if alternative financing is being used, pursuant to the commitments with respect thereto) have been satisfied (or, with respect to certificates to be delivered at the consummation of the Debt Financing, are capable of being satisfied upon consummation) (other than funding of the Equity Financing) and the Debt Financing will be funded at the Closing if the Equity Financing is funded at the Closing.

Debt financing

In many deals, the buyer is also subject to a separate back-to-back specific performance provision related to the debt commitment letter.

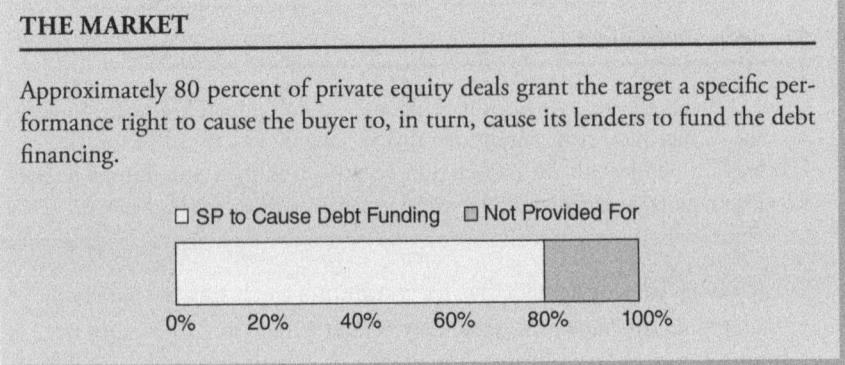

THE MARKET

Approximately 80 percent of private equity deals grant the target a specific performance right to cause the buyer to, in turn, cause its lenders to fund the debt financing.

☐ SP to Cause Debt Funding   ☐ Not Provided For

0%   20%   40%   60%   80%   100%

Under the specific performance provision, the target can require the buyer to enforce its rights against its lenders under the buyer's commitment letter. In this way, the target has more assurance that, if the conditions to the debt financing under the commitment letter are satisfied, the debt financing will actually be funded.

Sample Provision

The Company shall be entitled to seek specific performance to cause Parent to enforce the terms of the Debt Commitment Letter and cause the Debt Financing to be funded to fund the Total Common Stock Merger Consideration, including by demanding Parent to file one or more lawsuits against the sources of the Debt Financing to fully enforce such sources' obligations thereunder and Parent's rights thereunder, but only in the event that [...].

The back-to-back specific performance remedy for debt financing is also highly conditioned. It can only be used if, among other things:

The buyer's conditions to closing are satisfied.

The target has confirmed that its conditions to closing are satisfied.

The closing is required to occur under the terms of the acquisition agreement.

Sample Provision

(x) the conditions set forth in clauses (i) through (iii) of clause (A) above of this Section __ have been satisfied; and [...]

The conditions to the debt financing in the commitment letter have been satisfied—since it would be futile to seek specific performance against the banks if they did not have to fund under the terms of their commitment.

Sample Provision

(y) all of the conditions to the consummation of the financing provided for by the Debt Commitment Letter (or, if alternative financing is being used, pursuant to the commitments with respect thereto) have been satisfied (or, with respect to certificates to be delivered at the consummation of the Debt Financing, are capable of being satisfied upon consummation).

When the buyer grants the target a back-to-back specific enforcement right with respect to the buyer's lenders, the lenders often require that the acquisition agreement include a choice of forum clause that prevents the lenders from being sued in unfavorable states. These protective provisions for the banks normally require that any suits be brought in New York City courts under New York law.

Sample Provision

Notwithstanding anything in this Agreement to the contrary, each of the parties hereto agrees that it will not bring or support any action, cause of action, claim, cross-claim or third-party claim of any kind or description, whether in law or in equity, whether in contract or in tort or otherwise, against the Financing Sources and each of their respective Financing Source Representatives in any way relating to this Agreement or any of the transactions contemplated hereby (including, but not limited to, any such action, cause of action or claim against the Financing Sources or any Financing Source Representative arising out of or relating in any way to the Debt Commitment Letter, the Debt Financing or the performance thereof) in any forum other than the Supreme Court of the State of New York, County of New York, or, if under applicable law exclusive jurisdiction is vested in the Federal courts, the United States District Court for the Southern District of New York (and appellate courts thereof).

Specific performance usually requires an election of remedy. In other words, the target cannot both force the buyer to close and sue to collect the reverse breakup fee. That means that if the buyer can unilaterally trigger payment of the reverse breakup fee, it can prevent specific performance from being available to the target.

Sample Provision

For the avoidance of doubt, while the Company may pursue both a grant of specific performance of the type provided in the preceding sentence and the payment of the [reverse financing breakup fee], under no circumstances shall the Company be permitted or entitled to receive both a grant of specific performance of the type contemplated by the preceding sentence and monetary damages, including the [reverse financing breakup fee].

Damages

Liquidated damages

The reverse breakup fee normally acts as liquidated damages. Such provisions allow the parties to pre-agree on the measure of the target's damages. That measure then governs, whether actual damages are more or less. If the fee is paid, the target's damages claim has already been satisfied, so no further damages can be claimed.

Sample Provision

In the event that this Agreement is terminated and the Parent Termination Fee [the reverse breakup fee] is required to be paid, then (x) the Parent Termination Fee shall be deemed to be liquidated damages for any and all losses or damages suffered or incurred by any of the Company Parties in connection with this Agreement (and the termination hereof), the transactions contemplated hereby (and the abandonment thereof) or any matter forming the basis for the termination giving rise to the payment of such Parent Termination Fee and (y) [...]

Sole and exclusive remedy

If the reverse breakup fee is triggered and payable, it is normally the sole and exclusive remedy. The target cannot sue for specific performance to force the buyer to close, and cannot waive the fee and sue for additional damages in the hope that the award would exceed the reverse breakup fee amount.

Sample Provision

[...] and (y) the Company's rights under this Section __ shall be the sole and exclusive remedy of any of the Company Parties against the Buyer Parties for any loss or damage suffered as a result of the failure of the Merger to be consummated or for a breach (whether willful, intentional, unintentional, or otherwise) or failure to perform hereunder, and no Buyer Party shall have any further liability or obligation relating to or arising out of this Agreement or the transactions contemplated hereby (including the Financing).

Cap on damages

Instead of a reverse breakup fee, the buyer can be subject to damages for failure to close, with those damages capped at a specified amount. In contrast to a reverse breakup fee or liquidated damages provision, the target has to prove its damages. In light of the difficulty of proving damages, the target may end up settling for less than the cap in order to avoid litigation over the damage calculation.

War Story

The target gave the buyer the right to terminate the merger agreement if its financing failed, as long as it paid damages up to a cap of 7 percent of the deal price.

No sooner than the credit crunch had begun, the buyer's financing fell apart and it decided to walk. The target, despite being frustrated that it had ever agreed to the termination right in the first place, decided that it would not (and, indeed, could not) fight the buyer's right to terminate. It thought it would just take the 7 percent, lick its wounds, and go on with its business.

To its surprise, after the buyer walked, it added insult to injury by refusing to pay anything at all in damages. Arguing that the target had no real damages, the buyer challenged the target to prove and measure what harm had actually come to it in a lengthy court process.

The target was taken by surprise; it lost the deal and was now at risk of losing any recovery. Eventually, the target settled for an amount substantially less than 7 percent.

The cap can be used together with a reverse breakup fee, in which case it specifies that the reverse breakup fee is the maximum amount that can be collected in damages in any event. If the fee is paid, it counts toward the cap. The cap amount usually does not limit special expense reimbursement provisions included in the deal, such as reimbursement of the target company for expenses incurred to help support putting the buyer's financing package together.

If there is already an exclusive remedy provision, then the cap on damages would be to some extent duplicative. In the reverse breakup fee context, a cap on damages expresses the "belt and suspenders" concept that even if the right to claim damages under the agreement did not terminate with the agreement (which it does), even if the target company suffered additional damages (which the liquidated damages provision says have already been satisfied), and even if the target were entitled to pursue further damage claims (which it cannot on account of the sole and exclusive remedy provision), then those damages would be capped at the amount the target has already received under the reverse breakup fee payment.

Sample Provision

Notwithstanding anything herein to the contrary, the Company agrees that, to the extent it has incurred losses or damages in connection with this Agreement, (i) the maximum aggregate liability of Parent, Holdings, and Merger Sub for such losses or damages shall not exceed the Liability Limitation, provided that the sole obligations of Parent under and in respect of this Agreement and the transactions contemplated hereby shall be limited to the express payment obligations of Parent to pay the Reverse Termination Fee, if required, (ii) in no event shall the Company or any of its affiliates seek to recover any money damages or any other recovery, judgment, or damages of any kind in excess of the Liability Limitation. The "Liability Limitation" means an amount equal to $____ (inclusive of any payment of the Reverse Termination Fee).

No Recourse against Private Equity Buyer

As noted in 343 SPS § XII-B4, walk rights and other reverse breakup fees normally act as the sole remedy in the circumstances in which they apply. Most deals go on to include additional specific provisions that shield employees and other representatives of the buyer entity from any related litigation.

Anti-recourse provisions are rarely used in other deal contents, even though some of the concepts (e.g., no suits against employees) would be relevant. Anti-recourse provisions help ensure that any attempt at piercing the veil will fail. Such provisions are particularly relevant to private equity deals because special purpose vehicles (SPVs) function as the buyer's direct parties to the acquisition agreement. Private equity buyers usually structure the transaction so that a newly formed SPV (with no material assets) is party to the acquisition agreement; the private equity fund itself is not party to the agreement. The fund may enter into an equity commitment letter (committing equity to the SPV) and a guarantee of the liabilities the fund has specifically agreed to be bound by, such as the reverse breakup fee.

In the absence of a specific no-recourse provision, the buyer may be concerned that the target will seek to "pierce the corporate veil" of the SPV and directly sue the private equity fund for the full amount of damages for which the SPV is liable (but could not be expected to pay, since it has no assets). Veil piercing is very difficult to achieve even without anti-recourse provisions, but targets have sometimes argued that private equity SPVs have several characteristics of the "instrumentality" and "alter ego" theories that support veil piercing. They often have no assets, no employees, and no means of generating capital on their own. On the other hand, they usually observe all proper corporate formalities, and the target is well aware of the structure and intended distance being placed between them and the fund at the time of signing.

Sample Provision

This Agreement may only be enforced against, and any claims or causes of action that may be based upon, arise out of or relate to this Agreement, or the negotiation, execution, or performance of this Agreement, may only be made against the entities that are expressly identified as parties hereto, and no past, present, or future Representative of any party hereto shall have any liability for any obligations or liabilities of the parties to this Agreement or for any claim based on, in respect of, or by reason of, the transactions contemplated hereby.

Marketing Periods

In private equity deals, the buyer's financing will normally be committed by a lead bank. The lead bank will usually not plan to lend all of the proceeds itself. Instead, it will syndicate the loan to numerous other financial institutions. The syndication process takes time and requires support and information from the target (which is discussed further below).

The lead bank will work with the target and buyer to put together bank books of all the key information that potential syndicate members need to make a decision whether or not to participate in the transaction. The lead bank will also arrange for discussions with the target management. The syndication process, as a matter of practice, normally takes two to three weeks, depending on the size and the complexity of the deal.

If the conditions to closing the M&A deal were satisfied before the loan syndication is complete, it would place the buyer and its lead bank in a bind. The buyer would be forced to close once the conditions are met, but the lead bank would not be finished collecting the financing. A minimum marketing period addresses this timing concern, usually without indirectly creating a financing condition.

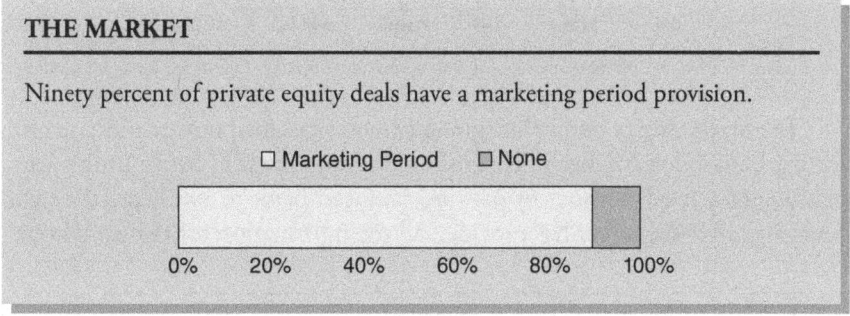

THE MARKET

Ninety percent of private equity deals have a marketing period provision.

☐ Marketing Period   ☐ None

0%   20%   40%   60%   80%   100%

In the absence of a marketing period, closing is required to occur shortly after the closing conditions are satisfied. The marketing period allows the required closing date to be pushed back, even if the conditions are already satisfied.

Sample Provision

The Closing will take place on the date following the Closing Condition Satisfaction Date that is the earlier of: (a) the first Business Day following the final day of the Marketing Period (but in any event prior to the Termination Date), or (b) such other date, time or place as may be agreed to in writing by the parties hereto.

In order to prevent the marketing period concept from turning into a closing condition, a deadline has to be set for the period to forcibly end, even if it has not expired by its terms. The number of days in the marketing period varies from deal to deal, but tends to center around a one-month period.

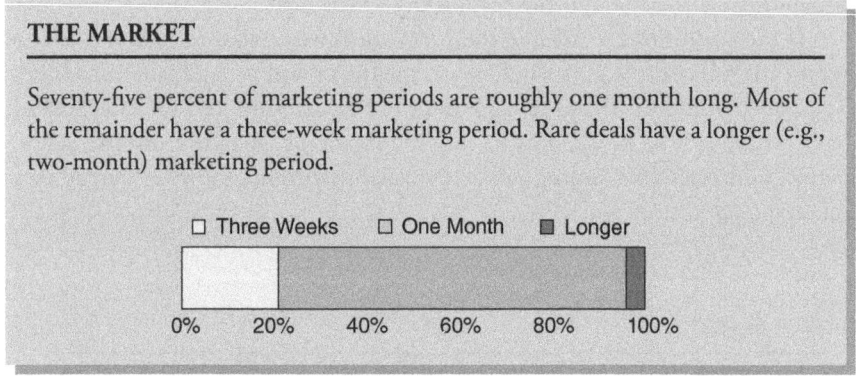

THE MARKET

Seventy-five percent of marketing periods are roughly one month long. Most of the remainder have a three-week marketing period. Rare deals have a longer (e.g., two-month) marketing period.

The marketing period will begin only when specified information needed for the bank book has been delivered to the buyer or lead bank. In this way, it provides a fixed number of days for the lead bank to syndicate the debt financing after the target has provided all the information for the bank book.

Sample Provision

"Marketing Period" shall mean the first period of [20] consecutive Business Days after [the date that the Proxy statement is cleared by the SEC for mailing to the stockholders of the Company].

—OR—

[the Stockholder Approval has been obtained] beginning on the [third Business Day after] delivery of the Required Information, throughout which Parent shall have the Required Information required to be delivered by the Company to Parent pursuant to Section __ (and throughout which the conditions set forth in Section __ have been satisfied or waived and nothing has occurred and no condition exists that would cause any of the conditions set forth in Section __ to fail to be satisfied assuming the Closing were to be scheduled for any time during such [20]-Business Day period); provided that [...].

Even if the bank book is finished early, syndication will usually begin only after the shareholder vote is successfully obtained. A successful vote makes the deal more certain, and allows syndicate lenders to take the transaction more seriously. In some deals, however, syndication occurs side-by-side with the merger vote process—during the month between delivering the proxy and holding the vote. In those cases, closing can normally occur shortly after the vote.

THE MARKET

In roughly 60 percent of mergers, the marketing period does not begin until all conditions have been satisfied, including the merger vote. In 25 percent, the marketing period does not begin until the merger proxy has been mailed to stockholders. In 15 percent, the marketing period can begin at any time after material for the bank book has been delivered.

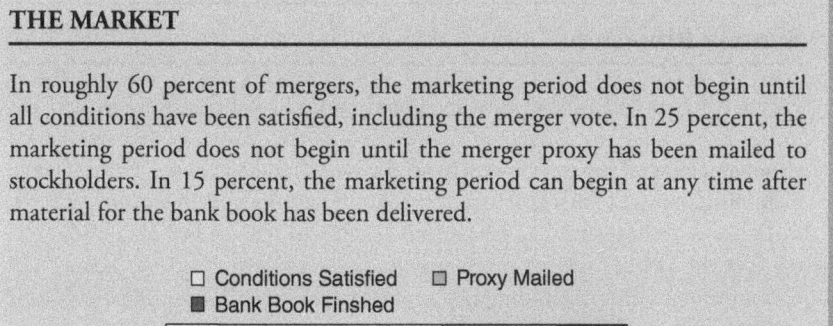

Financing Covenants

If a buyer requires financing, most deals include covenants designed both to ensure that the buyer fully seeks its financing and that the target provides support for the buyer's financing. The financing covenant usually requires the buyer to do whatever it takes to obtain equity financing. Of course, in a private equity acquisition, the party bound by this covenant is the buyer's acquisition vehicle and not the private equity fund itself. As a result, the impact is more or less limited to ensuring that the acquisition vehicle actually exercises its rights under the equity commitment letter it has from the private equity fund.

Sample Provision

Subject to the terms and conditions of this Agreement, each of Parent and Merger Sub shall take (or cause to be taken) all actions, and do (or cause to be done) all things, necessary, proper or advisable to […] obtain the Equity Financing contemplated by the Equity Commitment Letter on the terms and subject to the conditions thereof.

A similar but separate covenant is often included for the debt financing. In contrast to the equity financing covenant—which requires "all actions" (within the power of the buyer's acquisition vehicle) to be taken to obtain the equity financing—the debt financing covenant usually requires only reasonable best efforts to obtain the debt financing.

Sample Provision

Each of Parent and Merger Sub shall comply in all material respects with its obligations under the Financing Commitments and shall use their respective reasonable best efforts to cause their Affiliates to use, their respective reasonable best efforts to take, or cause to be taken, all actions and to do, or cause to be done, all things necessary, proper or advisable to arrange and obtain the proceeds of the Debt Financing on the terms and conditions described in the Debt Commitment Letter (including taking into account any market flex provisions applicable thereto), including [...].

Most financing covenants restrict the buyer's ability to amend the debt financing arrangements in a way that would be adverse to the target. Doing so is effectively deemed to be inconsistent with the effort to obtain the debt financing. More specifically, the buyer cannot reduce the commitment amount or add conditions in favor of the lenders (which would make it less likely that the debt will be funded).

Sample Provision

Neither Parent nor Merger Sub shall agree to any amendments or modifications to, or grant any waivers of, any condition or other provision or remedy under the Debt Commitment Letter if such amendments, modifications, or waivers would (a) reduce the aggregate amount of the Debt Financing, (b) impose new or additional conditions, or otherwise expand, amend or modify any of the conditions to the receipt of the Debt Financing in a manner adverse to Parent or the Company, or (c) amend, expand or modify any other terms in a manner that would reasonably be expected to (1) prevent, impede or delay, in any material respect, the ability of Parent to consummate the Merger, or (2) adversely impact the ability of Parent or Merger Sub to enforce its rights against the other parties to the Debt Commitment Letter.

In many deals, the buyer will ask for confirmation that its general "reasonable best efforts" covenant does not implicitly require it to seek additional equity financing or alternative debt financing at a higher interest rate. The buyer will also want clarity that it does not have to waive conditions or accept changes to the debt financing. Otherwise, it may not be clear what the general efforts covenant requires the buyer to do if the debt financing should fail.

These provisions often confirm that the buyer must accept the effect of any so-called "flex" terms in the debt commitment letter. Flex terms allow the lenders to change interest rates, and sometimes the structure, in order to get the loans syndicated. Sometimes, flex terms are not capped, so that the buyer must pay whatever rate it takes to get the debt placed.

Sample Provision

For purposes of this Agreement, "reasonable best efforts" shall not require Parent or Merger Sub to (x) pay (or agree to pay) more for the Debt Financing (whether in interest rate, fees or otherwise) than the terms set forth in the Debt Commitment Letter and any Fee Letter entered into by Parent and/or Merger Sub in connection with such Debt Commitment Letter (after giving effect to any increase in interest rate, fees or otherwise resulting from any lender exercising flex provisions contained in such Fee Letter), (y) seek more equity capital than is committed in the Equity Commitment Letter or (z) waive any condition or agree to any changes to the Debt Commitment Letter or Equity Commitment Letter.

The buyer is required to keep the target company informed on a current basis of any developments regarding the debt financing. The target wants an early warning if it appears that the lenders may not fund (whether because their conditions are not met or for any other reason).

Sample Provision

Parent shall keep the Company reasonably informed on a reasonably current basis and in reasonable detail of the status of its efforts to arrange the Financing. Without limiting the generality of the foregoing, Parent and Merger Sub shall give the Company prompt notice (x) of any breach or default by any party to any Financing Commitments of which Parent and Merger Sub become aware, (y) of the receipt by Parent or Merger Sub of any written notice or other communication from any Financing Source with respect to any breach, default, termination, or repudiation by any party to any Financing Commitments of any provisions of the Financing Commitments and (z) if for any reason Parent or Merger Sub believes in good faith that it will not be able to obtain all or any portion of the Financing on the terms, in the manner or from the sources contemplated by the Financing Letters.

The buyer is required to seek alternative debt financing if the original financing is not available. Usually, the buyer is not required to accept terms that are materially worse (e.g., more expensive) than the debt the buyer had originally planned to obtain. To determine whether the terms are materially worse, the buyer must take into account the market flex provisions in the original letter. If those flex provisions would have allowed unlimited changes in the rate that may be charged, the buyer may, in effect, have to take whatever deal it can find in the market.

Sample Provision

In the event that any portion of the Debt Financing becomes unavailable on the terms and conditions contemplated in the Debt Commitment Letter, promptly following Parent's Knowledge of the occurrence of such event, Parent and Merger Sub shall use their respective reasonable best efforts to arrange and obtain, and to negotiate and enter into definitive agreements with respect to, alternative financing upon terms and conditions not materially less favorable to Parent, Merger Sub, and the Company than those in the Financing Commitments (taking into account any market flex provisions thereof) [...].

The financing covenant requires the target to support the buyer's effort to finalize its debt financing. In leveraged buyouts, the earnings power and assets of the target company provide credit support for the buyer's acquisition financing. As a result, the lenders rely on the target's credit for repayment of the loan and need extensive information about the target company and its management team.

In addition, the buyer needs the target's management team to help it prepare financial details and join in-person meetings with the syndicate lenders. This covenant is highly detailed and negotiated in part by counsel to the lenders (rather than target's counsel), since the lenders have a specific interest in ensuring that they will have target support for the syndication process.

Sample Provision

Prior to and at Closing, the Company shall, and shall cause its Subsidiaries to, use its reasonable best efforts to provide, and to cause its and their Representatives to provide, to Parent and Merger Sub, at Parent's sole expense, such cooperation reasonably requested by Parent in connection with the arrangement of the Financing, including, without limitation, [litany follows].

Litigation Endnotes

1. *See* Chapter 11-A, Private Equity Deal Structures.
2. *See* Chapter 12-B4, Walk right; no further liability.
3. As one Delaware court explained: [A] "knowing and intentional" breach is a deliberate one—a breach that is a direct consequence of a deliberate act undertaken by the breaching party, rather than one which results indirectly, or as a result of the breaching party's negligence or unforeseeable misadventure. In other words, a "knowing and intentional" breach, as used in the merger agreement, is the taking of a deliberate act, which act constitutes in and of itself a breach of the merger agreement, even if breaching was not the conscious object of the act. *Hexion Specialty Chemicals, Inc. v. Huntsman Corp.*, 965 A.2d 715, 748 (Del. Ch. 2008).

CHAPTER 13

Topping a Public Merger

Overview of "No-Shop" Provisions

"No-shop" provisions in public mergers

"No-shop" provisions are customary in public company deals. They restrict the target company from taking actions that increase the likelihood that another bidder will make a competing offer to acquire the target.

In a public company merger, the buyer cannot close the transaction until the public shareholders vote to approve the deal. Until that vote occurs, a competing bidder can disrupt the original deal by convincing the target's shareholders that a better offer awaits them. A no-shop is a way for the buyer to reduce the risk of a competing bidder arising—by restricting the activities of the target company vis-à-vis competing bidders. The target cannot seek them out, negotiate a competing deal with them, or otherwise facilitate a competing bid.

The no-shop is not as harsh as it sounds in practice. It comes with an escape valve: the fiduciary out. A fiduciary out is an exception to the no-shop that is imposed by case law.[1] There are two primary fiduciary out exceptions. The first exception is relatively easy to satisfy, and allows the target company to provide diligence and negotiate with an unsolicited competing bidder. The second permits the target company to actually terminate the original merger agreement in order to enter into a competing deal on superior terms.

Exercising the fiduciary out termination right triggers an obligation for the target to pay the fiduciary out breakup fee. There is a wide range of fees among individual deals, but most range from 2 to 4 percent of the equity value of the target.

217

Responsibility for advisors

No-shop restrictions typically apply to both the target company and its advisors, including its bankers. In some agreements, the target company is strictly responsible for breaches by the advisors as if the breach were made by the company. In others, the target company is only responsible for using its efforts to prevent breaches by its advisors.

Sample Provision

[...] the Company and its Subsidiaries shall not, and shall [cause]
—OR—
[use commercially reasonable efforts to cause] their Representatives not to, directly or indirectly, [...]

Even without such a provision the target company can still be responsible for acts of its advisors, in particular if the target instructed its advisors to take actions that the target company itself would not be permitted to take. An explicit provision avoids the buyer needing to delve into contract theory to determine the target's liability. These provisions can also increase the target's responsibility as compared to underlying contract law, such as by providing strict liability for the acts of the target's representatives.

Private no-shop restrictions

Many private deals include no-shop restrictions on the target. In a public deal, the no-shop is justified because if the target identifies a better deal it can use the fiduciary out to terminate and take that better deal. As a result, the buyer should want to prevent the target from seeking out alternatives. In a private deal, the target does not have the benefit of a fiduciary out termination right. Nevertheless, some private deals still impose a no-shop on the target.

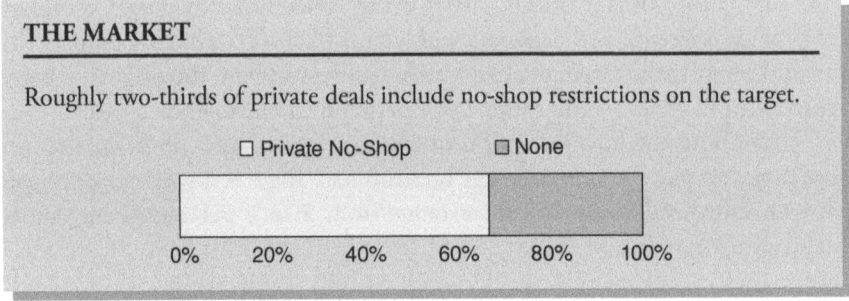

THE MARKET

Roughly two-thirds of private deals include no-shop restrictions on the target.

□ Private No-Shop   □ None

0%   20%   40%   60%   80%   100%

Types of Restrictions in No-Shop Provisions

Restriction on solicitation

The basic restrictions of the no-shop are designed to reduce the likelihood that a competing bid will emerge. The buyer cannot restrict the actions of a third-party bidder. But it can restrict the way in which the target company interacts with potential competing bidders, in order to hamper their ability to finalize a competing proposal. The first basic restriction prevents the target company from soliciting competing bids.

Sample Provision

[...] (i) initiate, solicit, or knowingly encourage any inquiry or the making of any proposal or offer that constitutes an Acquisition Proposal, [...].

In practice, it is hard to imagine that this restriction can have a significant impact. The target is by definition a public company, which must disclose the original deal in its filings with the Securities and Exchange Commission. Potential competing bidders will have notice of the deal in that way. The investment banking community will make sure that any potential bidders are aware that the target has signed a deal. This type of news travels quickly across Wall Street.

There is generally no fiduciary out exception to permit soliciting a competing bid. There are, however, negotiated go-shop provisions that permit soliciting competing proposals during an agreed window of time, which are discussed in a separate section below.

Restriction on discussions, negotiations, and diligence

If a potential competing bidder emerges despite the restriction on solicitation, the target company is restricted under the no-shop from negotiating or even discussing a competing offer with that bidder, and cannot share any diligence information. These provisions tend to be drafted as broadly as possible to tie the target down. It would be difficult for any serious competing bid to be formulated without any discussions with the target or basic due diligence.

> **Sample Provision**
>
> [...] (ii) engage in, enter into, continue or otherwise participate in any discussions or negotiations with any Person with respect to, or provide any nonpublic information or data concerning the Company or its Subsidiaries to any Person relating to, an Acquisition Proposal, [...]

These restrictions can be overcome relatively easily, however. If an unsolicited offer does come in, the target has the benefit of an exception which allows it to nevertheless discuss and negotiate the unsolicited offer and share diligence information with the bidder. To meet the terms of this exception, the target's board needs to conclude that the competing offer is either currently a "superior proposal" or that it is reasonably expected to eventually turn into one. The board also needs to conclude that not engaging with the potential bidder would likely violate its fiduciary duties.

The requirement that the offer is or may become a superior proposal is fairly easy to satisfy. It is rare for an offer at that stage—prior to receiving due diligence—to be firmed up sufficiently to actually constitute a superior proposal. It is relatively easy for a potential bidder to indicate in a nonbinding letter that it may be able to offer a superior deal if it receives appropriate diligence. A target company would normally find a general written statement to that effect from a credible bidder to be sufficient to satisfy this exception to the no-shop.

> **Sample Provision**
>
> [...] (x) the Company Board determines in good faith (after consultation with outside legal counsel) that failure to take such action would likely be inconsistent with the directors' fiduciary duties under applicable Law and (y) the Company Board determines in good faith based on the information then available (after consultation with its financial advisor and outside legal counsel) that such Acquisition Proposal either constitutes a Superior Proposal or [would reasonably be expected to] result in a Superior Proposal.

After the board determines that the potential offer would reasonably be expected to become a superior proposal, it must also conclude that failure to enter into negotiations and share diligence would violate its fiduciary duties. Since this is in the target board's own determination, it would be surprising if in practice a board concluded otherwise (particularly, if the potential competing bidder is credible and its lawyers have drafted an appropriate letter designed to satisfy this test).

In order to place some basic procedural limitations on the target board's discretion in making this fiduciary determination, this no-shop exception frequently requires the board's decision to be made after consulting with both its outside counsel and investment bankers. To satisfy its general fiduciary duty of care in connection with the deal, the target board would of course be expected to regularly consult with its advisors in any event.[2] So this procedural requirement tends to be a restatement of ordinary practice, rather than an incremental burden on the board.

Restriction on changing recommendation

A public company merger agreement requires the target board to recommend the deal to its shareholders for the shareholder vote. Another no-shop exception will allow the board to change its recommendation, subject to some restrictions.

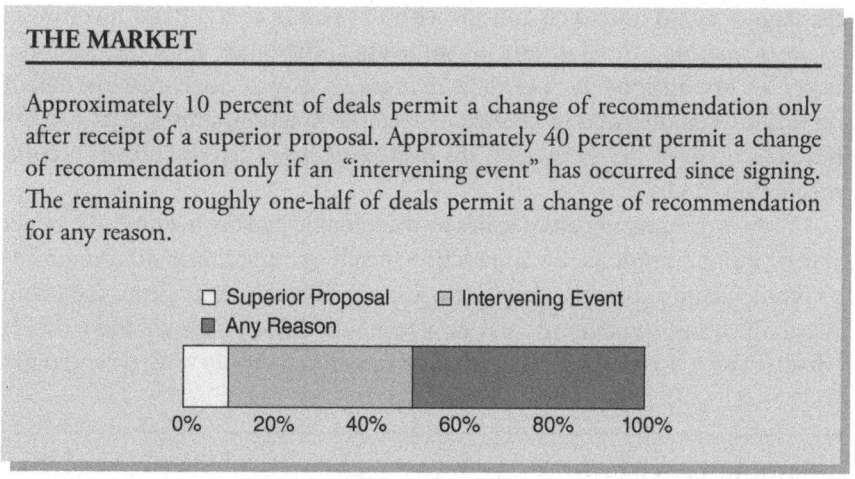

THE MARKET

Approximately 10 percent of deals permit a change of recommendation only after receipt of a superior proposal. Approximately 40 percent permit a change of recommendation only if an "intervening event" has occurred since signing. The remaining roughly one-half of deals permit a change of recommendation for any reason.

In a few deals, receipt of a superior proposal is required for a target to change its recommendation. In some deals, the board is only allowed to change its recommendation if it does so in response to an event that occurs after signing. This provision may be limited to intervening events that were not known to the board at the time that the merger agreement was signed which led the target board to conclude that the shareholders should no longer support the deal. The buyer will want to know that the target's board cannot change its view of the deal simply because it reevaluated the facts and came to a different conclusion.

Sample Provision

Prior to the time the Company Stockholder Approval is obtained, the Company Board may, in response to an (x) Acquisition Proposal made after the date hereof that did not result from a breach of this Section or (y) a material event, development, circumstance, occurrence or change in occurrence or facts not known to the Company board as of the date hereof (an "Intervening Event"), effect a Change of Recommendation [...]

The rise in popularity of the intervening event exception in the aftermath of the 2008 financial crisis (as compared to stricter provisions that only permit change of recommendation in light of a higher bid) can be seen as a reaction by targets to the hope that their prospects would quickly return to previous market highs.

The board's determination to change its recommendation is normally subject to the same procedural requirements described above. For instance, the target's board must first consult with its outside counsel and investment bankers regarding the decision. In some cases, the target must also give the buyer an opportunity to negotiate changes in its deal such that the board no longer feels the need to change its recommendation, in order to give the buyer an opportunity to sweeten the deal enough to keep the board's recommendation in place.

Even if the target board decides to recommend against the deal, the target usually cannot terminate the transaction merely because the board changed its recommendation. Instead, despite the change in recommendation, the board must still bring the current deal to a vote—letting the shareholders decide whether they wish to approve the deal despite the change in recommendation.

Sample Provision

Notwithstanding anything to the contrary in this Agreement, if the Company Board shall have made a Change of Recommendation, the Company shall nevertheless convene the Stockholders Meeting and solicit the Company Stockholder Approval at such Stockholders Meeting.

Actually changing the target board's recommendation against a deal may come at a cost to the target. It triggers a right for the buyer to terminate the transaction and collect the fiduciary out breakup fee. In that case, the target could lose the original deal, pay out the breakup fee to the buyer, and have nothing to show for it in terms of a higher-valued transaction.

In practice, a change in recommendation is only made if a better deal is available and ready to be signed. That superior proposal triggers a termination right (discussed below) for the target to terminate the current deal and actually sign up the competing deal. In that way, the target does not risk paying the termination fee until it has certainty that it has signed the next transaction.

Restriction on signing competing deals

The no-shop also prohibits the target from actually signing up a competing deal. Signing up a competing offer is a final and definitive step. As a result, the fiduciary out exceptions for actually signing a competing deal are harder to satisfy. In order to sign up a competing transaction, the original merger agreement has to be terminated. Most merger agreements permit termination upon the simultaneous execution of an acquisition agreement with the new buyer. Those that do not are referred to as "force the vote" transactions.

In force-the-vote deals, the target is permitted to change its recommendation (to recommend against the original deal and in favor of the new one), but cannot terminate the original merger agreement, even to accept a better offer from another bidder. Instead, the target must continue to move forward under the original merger agreement until the merger vote is held. At that point, if the original deal is rejected by shareholders, then the merger agreement can be terminated. If the shareholders vote for the original deal despite the better offer being potentially available, the original deal moves toward closing, and the fiduciary out exceptions expire (as they do upon the shareholder vote).

The target has control over the process of calling a shareholders' meeting and holding the vote. In force-the-vote deals, buyers must be careful to ensure that the documents pin down the target sufficiently to prevent it from scuttling that shareholder vote process on technicalities.

Force-the-vote deals tend to be limited to transactions in which a bidder is offering stock consideration. More specifically, they are mostly used in deals using fixed-ratio (variable priced) stock consideration. In those cases, the buyer may argue that investors cannot know the true value of the deal consideration until closer to the vote—given inherent fluctuations in the value of the stock consideration. Such uncertainty about relative value is the logical basis for the target to agree that it cannot terminate to take a better deal (before taking the first deal to a vote). Given the volatile equity markets experienced after the 2008 financial crisis, force the vote provisions have become more popular.

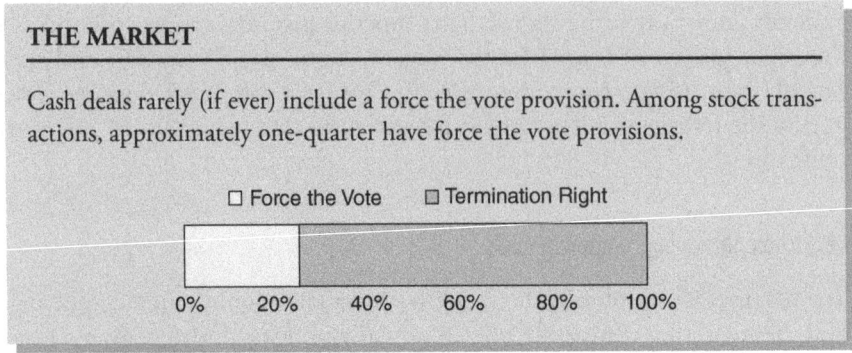

THE MARKET

Cash deals rarely (if ever) include a force the vote provision. Among stock transactions, approximately one-quarter have force the vote provisions.

In deals that have a fiduciary out termination right, the target can normally terminate to accept a competing offer only after meeting several requirements. The competing bidder must have made a "superior proposal." The soft exception discussed above for a proposal may become a superior proposal is not sufficient. To terminate, in order to take another deal, it must actually be a superior proposal.

To qualify as an actual superior proposal, it must have come to the target on an unsolicited basis. The target board also must conclude that its fiduciary duties require it to exercise the termination right. That determination, again, requires the board first to consult with its outside counsel and investment bankers regarding the decision. In a small subset of deals, the target is permitted to terminate the merger agreement if its board changes the recommendation for any reason—whether or not the target has received a superior proposal. For example, a change in the target's prospects, or improvement in the overall economy, can lead the target's board to change its view on the merger.

As noted above, the board usually has the ability to change its view. This termination provision allows the target to take its view a step further: to terminate the acquisition agreement and pay the breakup fee. Since the 2008 economic crisis, these provisions have become more popular, but still represent only a small minority of deals.

Definition of "superior proposal"

The merger agreement usually defines what is required for a competing bid to constitute a "superior proposal." The specific requirements that need to be met in order for a competing bid to qualify as a "superior proposal" differ from deal to deal, but the concepts share a few basic components.

Normally, the superior proposal definition starts with a general requirement that the competing bid constitute a majority deal (e.g., the competing bidder proposes to acquire at least a majority of the target's equity or assets). The target would not be permitted to terminate the merger agreement to accept a minority investment no matter what the price.

Sample Provision

"Superior Proposal" means a bona fide written Acquisition Proposal (with the percentages set forth in the definition of such term changed from 20 percent to [50] percent) that is not solicited or received in violation of Section __ [no shop].

The definition requires that the new deal be superior from a financial point of view in some way and be reasonably capable of being completed.

Sample Provision

[…] that the Company Board has determined in its good faith judgment, after consultation with outside legal counsel and its financial advisor, is (i) reasonably likely to be consummated in accordance with its terms, and (ii) if consummated, would be more favorable [from a financial point of view] to the Company's stockholders than the Merger and the other transactions contemplated by this Agreement.

In cash deals, the requirement for the new deal to be superior from a financial point of view normally translates into a higher price. When the drafting is done in this way—specifically requiring superior financial terms—then the target could not accept a lower or equal price in exchange for any other benefits, even a significant increase in deal certainty.

If the original deal has become uncertain, perhaps due to views expressed by regulators in a regulatory approval process, this restraint could bind the target to a deal that, everything considered (not just financial terms), is not as attractive. For that reason, some merger agreements leave the superior proposal definition more open ended, to permit judgment calls to be made by the target's board.

THE MARKET

Approximately half of public deals specifically require that a competing bid have superior financial terms.

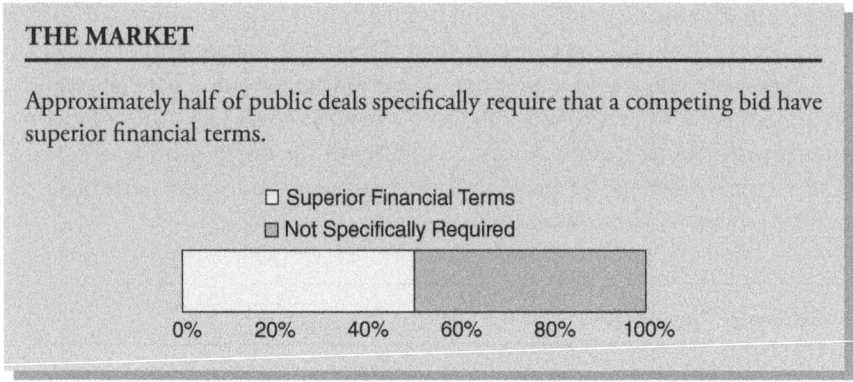

□ Superior Financial Terms
□ Not Specifically Required

0%   20%   40%   60%   80%   100%

In fixed ratio (variable price) stock deals, the value of the consideration may be harder to compare. If all consideration is in the form of publicly traded stock, the current price of the stock being offered can be used to compare the two. Other measures are relevant as well, such as average trading prices over the last 10 to 30 trading days. In addition, financial advisors may take into account growth trajectories of each of the buyer entities whose stock is being offered as consideration. All in all, this can turn into a process that is subject to a number of judgment calls.

The superior proposal definition also requires that the competing bid be reasonably capable of being consummated. That is not an issue in most deals. If the target and new buyer are close competitors in the same narrow industry, however, antitrust approval for the new deal could make it less than certain. The provision is usually written in an absolute form—"reasonably capable"—while the target would presumably want to take into account the relative certainty. One deal may have financing risk while the other has regulatory risk. The superior proposal definition does not actually require the new deal to have a higher or equal likelihood of completion, but simply requires it to be reasonably capable of being completed.

In some deals—and more frequently since 2008—the definition of "superior proposal" requires the competing bid to have committed financing. Sometimes it specifies that the terms cannot be less favorable than the current buyer's financing. In those cases, the target's board cannot use its judgment to balance a weaker financing package with a better price or overall better deal certainty in order to conclude that a competing bid is superior.

Match Rights

The buyer will normally insist on a "match" right, which entitles the buyer to match the price of a competing bid. If it matches, the target cannot terminate the merger agreement to accept the competing bidder's (matched) offer.

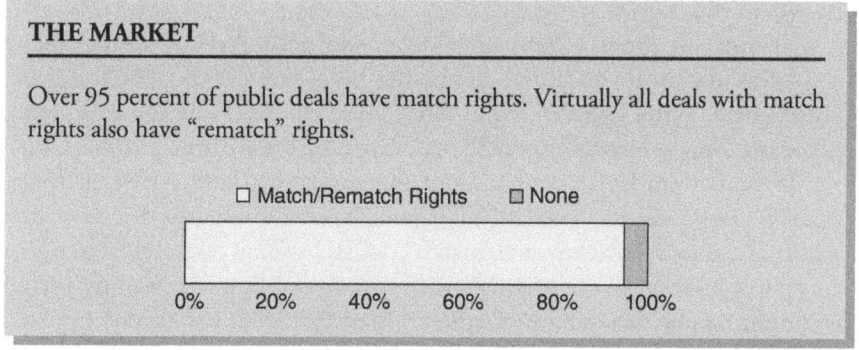

THE MARKET

Over 95 percent of public deals have match rights. Virtually all deals with match rights also have "rematch" rights.

☐ Match/Rematch Rights   ☐ None

0%   20%   40%   60%   80%   100%

If the buyer revises its purchase price to match, then the competing proposal is no longer "superior." By operation of the superior proposal definition, the target would no longer be permitted to (and presumably would no longer wish to) terminate in order to take the competing offer.

Sample Provision

(a) provided that prior to effecting any Change in Recommendation or termination of this Agreement pursuant to Section __: (i) the Company shall have delivered to Parent written notice at least [three] Business Days (the "Notice Period"), which notice shall (x) with respect to an Acquisition Proposal (A) state that the Company has received a Superior Proposal, and (B) include a copy of all relevant documents relating to the Superior Proposal and a written summary of the material terms and conditions of the Superior Proposal not made in writing and the identity of the Person or "group" making the Superior Proposal or (y) with respect to an Intervening Event, (A) state that an Intervening Event has occurred, and (B) specify in reasonable detail the basis for the Intervening Event.

The match right operates as a waiting period, giving the current buyer an opportunity to review and propose to change its price. The period starts when the target delivers notice to the buyer that the target has received a superior proposal. The target cannot act on the competing bidder's proposal (i.e., terminate the merger agreement) until the match period expires, which gives the buyer an opportunity to counter that superior proposal. The buyer is entitled to a copy of the competing bid in order to know what it is up against. A few deals have qualified match rights, in which the right may not apply if a competing bid tops the current deal price by a significant amount (such as 10 percent over the current bid), or may be eliminated for bidders who emerge during a go-shop period.

In order to support the match rights and generally provide the buyer with information on potential competing bids—even if the match right is not triggered—the target is required to notify the buyer of any competing proposals. Notice must be prompt in most cases, and often within 24 or 48 hours.

If the current buyer matches, but the competing bidder raises its price again in response, the current buyer will have the opportunity to match again. These are referred to as "rematch" rights. In some cases, rematch rights are simply a repeat of the original match right. In others, the waiting period is shorter for the rematch, on the theory that the buyer has already updated its financial analysis and had time to review the situation—and, thus, needs less lead time to decide whether to rebid or not.

Sample Provision

provided that any amendment to the material terms of any such Superior Proposal or any material change in the Intervening Event shall require compliance with [subsections (i) to (iii)] [match right] de novo, except that the Notice Period shall be reduced to two Business Days before the Change of Recommendation or termination of this Agreement pursuant to Section __.

Match rights frequently give the buyer three to five business days to consider the competing proposal and decide whether or not to match.

THE MARKET

Roughly 80 percent of deals have a three- to five-calendar-day match period. The range goes up to seven days (or five business days).

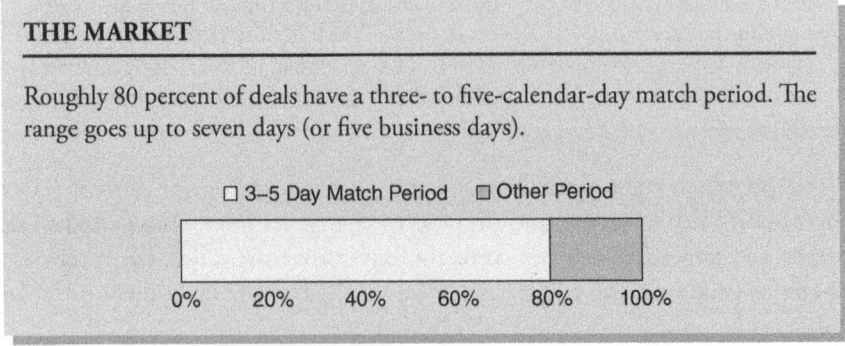

Sometimes the rematch period is the same length as the match period, but more often than not, the rematch period is a little shorter than the match period.

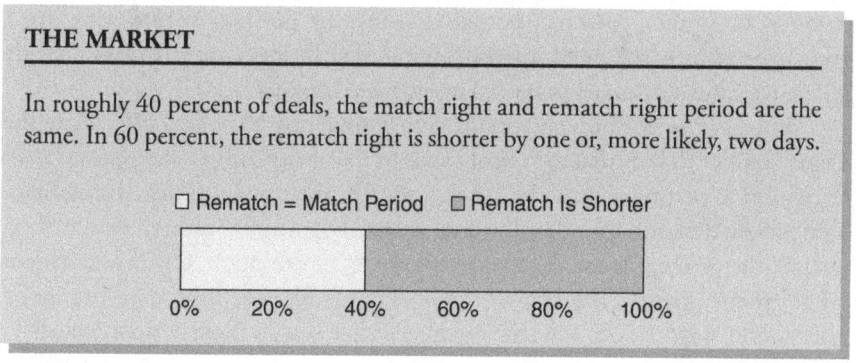

THE MARKET

In roughly 40 percent of deals, the match right and rematch right period are the same. In 60 percent, the rematch right is shorter by one or, more likely, two days.

In some deals, the competitive bidding process is done outside of the match procedure. Instead, bids and counterbids are made informally. Once the back and forth is done, the target initiates the formal match procedure. While the original buyer has a contractual right to notice and details of the competing bidder's proposals, the competing bidder does not have a contract guaranteeing it such information. That can sometimes lead the new bidder astray.

War Story

The target was a large public company in the consumer electronics industry. After a long period of disappointing results, and a challenging search for a buyer, the target eventually found a private equity buyer. The target had assumed that the only strategic buyers were its closest competitors, so the target had limited its search, for the most part, to private equity and ignored the strategics.

To its surprise, after publicly announcing the private equity deal, the target was approached by one of its closest competitors. Negotiations ensued, and the target eventually received an offer.

The target presented the new bid to the original private equity buyer. The private equity buyer declined to match. Nevertheless, the target was able to get the strategic buyer to bid against itself and raise its price. The private equity buyer was given the opportunity to raise its price again, and again declined. Somehow, the target was still able to get the strategic buyer to raise its price again.

Eventually, the strategic bidder had bid itself up to a substantial premium over the private equity buyer's deal price. The target then terminated to take the better deal.

Go-Shops

In a growing number of private equity deals, the no-shop period begins only four to six weeks after signing. This window before the no-shop begins is referred to as the "go-shop" period. During the go-shop period, the target may affirmatively solicit competing bids as well as negotiate with and provide diligence information to potential competing bidders.

None of the no-shop exceptions permit soliciting bids; they only allow the target to react to bids that are unsolicited. In that sense, the go-shop provides an exception to permit solicitation. The go-shop is often tied together with an auction process designed to end by the time the go-shop window expires. As a drafting matter, the go-shop is usually structured not as an exception, but as a statement of affirmative rights. The text of the no-shop is flipped. Instead of restricting solicitation, negotiation, and sharing diligence, it affirms them as permissible.

Sample Provision

Notwithstanding anything to the contrary contained in this Agreement, during the period beginning on the date of this Agreement and continuing until 12:01 A.M. (New York time) on the __ day after the date of this Agreement (the "No-Shop Period Start Date"), the Company and its Subsidiaries and their respective Representatives shall have the right to (i) initiate, solicit and encourage any inquiry or the making of any proposal or offer that constitutes an Acquisition Proposal and (ii) engage in, enter into, continue or otherwise participate in any discussions or negotiations with any Persons or groups of Persons with respect to any Acquisition Proposals and cooperate with or assist or participate in or facilitate any such inquiries, proposals, discussions, or negotiations or any effort or attempt to make any Acquisition Proposals.

The number of go-shop deals has increased since 2008, particularly among private equity deals.

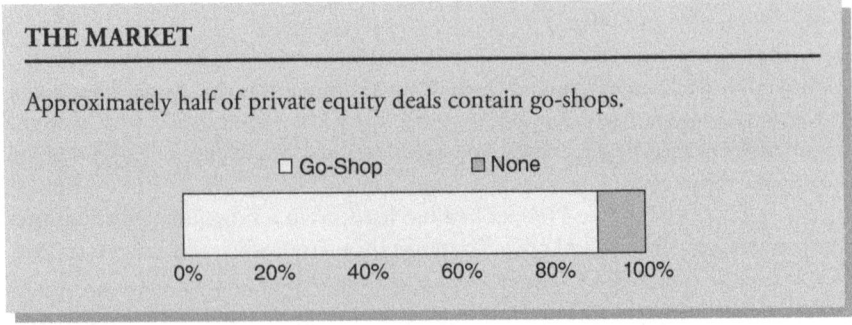

THE MARKET

Approximately half of private equity deals contain go-shops.

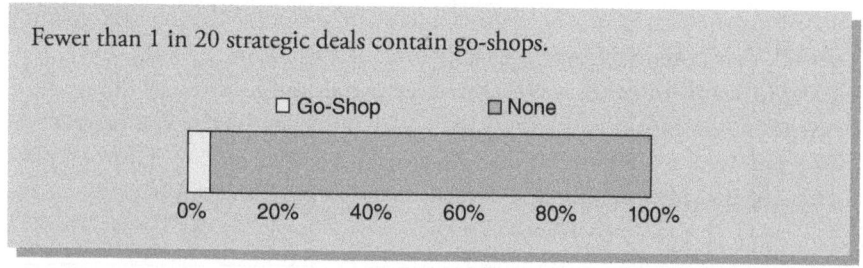

Fewer than 1 in 20 strategic deals contain go-shops.

Length of the go-shop period is negotiated. Go-shop periods have been slowly increasing in recent years, as go-shops have become more prevalent.

THE MARKET

The average go-shop period is just short of six weeks.

A third of go-shop deals have a go-shop period of approximately a month or a little less. One-half have a go-shop period of more than a month but less than six weeks. The remainder have go-shop periods of more than six weeks, but generally not more than eight weeks.

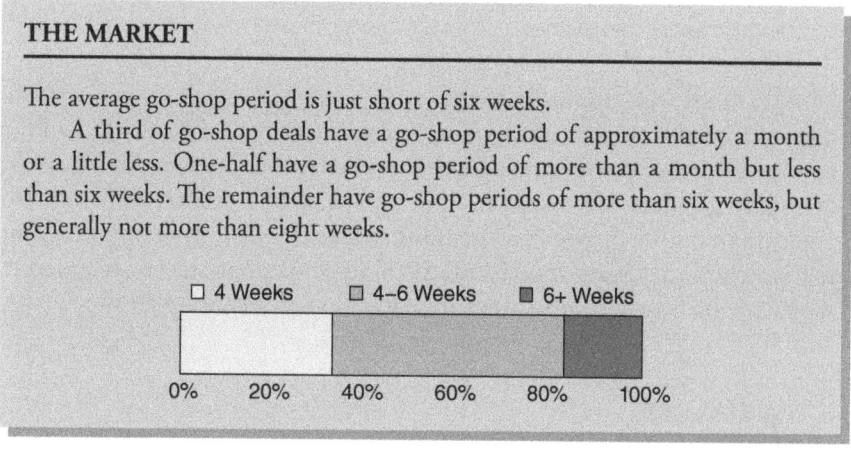

At the end of the go-shop period, the target is required to give the buyer a status update. The target provides a summary of the proposals it has received and the status of each.

Sample Provision

Promptly (and, in any event, within 48 hours) after the No-Shop Period Start Date, the Company will summarize all material facts regarding all proposals or offers that were received by, any nonpublic information that was requested from, or any discussions or negotiations that were sought to be initiated or continued with, the Company or any of its Subsidiaries or any of their respective Representatives during the period from the date of this Agreement until the No-Shop Period Start Date.

If a potential buyer submits a qualified proposal during the go-shop period, that potential buyer is usually excluded from the no-shop restrictions going forward. In other words, the target need not go through the no-shop exceptions to continue working with that potential buyer. For instance, it does not have to determine that its fiduciary duties require it to negotiate with and provide ongoing due diligence to that potential buyer.

Sample Provision

"Excluded Party" means any Person or group of Persons from whom the Company has received a written Acquisition Proposal after the execution of this Agreement [and prior to the No-Shop Period Start Date].

Go-shops were originally conceived as a method to help ensure that the target had fulfilled its fiduciary duties, particularly when the target had not conducted an extensive market check for a better deal prior to signing. Now, voluntary go-shops are common. They are negotiated deal terms, frequently appearing even in competitive auctions, where, by definition, a pre-signing market check has been conducted. Such go-shops that are not required to satisfy the board's fiduciary duties are referred to as voluntary go-shops.

THE MARKET

Approximately three-quarters of go-shops in private equity deals are voluntary. Since they follow a pre-signing market check, they are not motivated by fiduciary duty requirements. The others are presumed to be motivated at least in part by fiduciary concerns.

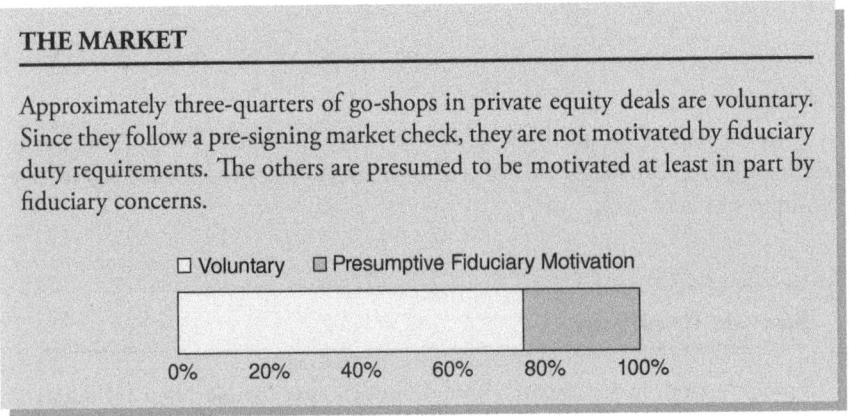

Voluntary go-shops parallel the trend toward lower fiduciary out breakup fees.[3] Each trend increases the ability for the target to benefit from a competing bid after the original deal is signed. The go-shop increases the likelihood of a competing bid in various ways. For one, it allows solicitation of competing bids (otherwise prohibited by the no-shop). Following a pre-signing auction, though, this may have little practical importance. For another, the disclosure statement for the merger vote is not filed until the go-shop period expires, increasing the time period over which a competing offer may arise.

A majority of go-shops provide for a smaller breakup fee (i.e., smaller than the no-shop breakup fee). This applies to bidders that present themselves during the go-shop period. In many deals, the target faces a deadline to benefit from the smaller go-shop breakup fee. It must actually complete and sign a deal by the end of the go-shop period. In other deals, the target benefits from the reduced breakup fee for bidders that emerge during the go-shop period, whether the deal with that bidder is signed before or after the go-shop expires.

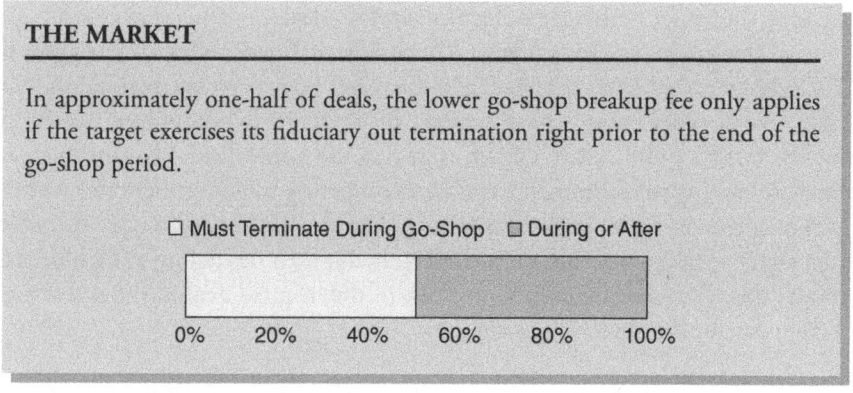

THE MARKET

In approximately one-half of deals, the lower go-shop breakup fee only applies if the target exercises its fiduciary out termination right prior to the end of the go-shop period.

☐ Must Terminate During Go-Shop   ☐ During or After

0%   20%   40%   60%   80%   100%

Recently, a few strategic deals have started including lower termination fees for competing bids that arise during an initial post-signing period. This is similar to a go-shop in terms of the fee structure, but—unlike a go-shop—does not permit affirmative solicitation of competing bids by the target.

Fiduciary Out Breakup Fees

Triggers for fiduciary out breakup fees

There are several ways in which a fiduciary out breakup fee can be triggered. All of them require that the original merger agreement be terminated. Whether the fee is triggered depends on the circumstances of termination.

Termination trigger

The target terminating the deal to accept a superior proposal is the primary fiduciary out breakup fee trigger. This trigger is relatively straightforward. There are hurdles to exercising the fiduciary out termination right—receiving an unsolicited superior proposal, the board determining that its fiduciary duties require it to accept the proposal, and so on.[4] Once those are met and the original deal is terminated, the fee is payable.

Change of recommendation trigger

Another trigger may apply if the target board changes its recommendation. The target is unlikely to change its recommendation until it is prepared to accept a superior proposal. Otherwise, the target could terminate in response to the change in recommendation and trigger the fiduciary out breakup fee, leaving the target with a fee obligation and no deal.

A change in recommendation is broadly defined under this trigger. It includes not only an actual change in the target board's recommendation, but also several other actions by the target or its board that could be perceived by the target's public shareholders as having the same effect.[5] For instance, it includes failing to recommend against a competing public tender offer within ten business days (the period provided under the SEC's tender offer rules for the target to take a position on the offer). It also includes failing to include the target board's recommendation in favor of the original deal in the disclosure statement for the shareholder vote.

Fee tail trigger

The so-called "fee tail" trigger applies if shareholders vote down the original merger agreement due to the likelihood that a better deal will arise and then, after termination, the target does actually sign or close another deal.

Sample Provision

If (x) this Agreement is terminated pursuant to Section __ [drop-dead date passing] or Section __ [vote down by shareholders], (y) any Person shall have publicly made a bona fide Acquisition Proposal or an Acquisition Proposal is publicly disclosed or publicly announced after the date of this Agreement but prior to the date the Stockholders Meeting, and in the case of termination pursuant to Section __ [vote down by shareholders] such Acquisition Proposal shall not have been publicly withdrawn prior to [the date that is five Business Days prior to the Stockholders Meeting] and (z) within [12] months after such termination the Company shall have consummated the transactions contemplated by [any] Acquisition Proposal [or entered into a definitive agreement with respect to any Acquisition Proposal] [...].

Usually, another potential deal must be publicly known before the original deal is voted down. Then, the target must sign up or close an alternative deal within a 12- to 24-month tail period after termination of the original merger agreement.

THE MARKET

Around 80 percent of deals have a 12-month tail period. In most of the remaining deals the tail is shorter (such as 9 months), but, in a few, the tail is longer (such as 18 months).

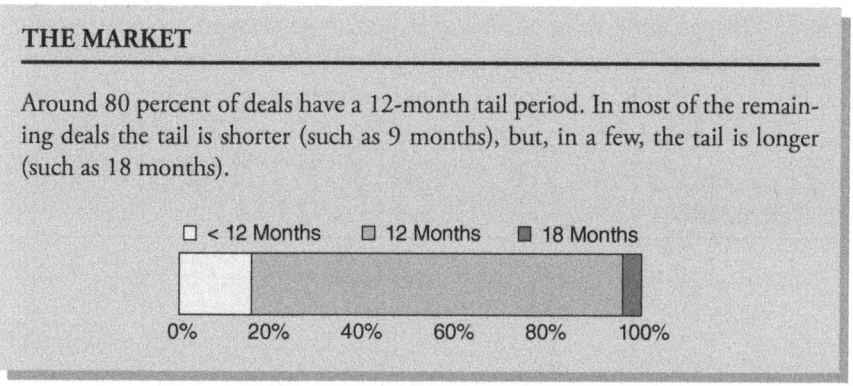

In most merger agreements, the alternative deal that is signed or closed need not be the same one that was publicly announced before the original deal was voted down. Any alternative deal during the tail period is sufficient to trigger the fee.

More often than not, the tail is triggered by actually closing the alternative deal in the tail period. In others, the tail is triggered by merely signing an alternative deal during that period. For deals in which closing (as opposed to just signing) the alternative deal is required, the tail on average tends to be slightly longer. If only signing is required, the target may have to pay the fee even if it never closes the alternative deal.

THE MARKET

In 70 percent of deals, the trigger for the tail fee requires closing an alternative deal during the tail period. In 30 percent, only signing is required during that period.

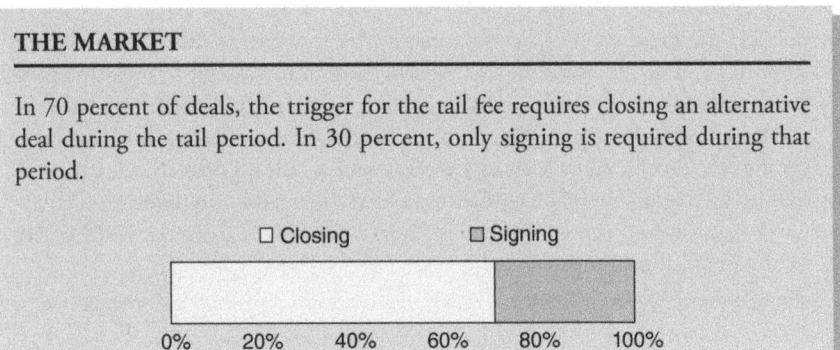

☐ Closing   ☐ Signing

0%   20%   40%   60%   80%   100%

Shareholder vote-down trigger

On occasion, a breakup fee is payable by the target upon a simple vote down by the target shareholders, whether or not a competing deal is signed or closed. This is fairly unusual, however, and puts pressure on the target to conclude that it has not placed an inappropriate burden on its shareholders to freely exercise their vote for or against the merger agreement.[6]

THE MARKET

Approximately 5 percent of deals have a breakup fee triggered by a vote down of the deal by the target's shareholders.

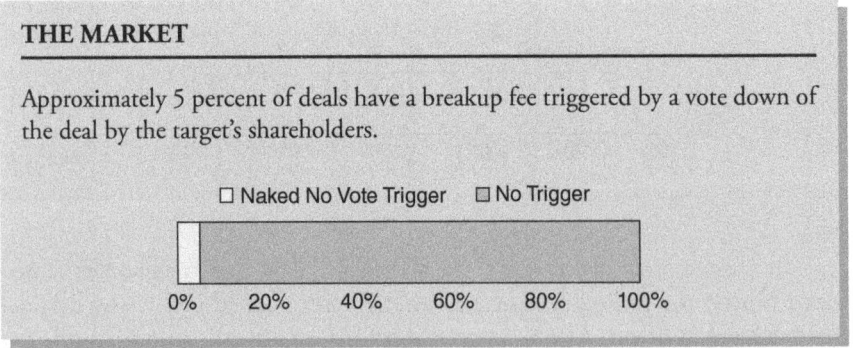

☐ Naked No Vote Trigger   ☐ No Trigger

0%   20%   40%   60%   80%   100%

When this trigger exists, the amount of the fee is usually equal to the amount of the fiduciary out breakup fee. The vote down itself is the trigger, and it does not have to be accompanied by a competing bid or a change in recommendation by the target's board. This is often referred to as a "naked no vote." It is much more common for a buyer to instead have its expenses reimbursed (but not a fee paid) by the target in the event of a vote down by the target's shareholders.[7]

Amount of fiduciary out breakup fees

The amount of fiduciary out breakup fees has trended downward over recent years, as fees have been restricted by judicial interpretations of corporate law. A high fee can be viewed as an unreasonable restriction on the target exercising its fiduciary out termination right. Practitioners generally believe that fees in the range of 2 to 4 percent of equity value are acceptable, with some deals having fees up to 5 percent or slightly higher.[8]

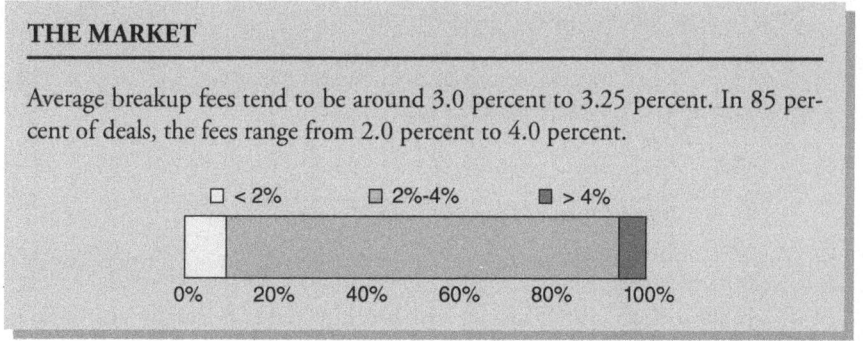

THE MARKET

Average breakup fees tend to be around 3.0 percent to 3.25 percent. In 85 percent of deals, the fees range from 2.0 percent to 4.0 percent.

☐ < 2%   ☐ 2%-4%   ■ > 4%

0%   20%   40%   60%   80%   100%

Usually, the breakup fee is measured as a percentage of the equity value of the target company, which is the value of all the company's equity, or market capitalization. Another measure of value is "enterprise value," which is the value of the target company, plus its debt, less any cash or other marketable securities. For instance, assume that a business would be worth $500 million (enterprise value) if it had no debt or cash. If it does have $50 million in debt, then a buyer would pay $450 million (equity value) to buy the stock of the target company. Alternatively, if the target would be worth $500 million if it had no debt or cash (enterprise value), but does have $50 million of cash, then a buyer may be willing to pay $550 million (equity value) for the stock of the target.

Purchase price (equity value) is the normal basis for measuring breakup fees. However, if the target has high leverage (debt), equity value is not the right measure for the breakup fee. If the company mentioned above would be worth $500 million if it had no debt, but actually has $400 million in debt, then the equity value is only $100 million. Thus, a $15 million breakup fee (3 percent of $500 million) would be 15 percent of the equity value, but only 3 percent of the enterprise value. If the buyer were limited to a percentage of equity value, then the breakup fee would be only around $3 million, which some buyers may view as too small for the effort required to get to signing of the merger agreement.

Courts will allow the parties to consider the enterprise instead of (or in addition to) the equity value when deciding upon an appropriate breakup fee when it is reasonable to do so under the circumstances.[9]

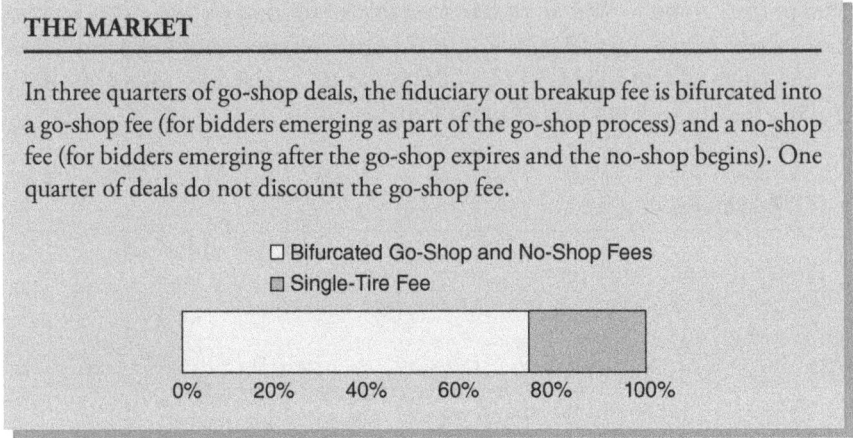

THE MARKET

In three quarters of go-shop deals, the fiduciary out breakup fee is bifurcated into a go-shop fee (for bidders emerging as part of the go-shop process) and a no-shop fee (for bidders emerging after the go-shop expires and the no-shop begins). One quarter of deals do not discount the go-shop fee.

☐ Bifurcated Go-Shop and No-Shop Fees
☐ Single-Tire Fee

0%   20%   40%   60%   80%   100%

In go-shop deals, the fiduciary out breakup fee is normally cut back in size if the buyer emerged during the go-shop period. This results in two tiers of fees; the lower fee is triggered by the target terminating to take a better deal from a bidder that participated in the go-shop process. If another bidder were to emerge after the go-shop period expires—which is unlikely—then the normal fiduciary out breakup fee applies. As a result, in addition to creating a post-signing auction context, practically speaking, a go-shop cuts the size of the fiduciary out breakup fee in half.

Expense Reimbursement

In many deals, the buyer is entitled to be reimbursed by the target for the buyer's expenses, up to a capped amount, if the deal does not close for various reasons.

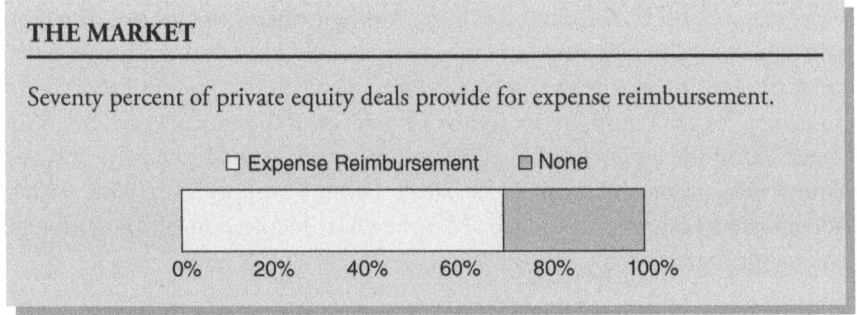

THE MARKET

Seventy percent of private equity deals provide for expense reimbursement.

☐ Expense Reimbursement   ☐ None

0%   20%   40%   60%   80%   100%

Expense reimbursement is normally triggered by the target shareholders voting down the deal. The pressure this places on shareholders to vote in favor of the deal is considered small and not too burdensome from a fiduciary duty perspective.

Sample Provision

If this Agreement is terminated pursuant to Section __ [vote down by shareholders], then the Company shall promptly, but in no event later than five Business Days after the date of such termination (without regard to whether the Company shall have entered into a definitive agreement with respect to an Acquisition Proposal or an Acquisition Proposal shall have been consummated) pay Parent or its designees all reasonable out-of-pocket fees and expenses incurred by Parent or Merger Sub in connection with this Agreement or the transactions contemplated hereby, in an amount not to exceed $__ [expense cap] by wire transfer of same day funds.

In some deals, a "naked no vote" is not sufficient to trigger reimbursement; the vote down must be due to the likelihood of a competing deal. Specifically, the vote down must be preceded either by a competing bid becoming known to the public shareholders or by the target's board changing its recommendation.

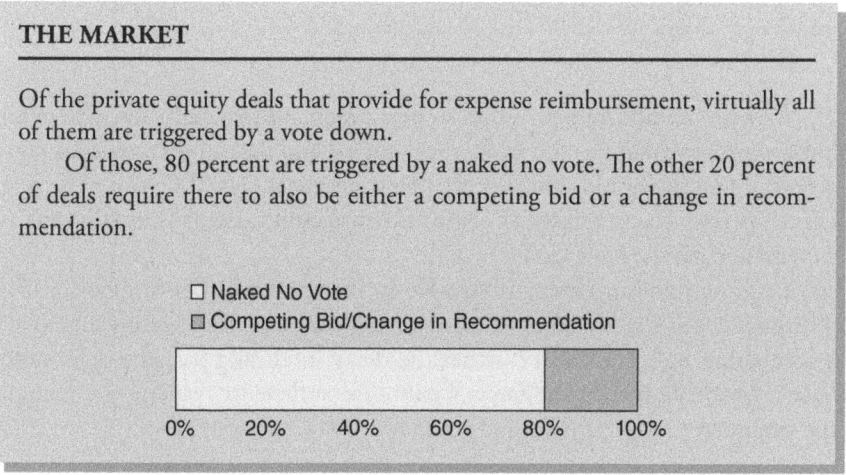

THE MARKET

Of the private equity deals that provide for expense reimbursement, virtually all of them are triggered by a vote down.

Of those, 80 percent are triggered by a naked no vote. The other 20 percent of deals require there to also be either a competing bid or a change in recommendation.

☐ Naked No Vote
☐ Competing Bid/Change in Recommendation

0%   20%   40%   60%   80%   100%

Sometimes expense reimbursement may be triggered if the buyer terminates the deal due to the target's breach of its representations or covenants.

THE MARKET

Among deals with an expense reimbursement trigger, breach of representations or covenants is a trigger in 60 percent.

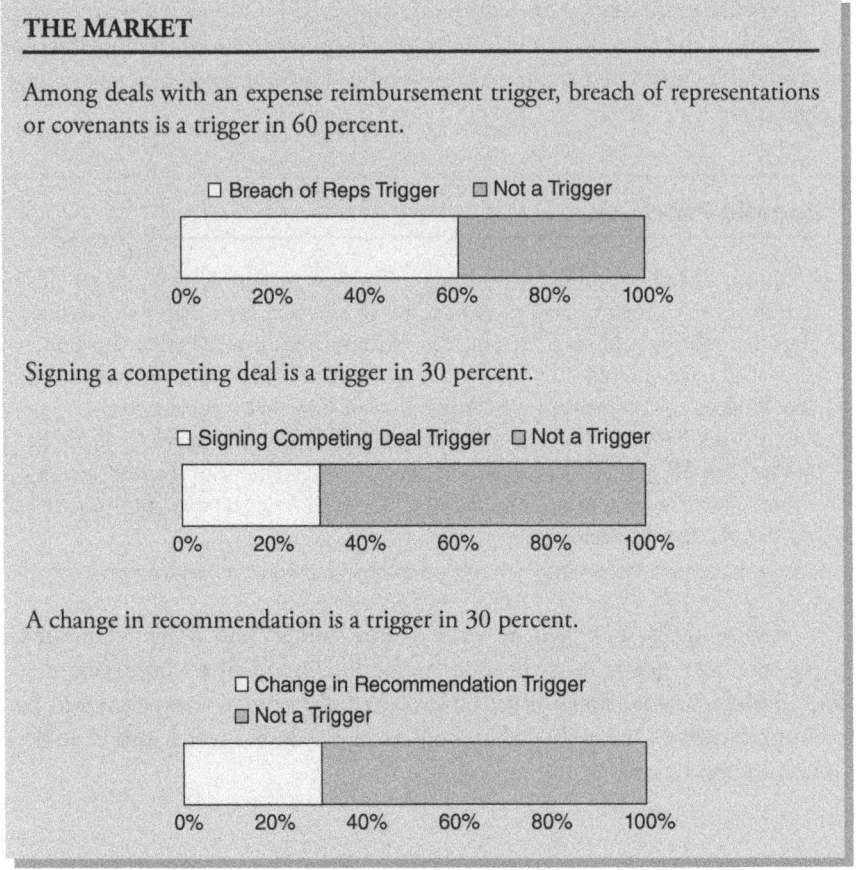

Signing a competing deal is a trigger in 30 percent.

A change in recommendation is a trigger in 30 percent.

Expense reimbursement can also be a precursor to a "tail" fee, where reimbursement would be paid upon termination and the tail fee would be payable if a competing bid that met the fee trigger was signed or closed during the tail period. In such cases, the prior expense reimbursement usually acts as a credit against the later fee.

Expense reimbursement is payable in some cases if the original deal is terminated because the drop-dead date passes following announcement of a competing bid. The theory is that the delay in closing past the drop-dead date is probably due to the target's failure to sufficiently pursue the vote or the deal.

Sample Provision

[…] if this Agreement is terminated pursuant to (x) Section ___ [drop-dead date] and any Person shall have publicly made an Acquisition Proposal or an Acquisition Proposal is publicly disclosed or publicly announced after the date of this Agreement but prior to the date of the Stockholders Meeting or (y) Section ___ [vote down by shareholders] […]

Finally, expense reimbursement may be triggered by the target exercising its fiduciary out termination right or by the target changing its recommendation. In those cases, the amount of expense reimbursement is usually added to the fiduciary out breakup fee. Both must be paid. In occasional deals, expense reimbursement is triggered by other events, such as a material adverse effect on the target or any failure to close by the drop-dead date.

Although larger deals do tend to be more expensive to negotiate for a variety of reasons, expense caps should theoretically not be directly dependent on deal size. They are intended to reimburse expenses rather than represent a fee. Nevertheless, expense cap amounts tend to be tied to the equity value of the deal, forming a hybrid, in a sense, between an actual expense estimate and a fee concept. The amount tends to center around 50 to 75 basis points (0.5 percent to 0.75 percent) of the equity consideration, but ranges from 25 to 125 basis points. The percent of equity value is somewhat smaller in larger than in smaller deals.

Litigation Endnotes

1. *See, e.g., Revlon, Inc. v. MacAndrews & Forbes Holdings, Inc.*, 506 A.2d 173, 184 (Del. 1986) (finding that a no-shop provision without exceptions would be an impermissible restraint on a board's duty to sell a company to the highest bidder, where the board of the target company implemented defensive measures, including a poison pill, in order to prevent a hostile takeover by a buyer). *See also McMillan v. Intercargo Corp.*, 768 A.2d 492, 506 (Del. Ch. 2000) (holding that no-shop provisions are permissible if they permit the board to consider unsolicited proposals more favorable to stockholders than the immediate one; stockholders had sued the directors of a target company for not attaining the highest reasonable value in the sale of the target as a result of a no-shop provision).
2. *See, e.g., Mills Acquisition Co. v. Macmillan, Inc.*, 559 A.2d 1261, 1280 (Del. 1989) (discussing fiduciary duty of care); *Smith v. Van Gorkom*, 488 A.2d 858, 872 (Del. 1985) (same).
3. *See* Chapter 13-E, Fiduciary Out Breakup Fees.
4. Chapter 13-B, Types of Restrictions in No-Shop Provisions.
5. *See, e.g., In re Compellent Techs., Inc. S'holder Litig.*, No. 6084-VCL, 2011 BL 317827 (Del. Ch. Dec. 9, 2011) (characterizing the fee triggers as "hair-trigger" events, and noting that (i) the definition of "change in recommendation" is generally governed by the agreements themselves and (ii) while courts can find definitions of change in recommendation to be unusually broad, they will generally respect an agreement between the parties).
6. In *In re Lear Corp. Shareholder Litigation*, the target's shareholders alleged that its directors had breached their duty of loyalty when they approved the sale of the target despite the fact that the shareholders were not likely to vote to approve the sale. They argued that this exposed the shareholders to a high risk of paying the naked no-vote termination fee that the directors had implemented to appease the buyer's doubts regarding a successful merger. The court found that there was no breach of the duty of loyalty because there were no facts supporting the allegation of bad faith. 967 A.2d 640 (Del. Ch. 2008).
7. *See, generally,* Chapter 13-F, Expense Reimbursement.
8. *See, e.g., McMillan v. Intercargo Corp.*, 768 A.2d 492, 505 (Del. Ch. 2000) (holding termination fee of 3.5 percent of deal value permissible, if tending toward high end of what was acceptable); *Goodwin v. Live Entm't, Inc.*, No. 15765, 1999 BL 128 (Del. Ch. Jan. 22, 1999), *aff'd*, 741 A.2d 16 (Del. 1999) (finding termination fee of 3.125 percent to be commonplace and within range of reasonableness). *See also La. Mun. Police Emps. Retirement Sys. v. Crawford*, 918 A.2d 1172 (Del. Ch. 2007) (overturning $675 million termination fee (3 percent of $23 billion equity value) and rejecting target's justification that it was appropriate because higher percentages of equity value had been previously upheld). The *Crawford* court's analysis emphasized—the real world risks and

prospects confronting [directors] when they agreed to the deal protections. ... That analysis will, by necessity, require the Court to consider a number of factors, including without limitation: the overall size of the termination fee, as well as its percentage value; the benefit to the shareholders, including a premium (if any) that directors seek to protect; the absolute size of the transaction, as well as the relative size of the partners to the merger; the degree to which a counterparty found such protections to be crucial to the deal, bearing in mind differences in bargaining power; and the preclusive or coercive power of all deal protections included in a transaction, taken as a whole. The inquiry, by its very nature fact intensive, cannot be reduced to a mathematical equation. Though a "3 percent rule" for termination fees might be convenient for transaction planners, it simply too blunt an instrument, too subject to abuse, for this Court to bless as a blanket rule. *Id.* at 1181 n. 10 (internal quotations omitted).

9. In *In re Cogent, Inc. Shareholder Litigation,* shareholders of the target company sued the board of directors for agreeing to pay a bidder a termination fee equal to 3 percent of its equity value. The target company had significant cash reserves, such that the termination fee was equal to 6.58 percent of the target's enterprise value. The shareholders argued that comparing the termination fee against enterprise value was the more relevant metric, in light of the company's cash position. The court stated that enterprise value might sometimes be an appropriate metric. 7 A.3d 487, 503–04 (Del. Ch. 2010). However, the court found that this argument would not likely be successful on the merits in this case and, thus, that the plaintiffs did not meet the standard for a preliminary injunction. *Id.* at 504.

CHAPTER 14

Indemnities

Indemnities in M&A Negotiations

Overview of indemnities

An indemnity shifts liabilities to the seller that would otherwise fall upon the buyer. Once the transaction closes, the buyer owns the target business and, by default, has economic responsibility for the target's obligations (in that the target's liabilities reduce the value of the target for the buyer). An indemnity is one mechanism for the buyer to shift liabilities back to the seller.

An indemnity is frequently used where the liability at issue is uncertain. If the amount of a liability is fixed, such as $100 million in debt or a $50 million fine that cannot be appealed, then it is easy enough for the parties to simply adjust the purchase price. By doing so, the shift in value occurs on the closing date. The buyer does not have to take any credit risk with respect to the sellers—that is, no risk that the sellers fail to pay the indemnity when due.

Where a liability is contingent and uncertain, however—such as outstanding litigation—there are two choices. If the buyer is willing to take the risk, the parties could adjust the purchase price by the expected value of the liability (plus a risk premium for the buyer). In that case, the buyer would forgo indemnity protection. If the buyer is not willing to bear the risk, the seller could instead provide an indemnity to the buyer.

Whether the buyer or the seller will want to take the risk of a contingent liability depends on a number of deal-specific factors. For instance, the seller may have more knowledge of the potential risk, and so may be able to better assess it. If that is the case, the seller may worry less about the risk than the buyer. In other cases, the target business will have significant influence over whether the liability actually arises or how extensive it is, so the seller will be reluctant to take on that type of risk without control over the situation.

War Story

A global software provider began an auction to sell one of its lines of business. It was a tough time to sell, because it was in the middle of complex litigation with all 50 U.S. states and several foreign countries over its pricing practices. As with many types of litigation, it was difficult for anyone—including the seller, regulators, and analysts—to estimate how much it would cost to eventually settle the lawsuits.

The seller worried: What if some bidders estimated the cost of the litigation at $50 million and some estimated it at $250 million? Would each bidder be willing to hire specialists and litigation advisors to help them estimate the risk of this highly technical lawsuit? And what if the most enthusiastic potential buyer was the most concerned about the litigation risk?

From the beginning of the auction, the seller and its advisors told bidders that they should not waste time valuing the litigation or reduce their bid prices on account of the risk. By affirmatively agreeing to take—rather than trying to push off—the litigation risk, the seller was able to create value and streamline the auction. The seller achieved this by offering a special indemnity covering that litigation.

The auction turned out to be quite competitive in that form. In fact, a couple of years later, the buyer regretted having gotten so involved in the deal because it felt (in retrospect) that it had significantly overpaid.

This chapter discusses indemnities from the perspective of the seller's indemnity to the buyer. The buyer also provides an indemnity for breaches by the buyer of its representations (and sometimes covenants). That indemnity is much less important to the deal as a practical matter in most cases, since the buyer's representations tend to be technical and highly unlikely to be breached. Nevertheless, the buyer's indemnity usually mirrors the terms negotiated for the seller's indemnity.

Types of indemnities

There are two types of indemnities. Under the basic indemnity, the seller agrees to cover after closing the buyer's losses that arise out of a breach of the seller's and target's representations in the acquisition agreement. This indemnity may also protect the buyer from breaches of covenants.

Under a special indemnity the seller agrees to pay for particular losses or liabilities, without regard to whether or not they arise from a breach. Special indemnities can be designed to cover any matters that the parties select. In particular, special indemnities are used to protect the buyer from matters that arise in its due diligence review.

Since the representations are qualified by the disclosure schedules, any adverse matter that the seller discloses on the appropriate schedules will not breach the representations. Without a breach of representation, the buyer cannot recover under the basic indemnity. A special indemnity tailored to a particular issue restores the right for the buyer to recover. There are several types of special indemnities that are commonly used in practice.

THE MARKET

Special indemnities are often used to cover:

Excess payments to dissenting shareholders under appraisal rights (80 percent of deals).

Taxes (60 percent of private deals).

Deal expenses and change in control payments (55 percent of private deals).

Deal-specific matters (40 percent of private deals).

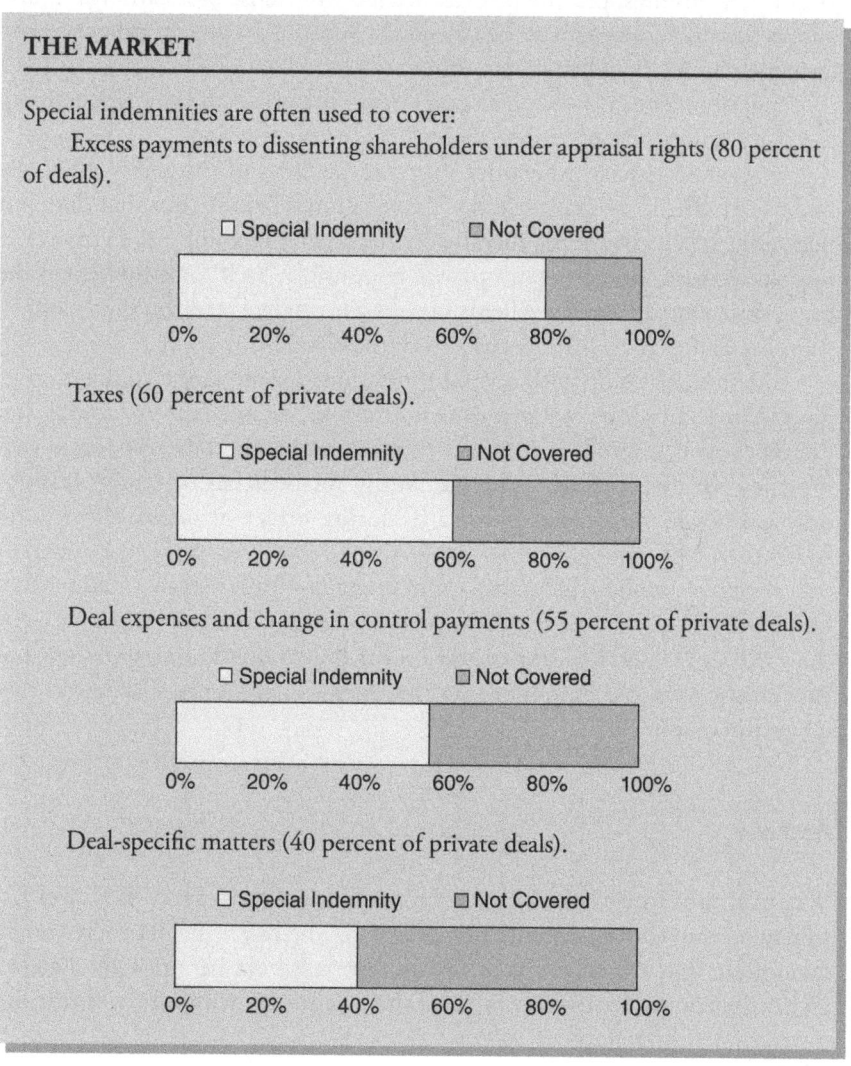

Special indemnities can protect the buyer from shareholders of the target exercising appraisal rights. Appraisal rights allow a shareholder to initiate a court process to receive fair value for their shares if they believe the price offered in a merger represents less than fair value. In that procedure, the value is determined by a court. The buyer will not want to take the risk that a court finds the agreed price to be inadequate, requiring payment of additional amounts to the dissenting shareholders.

Taxes that are owed (or may be owed) by the target are indemnified by the sellers in many deals. This ensures that the sellers, who received the benefit of past earnings, pay the taxes associated with those past earnings. It also allows the purchase price to be calculated without having to diligence and estimate potential tax liabilities.

Special indemnities may also cover deal expenses or the cost of obtaining any third-party consents under change in control provisions.

A separate special indemnity may run in favor of the seller, especially in an asset sale. In an asset sale the buyer assumes liability but that does not release the seller from being sued by the third party creditor if the buyer does not pay. Instead, it makes both parties responsible. So if for some reason the buyer does not pay and the seller is sued by the original creditor, the seller will want the ability to recover its costs from the buyer.

Indemnities come with several limitations on the sellers' obligation to pay. These limitations include: time limitations, de minimis exclusions, deductibles or thresholds, caps, and restrictions on the types of losses that may be collected.[1] Usually, the indemnity for breaches of representations only applies if the closing occurs. If closing does not occur, there is no indemnity.

The buyer would still retain a claim under law for misrepresentations that occur at signing, however. For those types of claims (outside of the indemnity), the variety of negotiated limitations on the indemnity do not apply, such as time restrictions and limitations on the types and amounts of damages that a buyer may seek.

Escrow

When an indemnity is included in an acquisition agreement, the buyer has to rely on the seller to actually pay as agreed. The buyer may not have much confidence that the seller's creditworthiness will hold up until the liability comes due; or the buyer may not trust the seller to pay without the threat and distraction of litigation.

If the seller does not pay under the indemnity, then the buyer would be "stuck in the middle"—required to cover the underlying liability, but unable to recover under the indemnity from the seller. Placing a portion of the purchase price into escrow with a third-party financial institution is a common solution to this sort of credit risk, but one that has a cost. This solution is not well received by the sellers in some circumstances, who would like access to as much of the purchase price as soon as possible.

THE MARKET

Over 90 percent of private deals have escrow arrangements.

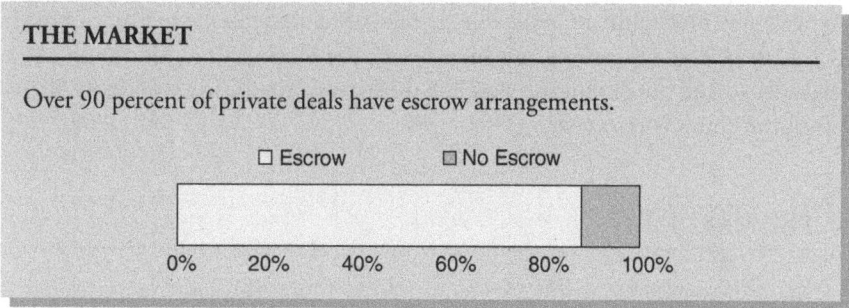

When an escrow is established, it is normally funded by the buyer out of the purchase price. For instance, 90 percent of the purchase price may be paid to the seller, with the remaining 10 percent of the purchase price placed into escrow at closing.

The size of the escrow depends on the potential and expected size of the indemnity. If the escrow supports the general indemnity for breaches of representations, then the escrow is unlikely to be larger than the cap on that indemnity. In many cases, the escrow will simply be equal to the cap. Likewise, if the escrow supports a special indemnity, the size will be tied to the liability under the special indemnity.

THE MARKET

The average escrow size is around 10 to 15 percent of deal value. Approximately 85 percent of escrows hold back between 5 percent and 20 percent of deal value.

In roughly one-half to three-quarters of deals, the size of the escrow is equal to the cap under the indemnity for breaches of basic representations and warranties.

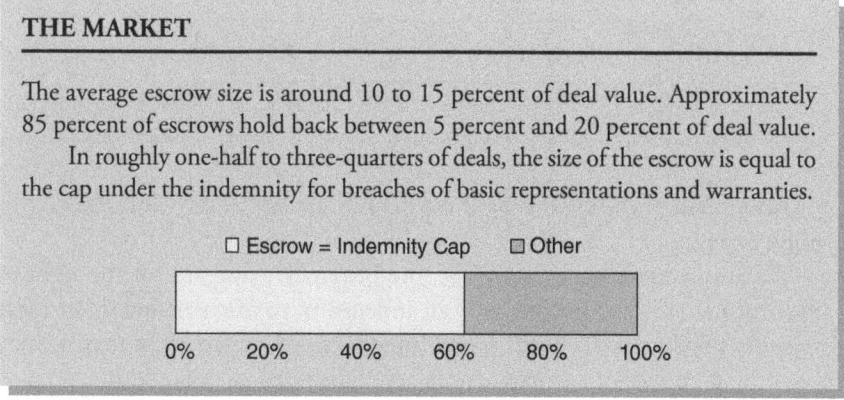

The escrow holding period varies from deal to deal, primarily depending on when underlying liabilities are likely to be payable. An escrow supporting a basic indemnity is likely to expire at the end of the survival period for the representations. Unless there has been a claim against the buyer in the meantime, it will then be paid out to the sellers at expiration of the survival period.

The amount in escrow may ratchet down as the expiration date approaches. For example, an 18-month escrow supporting an indemnity for breach of representations could be paid out in one-third increments at the 6-month, 12-month, and 18-month anniversaries of the closing. If a good faith claim is made before the expiration date for the escrow, the funds remain in escrow until the claim is resolved.

THE MARKET

The average escrow period is 18 months, which is approximately the same length as the survival period for breach of basic representations.

The escrow period range is wide when the escrow supports special indemnities.

Claims are frequently made against the escrow for breaches of representations.

THE MARKET

Claims are made by the buyer against the escrow for breaches of representations in roughly one-third to one-half of deals.

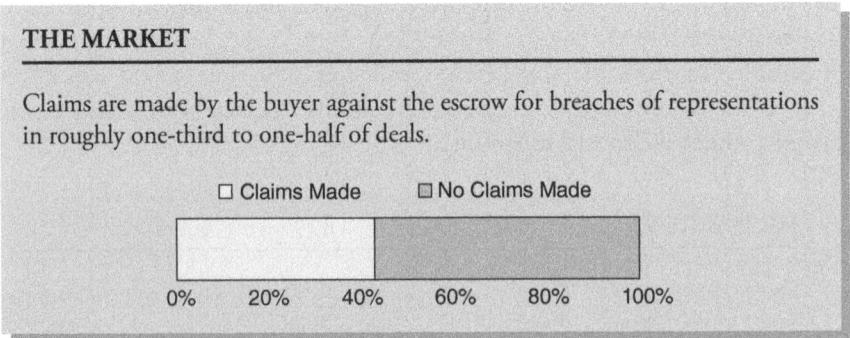

About half of the claims made are filed in the last week before the escrow period expires.

If a transaction has an earn-out, the buyer may bargain for the right to offset future earn-out payments if an indemnity payment is owed. In these cases, the pressure to have an escrow is reduced. The offset right may or may not apply if an indemnity payment is being disputed in good faith.

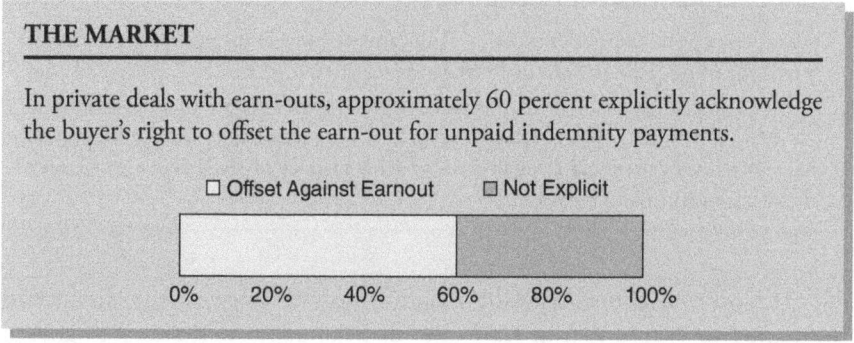

THE MARKET

In private deals with earn-outs, approximately 60 percent explicitly acknowledge the buyer's right to offset the earn-out for unpaid indemnity payments.

☐ Offset Against Earnout   ☐ Not Explicit

0%   20%   40%   60%   80%   100%

Survival Periods

Indemnities for breaches of representations are limited in time by a provision that states that the representations "survive" the closing, but survive only for a specific period. The concept of "survival" is really a way to address the period during which the buyer can make a claim for breaches of representation.[2]

Although the documents speak of the representation surviving, the representation is still only made (and only has to be true) as of specific dates, such as signing and/or closing. It is actually the right to sue for breach of that representation rather than the representation itself that survives.

A claim for breach can be made during the survival period. After expiration of the survival period for a representation, no claim may be made under the indemnity for breach (though claims submitted by the deadline may be pursued until they are resolved).[3] Some courts have held that a claim can be made for breach even after the survival period expires as long as the claim arises during the survival period.[4]

Others have held that the survival period does not shorten the amount of time a party has to file a lawsuit under the statute of limitations, unless it is explicit that this is the result.[5] To avoid that interpretation, most acquisition agreements now specify that no claim may be made after the survival period expires.

Sample Provision

The representations and warranties of the Sellers and the Buyer contained in this Agreement shall survive the Closing for the period set forth below. All representations and warranties contained in this Agreement and the ability to make any claims under this Article __ with respect thereto shall terminate on the date that is __ months after the Closing Date, except that the representations and warranties contained in Sections ___ [fundamental representations] shall survive [until the applicable statute of limitations expires] [indefinitely], provided that if notice of any claim for indemnification has been given within the applicable survival period, then the representations and warranties that are the subject of such indemnification claim shall survive with respect to such claim until such claim has been finally resolved.

The survival period typically ranges from one to two years. It is often structured to ensure that at least one financial audit of the target's annual financial statements is completed prior to the expiration of the survival period. The idea is that the buyer's accountants are likely to uncover any errors in the target's financials during the process of completing the next audit.

THE MARKET

Roughly three-quarters of deals have survival periods for basic representations that are between 12 and 18 months.

Roughly a quarter of deals have 12-month survival periods. Roughly one-half have 18-month survival periods. Fifteen to 20 percent have 24-month survival periods. Most of the rest fall between 12 and 18 months.

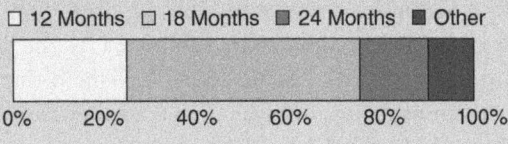

Fundamental representations usually have longer survival periods. Extended survival periods are sometimes measured in years (e.g., five years) and are sometimes measured by reference to the relevant statute of limitations. For example, tax representations may survive until the statute of limitations expires for the applicable tax returns.

On occasion, some representations are said to survive indefinitely. It may not be clear whether those provisions permit claims forever, or only during the statute of limitations provided by law. Some courts have concluded that the survival provision can only shorten, but not extend, the statute of limitations provided by law for breach of representations.

The list of representations to receive special treatment as fundamental representations are negotiated in each deal. In addition to tax representations, the parties may include representations regarding authority to enter into the transaction agreements, ownership of the equity being sold (in a stock sale), the absence of brokers that will need to be paid from the deal proceeds, and other representations that are of particular importance in a transaction.

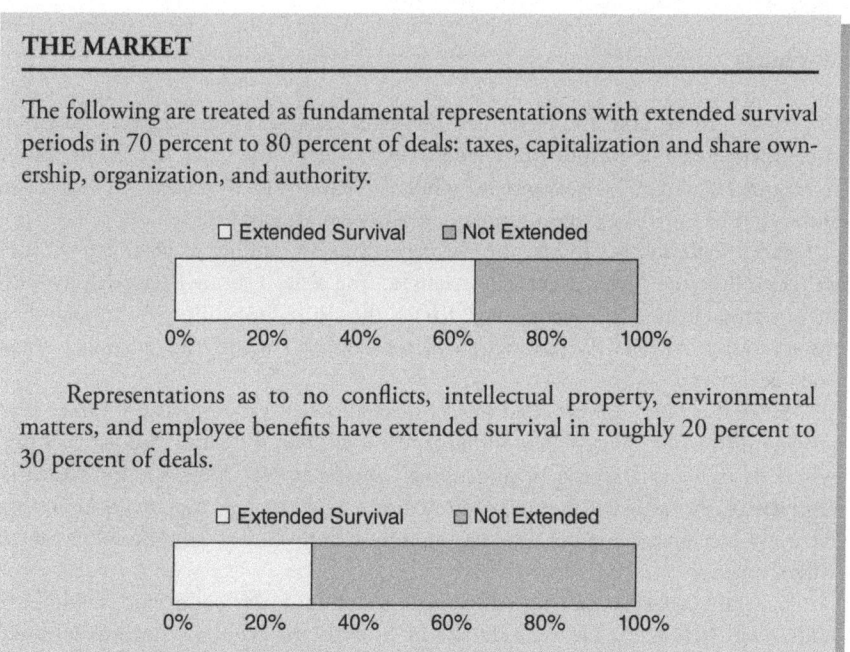

THE MARKET

The following are treated as fundamental representations with extended survival periods in 70 percent to 80 percent of deals: taxes, capitalization and share ownership, organization, and authority.

☐ Extended Survival   ☐ Not Extended

0%   20%   40%   60%   80%   100%

Representations as to no conflicts, intellectual property, environmental matters, and employee benefits have extended survival in roughly 20 percent to 30 percent of deals.

☐ Extended Survival   ☐ Not Extended

0%   20%   40%   60%   80%   100%

Special indemnities also have a time limitation in most cases. This time period is tied to the horizon of the underlying liabilities, rather than being tied to the target's audit cycles.

If the parties do not intend for the buyer to have an indemnity for breaches of representations, simply deleting the indemnity article does not work because indemnity would be provided by default as a matter of underlying contract law. The seller would instead need to ensure that the acquisition agreement includes a provision clearly stating that the representations and warranties do not survive closing.

Sample Provision

The representations and warranties of the Sellers and the Buyer contained in this Agreement shall not survive the Closing. For the avoidance of doubt, after the Closing neither party shall be entitled to make any claim based on the breach of any representation or warranty in this Agreement and each party waives any rights to make any such claims.

Underlying contract law provides remedies for breach of representations, which would be given effect in the absence of any statement to the contrary,[6] as discussed further under the exclusive remedies section below.

War Story

In a small private deal, the buyer and the seller engaged in an intense negotiation over whether or not an indemnity would be provided. The seller wanted the buyer to acquire the target "as is, where is," while the buyer wanted customary protection allowing it to sue if the target's representations were breached.

Faced with another bidder for the target who was willing to go ahead without an indemnity, the buyer eventually relented. The seller's counsel were happy with their success. In one fell swoop, they deleted the entire indemnity article, including the survival provision. The parties quickly moved on to finalize the remainder of the open deal points.

Since the seller's lawyers had simply deleted the survival provision, rather than revising it to make the representations expire at closing, the buyer had actually preserved its rights as a matter of underlying contract law. It could sue for breach of representations until the statute of limitations, without any cap or limitation on recovery. The buyer's counsel thought carefully about whether they should reveal the sellers' mistake.

Several years after closing—long after a standard survival period would have ended, yet before the six-year statute of limitations expired—the buyer raised a claim. It would have been too late for that claim to be valid if the lawyers had simply clarified that there was no survival, rather than deleting the survival provision.

The same survival issue applies to breaches of covenants. Claims for breaches of covenants that occur before closing normally survive the closing. Covenants do not usually have a specific survival period after which they expire. If there is no survival period stated, then the survival period is the statute of limitations provided by underlying law. In other cases, survival through to the statute of limitations is specifically agreed.

Sometimes a problem can be classified as both a breach of representation (subject to survival limitations) and a breach for failure to operate in the ordinary course (with no limit on survival). In many cases, claims for breaches of covenants are also not subject to a cap on the amount of recovery as breaches of representations are. In that way, a loss suffered by the buyer can form the basis for both a claim for breach of representations and a claim for breach of the operating covenants.

To address this concern, in some deals the seller may want to limit the survival period for breaches of operating covenants so that those do not survive closing, or survive for only a limited period of time.

Indemnity Amounts, Limitations, and Calculations

Per claim de minimis exceptions

The de minimis exception is designed to be the amount per individual claim that is so small that the buyer should not go through the trouble of making the claim. It is usually structured as a dollar threshold per claim. Below that amount, the buyer is not permitted to pursue the claim, so it basically works like a per-claim deductible.

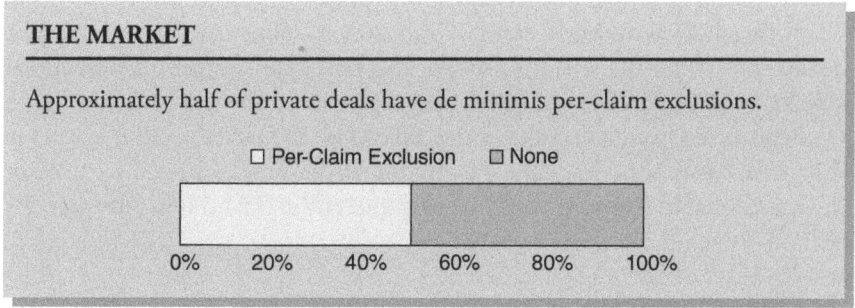

THE MARKET

Approximately half of private deals have de minimis per-claim exclusions.

☐ Per-Claim Exclusion   ☐ None

0%   20%   40%   60%   80%   100%

If a series of similar claims arise, the provision usually aggregates those amounts. This helps ensure that the de minimis threshold does not inadvertently exclude claims that are, as a group, meaningful enough to be worth pursuing. For instance, a customer claim for $1,000 will probably fall below the de minimis threshold. A series of 1,000 customer claims based on the same or similar underlying facts, in contrast, would be sufficiently material and dealt with as one matter.

Deductibles and "dollar-one" thresholds

In addition, the ability of the buyer to recover under the indemnity is limited by a "deductible" or "threshold" amount. This deductible or threshold applies across all claims in the aggregate.

A deductible is an initial amount of loss that the buyer cannot recover. It operates much like a deductible under insurance policies. If the deductible is $1 million and the buyer suffers indemnifiable losses equal to $3 million, then the buyer can only recover $2 million.

Sample Provision

Seller shall not be liable to the Buyer Indemnified Parties for any Losses with respect to the matters contained in Section __ [indemnity for breach of representations] unless the Losses therefrom exceed an aggregate amount equal to $__, and then [only for Losses in excess of that amount]
   —OR—
   [for all Losses including the Losses not in excess of $__] (but not in excess of the Cap).

A threshold is an initial hurdle to making a claim, but does not act as a deductible. If the threshold is crossed, the buyer can recover its indemnifiable losses from "dollar one." In the example above, if the $1 million figure were converted from a deductible to a threshold, the buyer could not recover if its total losses were less than $1 million. If the buyer suffered $3 million in indemnifiable losses, it could recover the entire $3 million (not just $2 million, as was the case for a deductible).

THE MARKET

Deductibles are used in roughly a third to a half of deals. Thresholds are used in roughly a half to two thirds of deals. A small handful of deals use a hybrid.

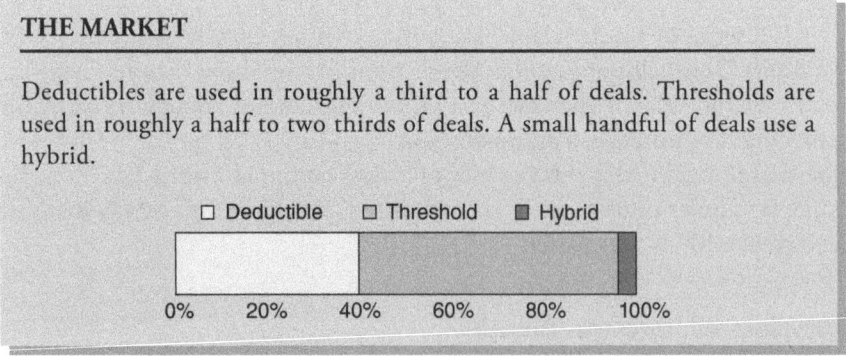

A deductible and a threshold can be combined into a hybrid. If the losses exceed the threshold amount, the buyer recovers a percentage (e.g., 50 percent) of the losses up to the threshold. It recovers all losses in excess of the threshold. The amount of the deductible or threshold varies from deal to deal.

THE MARKET

The most common deductible/threshold amount is 0.5 percent of the deal consideration.

In roughly half of deals, the deductible/threshold amount represents 0.5 percent or less of the deal consideration. In roughly a third of deals, the deductible/threshold is 0.5 percent to 1 percent. In most of the remainder, the deductible/threshold is 1 percent to 2 percent.

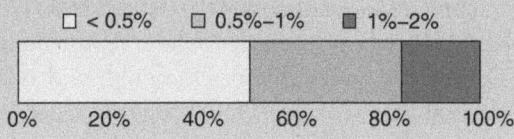

The deductible or threshold applies to the indemnity for breach of basic representations, but usually does not apply to breaches of fundamental representations. In some deals, it applies to the indemnity for breach of covenants and, in a few cases, it applies to special indemnities.

Whether the deductible or threshold should apply to breach of covenants is sometimes debated. For instance, the target may be subject to a covenant to extinguish all debt at closing, or to pay all deal-related expenses of its bankers and lawyers at or before closing. If there is a $1 million deductible that applies to breaches of those covenants, the target could simply fail to pay a small portion of the debt or deal expenses. If the debt and deal expenses are obligations of the target company, those unpaid obligations would effectively shift to the buyer.

Absent any other claims, the buyer could not recover because of the deductible (unless it pursued specific performance). In most cases, that would not be viewed as the intended outcome for an intentional breach. When negotiating survivability of covenants, the parties are often focused on giving relief to the seller only for the ordinary course operating covenants. Those do not have the characteristic of unfairly shifting an economic burden from one party to the other.

THE MARKET

Approximately one quarter of private deals apply the deductible or threshold to breaches of covenants.

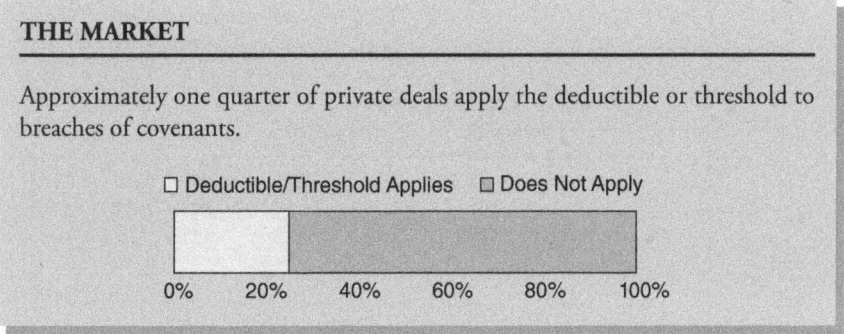

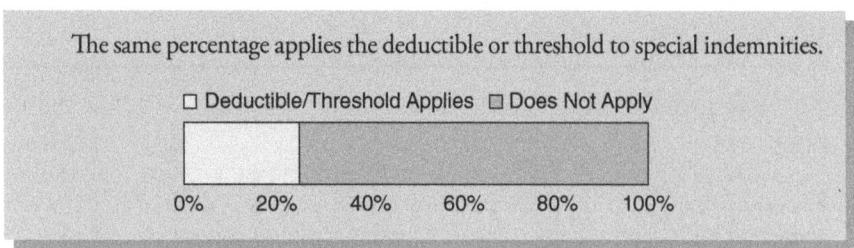

The same percentage applies the deductible or threshold to special indemnities.

☐ Deductible/Threshold Applies   ☐ Does Not Apply

0%   20%   40%   60%   80%   100%

Fundamental representations are often carved out from the deductible or threshold. If a claim is based on a breach of those representations, the claim does not count against the deductible or threshold, and is not limited by them. The fundamental representations for this purpose generally tend to be the same representations that have extended survival periods.

THE MARKET

Approximately 60 percent to 70 percent of private deals exclude the following representations from the deductible or threshold: capitalization and ownership of shares, due authority, due organization, and taxes.

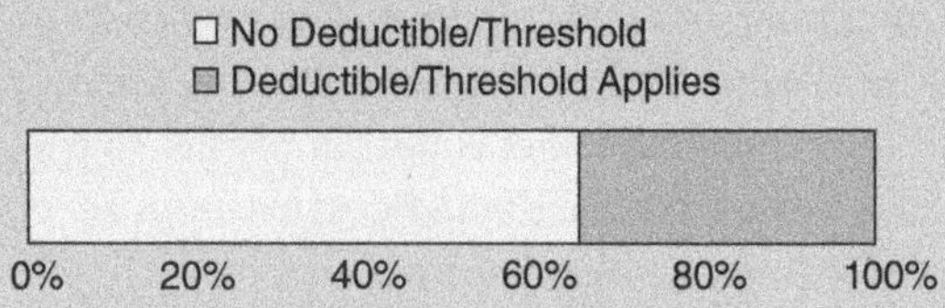

☐ No Deductible/Threshold
☐ Deductible/Threshold Applies

0%   20%   40%   60%   80%   100%

Fraud is excluded in 90 percent of deals

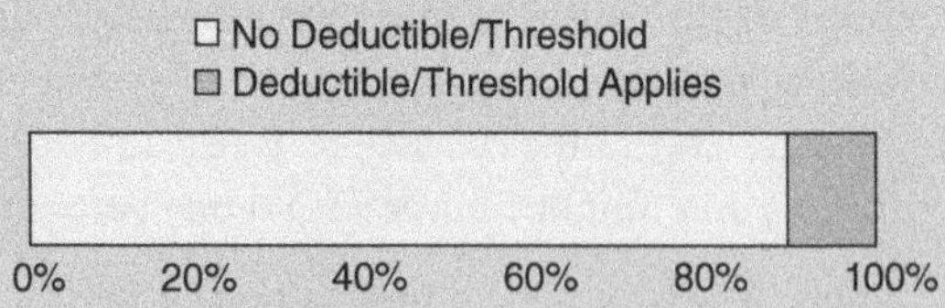

☐ No Deductible/Threshold
☐ Deductible/Threshold Applies

0%   20%   40%   60%   80%   100%

Intentional breach is excluded in a majority to 60 percent of deals.

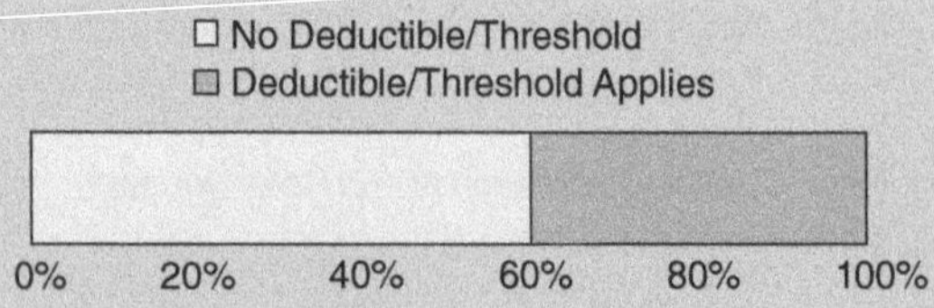

☐ No Deductible/Threshold
☐ Deductible/Threshold Applies

0%   20%   40%   60%   80%   100%

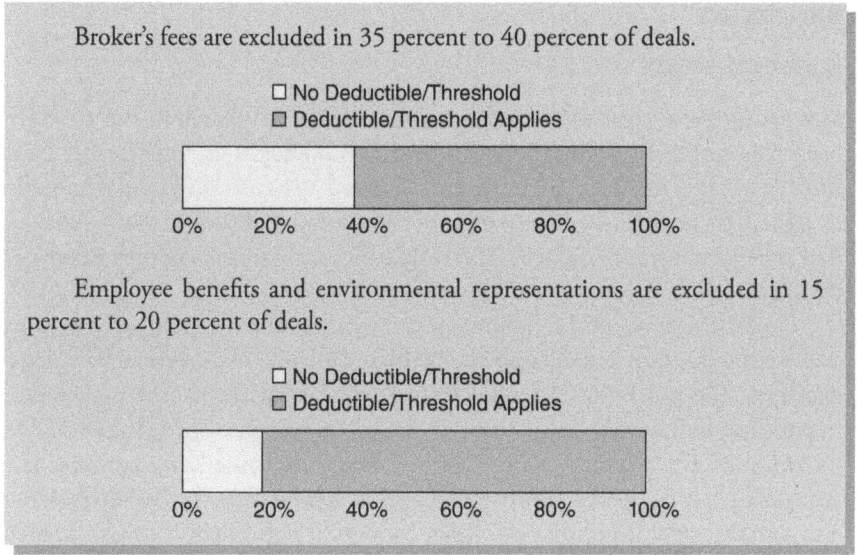

Broker's fees are excluded in 35 percent to 40 percent of deals.

☐ No Deductible/Threshold
☐ Deductible/Threshold Applies

0%   20%   40%   60%   80%   100%

Employee benefits and environmental representations are excluded in 15 percent to 20 percent of deals.

☐ No Deductible/Threshold
☐ Deductible/Threshold Applies

0%   20%   40%   60%   80%   100%

Caps on recovery

The indemnity for breaches of representations normally places a cap on the aggregate amount the buyer can recover. In most deals, the buyer can recover more than the pre-agreed cap if the seller engaged in actual fraud (which is a difficult claim to prove). The cap and the deductible mean that the buyer is basically expected to take some business risk as to breaches of representations.

The general cap on recovery applies to breaches of basic representations. The indemnity for breaches of fundamental representations is capped at a higher amount—often the total purchase price. In other deals, the indemnity for breaches of fundamental representations may be uncapped.

THE MARKET

Caps for breaches of basic representations average a little over 10 percent of deal value for sales to private equity buyers and close to 20 percent of deal value for sales to strategic buyers.

Two-thirds of deals have caps between 10 percent and 15 percent of deal value, although caps commonly range up to 30 percent, and, in rare cases, may exceed 50 percent.

Measuring Loss

Inclusions and exclusions

If a commercial contract without an indemnity is breached, the party in breach is responsible for the counterparty's damages as a matter of contract law. The measure of damages is based on case law, and generally designed to put the counterparty in the position it would have been in had the breach not occurred. The indemnity contains its own measure of damages.

Under the general U.S. approach to litigation costs—each party pays its own way—contract damages normally do not include reimbursement of legal expenses. The indemnity provided by the seller in an acquisition agreement, in contrast, requires the seller to cover the buyer's defense costs. In particular, indemnities may exclude many types of damages. Underlying contract law permits a party to sue for punitive damages in special cases. Indemnities, however, usually exclude punitive damages. More or less speculative damages, such as lost profits, consequential, special, indirect, or incidental damages, may also be excluded.

Sample Provision

Notwithstanding anything to the contrary contained in this Agreement, no Person shall be liable under this Article __ for any [consequential], [punitive], [special], [incidental] or [indirect damages], [including lost profits], except to the extent awarded by a court of competent jurisdiction to a third party in connection with a Third-Party Claim.

THE MARKET

Approximately three-quarters of private deals exclude punitive damages.

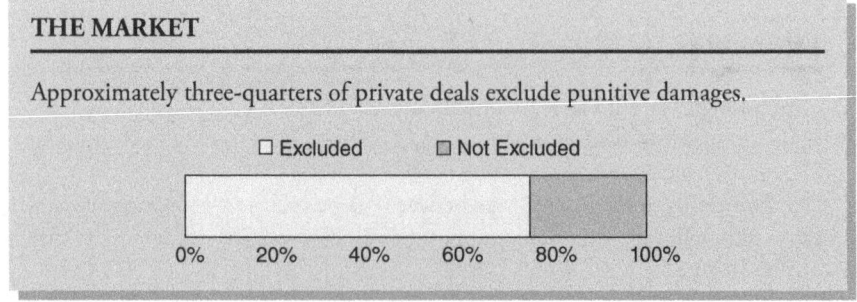

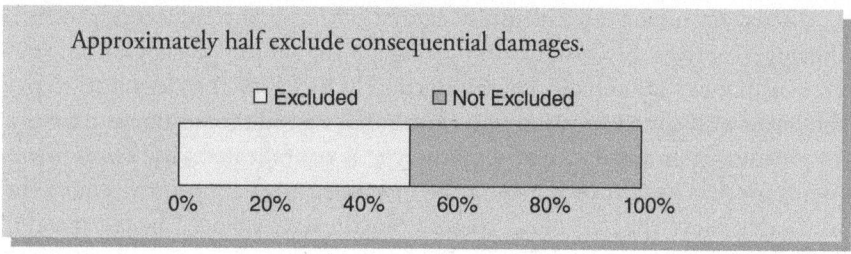

Approximately half exclude consequential damages.

Buyers often calculate the purchase price based on a multiple of earnings (say 6× the target's trailing 12-month earnings before interest, taxes, depreciation, and amortization [EBITDA]). The buyer derives the appropriate multiple by taking into account a wide range of factors, including the assets on the balance sheet and future growth prospects.

A question may arise as to the amount of loss a buyer suffers if the sellers misrepresent the earnings of the target by $10 million. A buyer may argue that the loss is $60 million, because it calculated the purchase price based on a 6× multiple. On the other hand, if the $10 million in additional expense was a one-time, unusual charge, the $10 million may have actually had no impact on the future expected earnings of the target. In that case, the sellers may argue that there is no actual loss.

On occasion, a seller will clarify in the indemnity that no multiples will be used to calculate damages; sometimes a buyer will clarify that multiples can be used. More often than not, the parties leave it for courts and litigation to determine the amount of loss based on the facts and circumstances.

A less direct way of addressing this issue is to exclude diminution in value from indemnifiable losses. Diminution in value is a broad concept that may or may not be appropriate to exclude depending on the type of expected losses.

Offsets

Contract law generally implies a duty to mitigate losses suffered due to a breach of contract.[7] Occasionally, this requirement is specified in the indemnity, but usually it is not.

The indemnity may reduce the damages a buyer can claim based on tax offsets. For instance, if a company incurs $100 million in indemnified expenses, those expenses reduce its taxable profits, so it may save $25 million in taxes. The seller will argue that it should only be required to pay the buyer $75 million in order to make the buyer whole.

Recovery under the indemnity can be offset by any insurance proceeds the buyer receives. For instance, if the target is the subject of a lawsuit, the target's insurance may actually cover a portion of its losses. A seller wants to pay the buyer only for the portion of its losses that exceed the insurance recovery.

Including an insurance offset, however, is complicated. The buyer wants to ensure that its cost of pursuing the insurance recovery counts against the recovery (that is, the buyer only passes along the net benefit). The buyer wants to make sure it has some ability to decide whether or not to pursue insurance recoveries, based on the likelihood and costs of recovery—as any reasonable party would do if it were pursuing insurance recoveries for its own benefit. In some cases, the buyer may want a reasonable estimate of future increased premiums reflected as a cost of obtaining an insurance recovery.

Combining indemnities and adjustments

The seller wants to avoid double counting between an indemnity claim, on the one hand, and a working capital or other purchase price adjustment, on the other. For instance, if a $10 million liability reduces working capital and thereby reduces the purchase price by $10 million under a working capital adjustment, the buyer has already been made whole.

Presumably, that would be taken into account in any event in the measure of the buyer's losses. While a buyer could claim that it is separately entitled to recover under the indemnity, many sellers would view that as double counting.[8]

In some cases, a no-double-counting provision is included in the acquisition agreement in broad form. It may say that if a topic was already dealt with in the working capital adjustment, then it cannot be the source for another claim under the indemnity—even if the buyer were not already made whole.

For example, assume that there is a breach of representation related to an unexpected lawsuit filed against the target. The target accrues $10 million as a current liability toward settlement costs, which reduces working capital and the purchase price by $10 million.

If that suit ultimately settles for $100 million, the buyer will want full protection. The seller may use the drafting of this exclusion to argue that the buyer has no remedy because the topic was already addressed (albeit with inadequate results) in its working capital adjustment remedy. The seller may claim the buyer should not have "two bites at the apple."

Representations

Reading out qualifiers

Representations are limited by a variety of qualifications. These include materiality qualifiers, knowledge qualifiers, exceptions in the disclosure schedules, and several others discussed in 343 SPS § VI.

Materiality qualifiers

In many cases, materiality qualifiers in the representations are ignored, or "read out," for purposes of the indemnity. A representation may state that the target is in compliance with law in all material respects. If the materiality qualifier is ignored, the buyer can sue under that representation as if it stated that the target is in compliance with law in all respects.

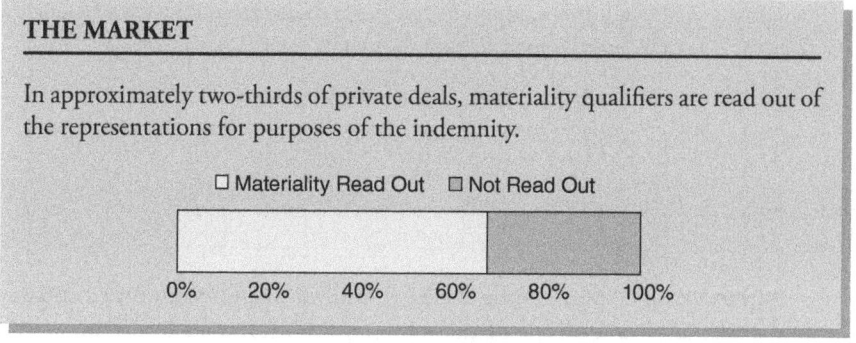

THE MARKET

In approximately two-thirds of private deals, materiality qualifiers are read out of the representations for purposes of the indemnity.

☐ Materiality Read Out   ☐ Not Read Out

0%   20%   40%   60%   80%   100%

Reading out a materiality qualifier results in more indemnifiable losses. Assuming, for the sake of argument, that $2 million is material for this purpose in a particular transaction, then the representations will not be breached by a failure to comply with law that results in $1.5 million in losses. If the materiality qualifier is read out of the representations for purposes of the indemnity, however, then the entire $1.5 million would be indemnifiable (subject to the deductible or threshold, and other limitations described earlier),[9] even though the loss was actually too small to breach the representation as written.

Sample Provision

[…] it being understood that for purposes of this Section ___ any qualifications relating to materiality, including the term "Material Adverse Effect," contained in such representation or warranty shall be disregarded for purposes of determining [whether such representation or warranty was breached] [and for purposes of determining any Losses].

In some transactions, the use of a deductible (as opposed to a threshold) goes hand-in-hand with reading out materiality qualifiers. In a sense, the deductible quantifies and aggregates materiality exceptions for purposes of the indemnity.

THE MARKET

In approximately one-half of deals in which materiality is read out of the representations, it is read out only for purposes of determining damages. In approximately the other half, it is read out for purposes of determining both whether a breach has occurred and for calculating the extent of damages.

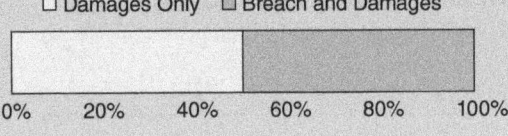

□ Damages Only   □ Breach and Damages

0%   20%   40%   60%   80%   100%

In the example above, while the $1.5 million would be an indemnifiable loss if materiality is read out of the representations, the $1.5 million would nevertheless not be collectible by the buyer (in the absence of other losses), assuming $1.5 million is less than the deductible.

In some deals, materiality is read out only for purposes of determining damages. In that case, a representation containing a materiality qualifier has to be breached as written (giving effect to the materiality qualifier) before any indemnity claim can be made. But if breached, once a claim can be made, the damages are calculated from "dollar one" as if there were no materiality qualifier in the relevant representation.

Knowledge qualifiers

Occasionally, knowledge qualifiers are read out of the representations for purposes of the indemnity. If read out, a knowledge qualifier will be ignored for purposes of determining whether the buyer is entitled to recover for a loss under the indemnity.

For example, a representation may state that, to the seller's knowledge, there is no threatened litigation against the target company. If the target ends up having liability under litigation that had been threatened, but was unknown to the seller's knowledge persons, than the representation is not breached. If knowledge qualifiers are read out of the representations for purposes of the indemnity, however, the buyer is entitled to recover for those litigation losses whether or not the threats were known to the seller's knowledge persons.

Knowledge qualifiers essentially transfer risk to the buyer for unknown liabilities. Such liabilities are not taken into account to reduce the purchase price because they are, by definition, unknown. By reading knowledge qualifiers out of the representations for purposes of the indemnity, the parties are effectively saying that while the buyer may still be required to close over such liabilities, the buyer can still recover from the seller for such losses.

When representations are made

The seller takes responsibility in one form or another for the accuracy of the target's representations as of each date they are made. Representations can be made as of the signing of the acquisition agreement, as of the closing of the transaction, or both. Two separate provisions govern the date or dates on which representations are tested for purposes of the indemnity.

First, the representations themselves usually state that they are made when the acquisition agreement is signed. In some cases, the representations state that they are also made at closing. In that structure, the representations are simply repeated at closing in the same form in which they are written in the agreement. Second, the indemnity may treat the representations as if they were repeated at closing, even though they are only made at signing.

Most acquisition agreements test the representations as of signing for purposes of the indemnity. This gives the buyer the benefit of the bargain it signed up for when the acquisition agreement was executed. In addition, many acquisition agreements test the representations at closing. Making the seller responsible for the accuracy of the representations at closing puts the risk on the seller for adverse developments in the business between signing and closing.

In some transactions, the representations are tested only at closing for purposes of the indemnity. In this structure, the buyer is entitled at closing to the benefit of the bargain it agreed to at signing. If the representations were not true at signing, but the target was brought into compliance in the meantime, the buyer has no claim under the indemnity.

Claims, Remedies, and Related Issues

"Sandbagging" and closing over breaches

On occasion, the buyer knows at signing that the target has failed to disclose a problem in its disclosure schedules. This is rare. When it does occur, it is usually because the target's lawyers and business teams inadvertently omitted to put the item on the disclosure schedules. When that happens, the question arises whether the buyer should be entitled to make a "gotcha" claim under the indemnity (and/or exercise remedies under the closing condition to avoid closing). Such a claim is generally referred to as "sandbagging."

The parties' sense of business fairness may dictate that the buyer cannot make such an indemnity claim. If the buyer knows about the problem, the seller will argue that the buyer must have factored it into its purchase price. If the risk was taken into account in the price, the seller will not want the buyer to nevertheless recover under the indemnity.

The buyer may argue that it did not factor the problem into the price because it believed it was covered by the indemnity. If the parties plan to sign an agreement knowing that the buyer will have an indemnity claim at closing, using a special indemnity is a better technique to achieve clarity on such issues. General indemnity claims for breach of representations are usually reserved for matters that surprise the parties.

Even though sandbagging may conflict with the parties' sense of fairness, nevertheless it is usually allowed, and often explicitly so.

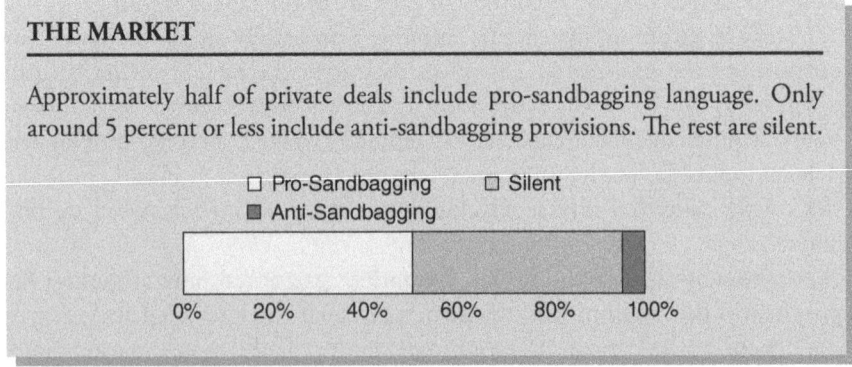

THE MARKET

Approximately half of private deals include pro-sandbagging language. Only around 5 percent or less include anti-sandbagging provisions. The rest are silent.

Buyer-friendly language regarding sandbagging comes in the form of a provision confirming that the buyer can recover for breaches of which it had knowledge. This is sometimes referred to as a pro-sandbagging provision.

Sample Provision

The representations, warranties, covenants, agreements, and obligations of each of the Buyer and the Sellers and any rights to indemnification with respect thereto shall not be affected or deemed waived by reason of any investigation made by or on behalf of such Person (including by any of its Representatives) or by reason of the fact that such Person or any of such Representatives knew or should have known that any such representation or warranty is, was, or might be inaccurate.

In rare cases, the seller includes anti-sandbagging language in the agreement. The buyer usually resists this for fear that any claim it makes under the indemnity will be challenged under a vague argument that the buyer knew of the breach beforehand. Buyers are concerned that anti-sandbagging provisions create a burden of proof problem for the buyer that harms its ability to make legitimate (including non-sandbagging) claims under the indemnity.

Some courts require reliance on the accuracy of representations in order for a buyer to pursue an indemnity remedy.[10] If that were the case, the buyer may not be able to recover for a breach of representation if it had knowledge of the breach. A special indemnity may be a more appropriate solution to that drafting concern. Special indemnities do not rely on breach of representations as the basis for a claim.

In some deals, a seller may ask the buyer to choose its remedy for breaches of representations: either refuse to close or close without the ability to sue under the indemnity. The seller will argue that the buyer should not be allowed to waive and close over a known breach of representations, yet still sue under the indemnity. The buyer will not want to waive any remedy for which it has bargained. It does not want to be forced to choose between losing the deal and losing a legitimate claim.

This protection for the buyer is often drafted in the form of a confirmation that indemnity claims will not be affected by waiving any closing condition.

Sample Provision

[Indemnity...] shall not be affected or deemed waived by reason of the waiver of any condition based on the accuracy of any representation or warranty, or on the performance of or compliance with any covenant, agreement, or obligation.

Without such a provision, some courts have found that if a buyer closes over a known breach of representation, the buyer has, by implication, waived its right to rely on that representation.[11] This approach has the risk of undermining the indemnity claim by the removing reliance as a basis for claiming against the underlying breach of representation.

Exclusive Remedy

The indemnity usually serves as the exclusive remedy for monetary damages for the type of claims that it covers. In other words, the buyer cannot sue under the indemnity for a breach of representations, then sue at the same time under additional theories of contract law for the same problem.

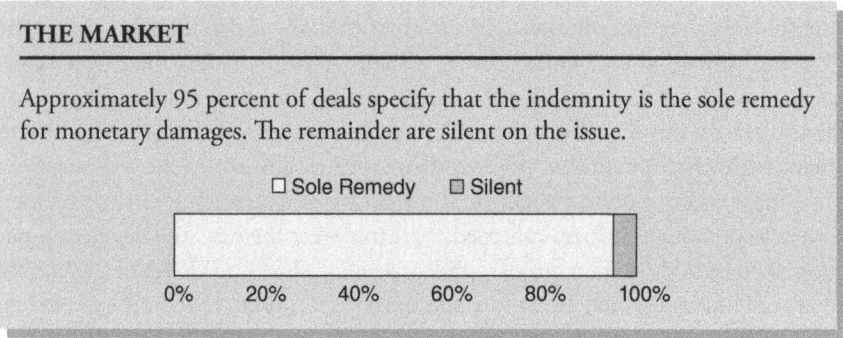

THE MARKET

Approximately 95 percent of deals specify that the indemnity is the sole remedy for monetary damages. The remainder are silent on the issue.

☐ Sole Remedy   ☐ Silent

0%   20%   40%   60%   80%   100%

Without an indemnity, the buyer could, for instance, sue for a general breach of contract, or pursue claims for misrepresentation, reformation of the contract, or tort remedies such as fraud in the inducement.

Sample Provision

The rights and remedies of Seller and the Buyer under this Article __ [indemnity] are exclusive and in lieu of any and all other rights and remedies which Seller and the Buyer may have under this Agreement or otherwise against each other with respect to the Transaction for monetary relief with respect to any breach of any representation or warranty or any failure to perform any covenant or agreement set forth in this Agreement, other than in the case of fraud.

If a contract claim falls outside the indemnity, it would escape the negotiated limitations on recovery under the indemnity, such as the cap, the deductible or threshold, and the prohibition on pursuing punitive and speculative damages.

Some nonindemnity claims do survive the exclusive remedy provision. Fraud, for instance, is often carved out of the exclusive remedy provision. Even if fraud is not carved out, some courts may permit a fraud claim to proceed outside of the indemnity (e.g., not subject to its caps or other limitations) notwithstanding the exclusive remedy provision.[12]

Joint and several liability

If there are multiple sellers, the indemnity needs to address which seller is responsible for which losses. Sometimes, separate sellers are separately responsible for losses arising from their own breach (several indemnity). Sometimes, all sellers are equally responsible for all losses (joint and several indemnity).

One seller will not want to be held responsible for the obligations of the other sellers. The buyer will not want to have to pursue each and every seller for what it believes should be collective responsibilities. The buyer would rather that the sellers work out common liability among themselves.

A hybrid structure forms a common resolution. Each seller gives representations about itself (e.g., such seller has good title to its shares of stock being sold and such seller has authority to sell its shares of stock). The buyer has to accept several (and not joint) liability for breach of those representations that relate to a particular seller. Representations that relate to the business of the target company, in contrast, are indemnified by all of the sellers collectively, on a joint and several basis.

These include, for example, representations as to accuracy of the target's financial statements and the target's compliance with law. The sellers provide joint and several indemnity for breaches by the target of those types of representations. The target may be the party that gives those representations about the business, but the target itself does not provide the indemnity. Otherwise, after closing, the buyer would be suing its own subsidiary to recover (rather than the sellers).

Litigation Endnotes

1. *See* Chapter 14-D, Indemnity Amounts, Limitations, and Calculations.
2. As the court noted in *GRT, Inc. v. Marathon GTF Technology:* [A] survival clause … that expressly states that the covered representations and warranties will survive for a discrete period of time, but will thereafter "terminate," makes plain the contracting parties' intent that the non-representing and warranting party will have a period of time, i.e., the survival period, to file a claim for a breach of the surviving representations and warranties, but will thereafter, when the surviving representations and warranties terminate, be precluded from filing such a claim. No. 5571-CS, 2011 BL 185693, at *17 (Del. Ch. July 11, 2011).
3. *See, e.g., GRT,* 2011 BL 185693, at *18 (finding that a clause which limited the period of time a representation survives closing acted as a statute of limitations on the buyer's ability to commence litigation for breach). *See also ENI Holdings, LLC v. KBR Grp. Holdings, LLC,* No. 8075-VCG, 2013 BL 332008, at *1 (Del. Ch. Nov. 27, 2013) (reiterating Delaware's recognition of the right of contracting parties to impose a shorter period of limitation than that provided for by statute and noting that "it is clear [that contracting parties] are in a better position than legislators to know what result is called for by those circumstances peculiar to their relationship").
4. *See W. Filter Corp. v. Argan, Inc.,* 540 F.3d 947 (9th Cir. 2008) (finding that a survival clause permitting representations to survive for one year after the closing of an acquisition did not unambiguously state the parties' intent to contractually reduce the applicable California statute of limitations to the one-year survival period, since the survival clause's one-year limitation served only to specify when a breach of representations and warranties would occur, but not when an action was required to be filed). *See also Herring v. Terradyne, Inc.,* 256 F. Supp. 2d 1118 (S.D. Cal. 2002), *rev'd,* 242 F. Appx. 469 (9th Cir. 2007) (holding that when a contract does not provide for the representations therein to survive the closing of a transaction, such representations are treated as extinguished, as of the closing date, and cannot thereafter give rise to liability).
5. In *Hurlbut v. Christiano,* a New York court held that survival clauses should be read with strictness against the party invoking them because such clauses are in derogation of the statutory limitation. 405 N.Y.S.2d 871 (N.Y. App. Div. 1978). Even so, the court allowed a claim brought after the end of the survival period to proceed because the survival clause in the contract at issue was "clear and unambiguous." *Id.* at 1117.
6. There are principles in other areas of law, however, that prevent the survival of representations past closing. Real estate law often does not permit survival after transfer of the deed to the property being sold. *See, e.g., Wells v. Burroughs,* 65 S.W.2d 396, 397 (Tex. Civ. App. 1933) ("All contracts prior to the execution of the deed are presumed to have been merged in the deed, which expresses all the agreements of the parties."). This doctrine is not directly applicable to the sale

of a business, but it does highlight the importance of being specific about the intent of the parties as to whether the buyer can sue after closing for breaches of representations.

7. *See, e.g., W. Willow-Bay Ct., LLC v. Robino Bay Ct. Plaza, LLC,* No. 2742-VCN, 2009 BL 38745 (Del. Ch. Feb. 23, 2009).

8. *See Brim Holding Co., Inc. v. Province Healthcare Co.,* No. M2007-01344-COA-R3 (Tenn. Ct. App. May 28, 2008) (affirming a lower court decision that awarded the buyer damages for an indemnity claim covered in a working capital adjustment because the contractual language of the indemnity was unambiguous, and stressing that courts will not try to ascertain "unstated intentions" when there is an "express and unequivocal agreement" concerning the point).

9. *See* Chapter 14-D, Indemnity Amounts, Limitations, and Calculations.

10. *See, e.g., Kelly v. McKesson HBOC Inc.,* No. 99C-09-265 (Del. Super. Ct. Jan. 17, 2002) (finding, in a shareholder suit for breach of warranty against an acquiring corporation for alleged accounting irregularities that rendered a representation untrue, that the plaintiff must establish reliance as a prerequisite for such a claim).

11. In *Galli v. Metz,* as part of an extensively negotiated sale of a company, a seller represented that it had not mortgaged or encumbered any of its property, business or assets. 973 F.2d 145 (2d Cir. 1992). Prior to the closing of the transaction, the seller's lawyer disclosed a security interest to the buyer's lawyer. Nevertheless, the buyer closed the transaction without explicitly reserving its rights. The Second Circuit held that the buyer had implicitly waived its right to rely on the representation at issue because it failed to expressly reserve its rights after learning of the breach before closing. *Id.* at 151.

12. *See ABRY Partners V, LP v. F&W Acquisition LLC,* 891 A.2d 1032 (Del. Ch. 2006) (permitting a rescission claim to proceed outside of the indemnity, despite a provision stating that the indemnity was the exclusive remedy).

CHAPTER 15

Dispute Resolution

Types of Dispute Resolution Provisions

Dispute resolution provisions are part of the "boilerplate" of an acquisition agreement. Many lawyers stop reading at the beginning of the boilerplate section, viewing these provisions as relatively unimportant. Others argue that boilerplate is comprised of those provisions which are so critical that they have to show up in every deal. Many key dispute resolution provisions can be negotiated, as discussed below.

Governing law

U.S. state laws generally allow the parties to choose the law that governs the contract. Some relevant laws are mandatory, however. The corporate law of the state in which the target is incorporated governs corporate law matters, such as the merger itself (in the case of a merger), and the fiduciary duties of the target's board.[1]

In public company mergers involving a target incorporated in Delaware, parties almost always choose Delaware law to govern the contract, though a few will choose New York. If the public target is not incorporated in Delaware, the choice of law varies, with Delaware, New York and the target's state of incorporation being the most common. In private deals, the target's state of incorporation plays a less significant role.

Governing law provisions usually cover contract disputes only but can also govern torts committed in connection with the agreement. A party with this preference would negotiate for language such as "the laws of Delaware govern any matter that relates to this transaction."

Litigation or arbitration

Unless the parties specify a choice of arbitration in the contract, any disputes will be governed though litigation. In private deals with a purchase price adjustment, some type of arbitration of the adjustment is common (roughly 90 percent of deals). An accounting firm usually is tasked with reviewing the parties' submissions and determining the adjustment. The parties usually view an accounting firm as more capable of arriving at the correct answer, given that most adjustment disputes relate to the appropriateness of a calculation or characterization of an asset or liability under relevant accounting standards.

The accounting firm process is much faster than litigation would be. And it is more definitive, since courts do not generally second-guess the arbitrator's decision absent an evident material mistake.[2] The accounting firm's resolution of a purchase price adjustment is usually meant to be final. The acquisition agreement usually says something to the effect that the accounting firm's decision is final and binding, but they usually do not specify that the accounting firm's decisions have the weight of an arbitration decision, and they usually do not specify that the accounting firm's review is the sole means for resolving a dispute over the purchase price adjustment.[3]

Arbitration of the whole contract is rare in public deals but chosen in roughly 20 percent of private deals. In particular, arbitration is more often selected in cross-border than in domestic deals.

Arbitration awards can be kept confidential. For public policy reasons, court proceedings are public. One party may prefer arbitration for the confidentiality benefit; one party may prefer litigation if they feel it would create pressure on the counterparty to settle a public dispute.

An arbitration provision should set forth a number of relevant details. First, the scope should be defined. For example, arbitration may be the dispute resolution mechanism for any dispute relating to an acquisition, or may only be available for a particular subset of disputes that might arise. Next, the provision should also specify the process for selecting an arbitrator, as well any arbitrator qualifications.

For deals in highly technical or specialized sectors of the economy, parties might want to specify arbitrators with the requisite knowledge and expertise to adequately analyze complex issues. Last, the arbitration provision will usually set forth procedural rules for the arbitration itself, such as time frame for conducting the process, choice of forum for the arbitration, and the extent of discovery that will be available to the parties.

Court

The parties may select the state or federal court in which a claim may be litigated, and may select the arbitration rules that would govern an arbitration (e.g., AAA). Delaware, followed by New York, courts are the most common choices. Delaware is often selected when the matter would fall within the chancery court's jurisdiction (mergers and stock purchases), and less so when the matter would fall to the superior court (asset purchase). New York is the most frequent choice for asset sales.

Location

The parties may select the city in which the claim will be handled. One party may want to ensure litigation or arbitration on its home turf, or may want to avoid having to travel to a more remote location for manage a dispute.

Waiver of jury trial

Provisions waiving the right to a jury trial are commonplace in today's merger and acquisition (M&A) landscape. Large corporations might negotiate for such a waiver, trying to avoid a potentially unsympathetic jury. Both parties might also prefer such a waiver in a contract setting forth a complex transaction, litigation over which might be beyond a lay juror's grasp.

> **THE MARKET**
>
> Around 80 percent of deals incorporate a waiver of jury trial.

A waiver of the right to a jury trial should be set forth prominently in the contract, and should be articulated clearly. The waiver needs to be knowing and voluntary in order to be enforceable.

Public vs. Private Company Deals

Public company deals

In public company deals, lawsuits brought on behalf of shareholders of the target are commonplace. They have increased in frequency over the years, such that now virtually every deal is subject to on average five shareholder lawsuits.

Most of these lawsuits are filed within two weeks after announcement of the deal. Some plaintiff firms announce "investigations" within hours of the announcement. These suits are usually filed in state rather than federal court. They are often filed in multiple state jurisdictions. Almost all of these suits are settled or voluntarily dismissed. Only a handful make it to a court decision, such as a dismissal or judgment.

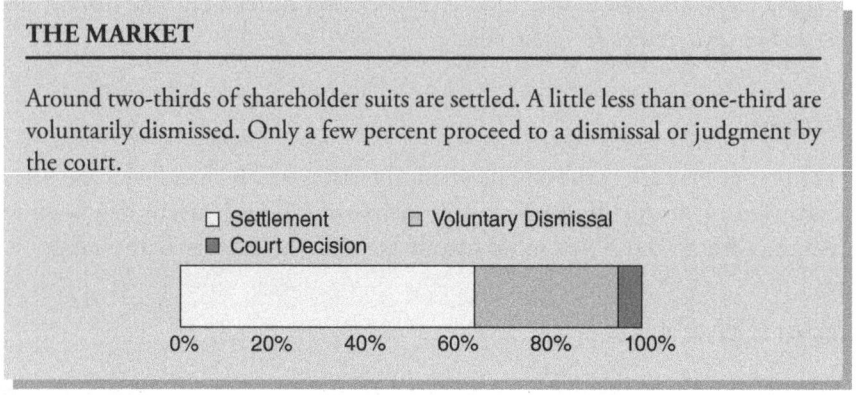

THE MARKET

Around two-thirds of shareholder suits are settled. A little less than one-third are voluntarily dismissed. Only a few percent proceed to a dismissal or judgment by the court.

Most settlements are so-called disclosure settlements, in which the target provides additional disclosure to the shareholders in advance of the shareholder vote. Only a few settlements provide some economic benefit. The breakup fee is reduced in some settlements.

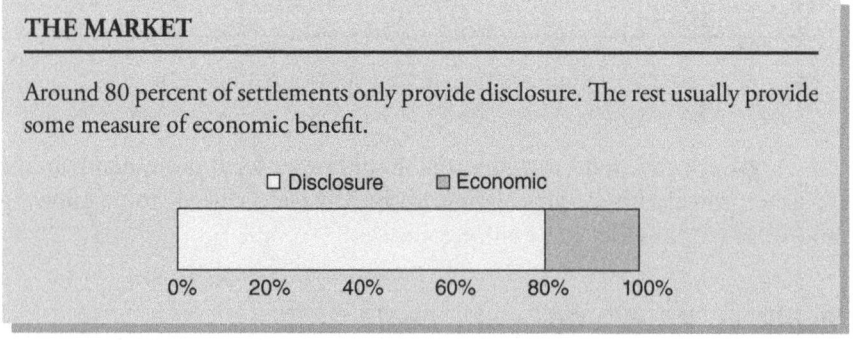

THE MARKET

Around 80 percent of settlements only provide disclosure. The rest usually provide some measure of economic benefit.

When monetary settlements do occur, they are most common when a conflict of interest presents itself that was not appropriately dealt with through the corporate governance process. The target reimburses the plaintiffs' lawyers for their fees in most settlements. The average fee award is roughly $500,000.[4]

In terms of litigation by the parties themselves, public company deals generate a limited amount of litigation surrounding the buyer's obligation to close. This is relatively uncommon during stable economic times, but quite common during an economic downturn.

Private equity deals generate litigation surrounding the use and availability of the financing provisions (such as the reverse breakup fee). Public company deals do not have purchase price adjustments or indemnities for the parties to fight over.

Private company deals

In private company deals, disputes regarding purchase price adjustments and indemnity claims for breach of representations are commonplace. For instance, claims are frequently made against the purchase price escrow (discussed above in the indemnity chapter) for breaches of representations.

THE MARKET

Claims are made by the buyer against the escrow for breaches of representations in roughly one third to one half of deals.

Litigation Endnotes

1. The corporate law governing the target can also be chosen by the target through its selection of its state of incorporation. At the point of a deal, however, that matter is already set.

2. The Federal Arbitration Act (FAA) permits arbitration awards to be vacated only—(1) where the award was procured by corruption, fraud, or undue means; (2) where there was evident partiality or corruption in the arbitrators, or either of them; (3) where the arbitrators were guilty of misconduct in refusing to postpone the hearing, upon sufficient cause shown, or in refusing to hear evidence pertinent and material to the controversy; or of any other misbehavior by which the rights of any party have been prejudiced; or (4) where the arbitrators exceeded their powers, or so imperfectly executed them that a mutual, final, and definite award upon the subject matter submitted was not made. 9 U.S.C. § 10(a). The FAA permits modification or correction of an arbitrator's award—(a) Where there was an evident material miscalculation of figures or an evident material mistake in the description of any person, thing, or property referred to in the award[;] (b) Where the arbitrators have awarded upon a matter not submitted to them, unless it is a matter not affecting the merits of the decision upon the matter submitted[; or] (c) Where the award is imperfect in matter of form not affecting the merits of the controversy. 9 U.S.C. § 11. The statutory grounds for vacating or modifying an award under the FAA cannot be expanded by contract. *See Hall St. Assocs., LLC v. Mattel, Inc.,* 552 U.S. 576, 578 (2008); *AT&T Mobility LLC v. Concepcion,* 131 S. Ct. 1740, 1752 (2011). State arbitration laws differ to the extent that they follow the FAA and federal law. *Compare In re Johnson (Summit Equities, Inc.),* 864 N.Y.S.2d 873, 885 (N.Y. Sup. Ct. 2008) ("The provisions of the FAA and of New York's counterpart statute, CPLR Article 75, are very similar, especially with respect to judicial review of arbitration awards. Hence, both federal and New York state law relating to standards of review afford guidance to the court in these proceedings.") (citations omitted), *with Cable Connection, Inc. v. DIRECTV, Inc.,* 190 P.3d 586, 599, 602 (2008) (finding that "the *Hall Street* holding is restricted to proceedings to review arbitration awards under the FAA, and does not require state law to conform with its limitations" and that "[t]he scope of judicial review is not invariably limited by statute" and that parties "may expressly agree to accept a broader scope of review").

3. In *Viacom International, Inc. v. Winshall,* the acquirer disputed the accountant's resolution of the earn-out, arguing that "the Resolution Accountants erred by refusing to consider an alternative approach to determining the earn-out that the acquirer originally raised in a preliminary calculation of the earn-out, but ultimately did not include in its contractually-mandated calculation of the earn-out." No. 7149-CS, 2012 BL 204765, at *1 (Del. Ch. Aug. 9, 2012), *aff'd* 72 A.3d 78 (Del. 2013). The parties in the *Winshall* case agreed that the FAA applied to the "Resolution Accountants' Determination." *Id.* at *12. The court

held that the acquirer was not entitled to de novo judicial review, and upheld the Resolution Accountants' decision strictly to abide by the calculation method agreed to by the parties in the Earn-Out Statement. *Id.* at *20–21. Affirming the court's decision in *Winshall,* and overruling contrary decisions, the Delaware Supreme Court provided guidance as to the scope of an arbitrator's discretion in deciding matters such as earn-out valuations: Whether an arbitration provision is branded "narrow" or "broad," the only question that the court should decide is whether the subject matter in dispute falls within it. If the subject matter to be arbitrated is the calculation of an earn-out, or the amount of working capital, or the company's net worth at closing, all issues as to what financial or other information should be considered in performing the calculation are decided by the arbitrator. In resolving those issues, the arbitrator may well rely on the terms of the underlying agreement, and the arbitrator's interpretation of the contract is likely to affect the scope of the arbitration. Nonetheless, those decisions fall within the category of procedural arbitrability. They are not "gateway" issues about whether the particular dispute should be arbitrated at all. Rather, they are questions about how the subject of the arbitration should be decided. *Winshall,* 72 A.3d at 83–84.

4. *See* Matthew D. Cain & Steven M. Davidoff, *Takeover Litigation in 2013,* at 3 (Ohio St. Univ., Pub. L. Working Paper No. 236, 2014) (finding a median fee of $485,000 in 2013).

CHAPTER 16

Structuring M&A Deals

Building Blocks for Structuring an M&A Deal

The basic building blocks for structuring merger and acquisition (M&A) deals are: asset sales, stock sales, and mergers. All are legal means to transfer ownership of a business from a seller to a buyer. All have unique characteristics in a deal structure, which can be used to achieve or avoid particular results.

In addition to the corporate structuring issues discussed in this chapter, tax analysis plays a critical role in structuring the transaction. Tax is a complex and separate topic that is not dealt with in this book. Industry-specific regulatory regimes, such as banking or public utility regulation, also play important roles in structuring deals for regulated companies.

Asset Purchase

To purchase a business, the buyer could acquire all the assets and rights related to the business that the target owns. In an asset sale, specified assets and liabilities of a target are transferred to the buyer. The target company (rather than its shareholders) is the counterparty to the agreement, since the target is directly selling its own assets. As a result, the target (rather than its shareholders) is entitled to the deal consideration. The target may use the proceeds for other business purposes, or may distribute the proceeds to its shareholders.

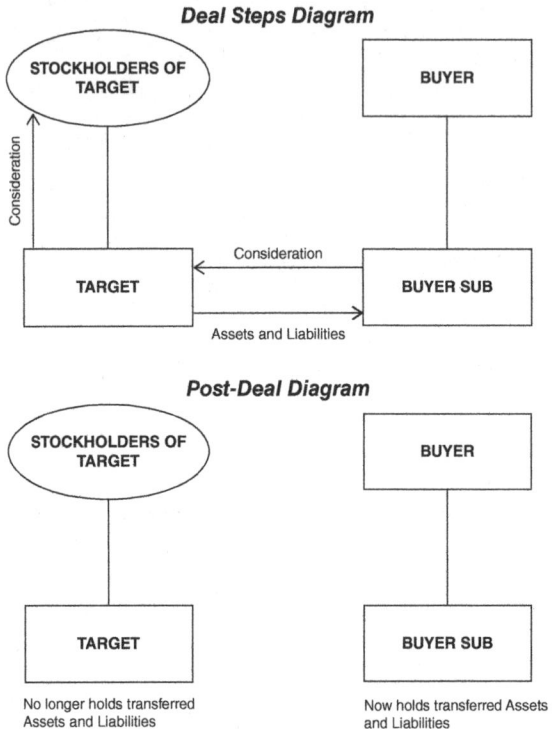

Deal Steps Diagram

Post-Deal Diagram

What assets?

An asset sale requires the parties to specify which assets are to be sold. If all the assets are being acquired, the parties can simply provide in general terms for the transfer of all the target's assets.

An asset sale is basically the only way for a target company to sell one line of business separate from its other lines of business.[1] In some deals, only one of several lines of business is being acquired. If that line of business is operated through its own separate legal entity that separate entity can simply sell all its assets.

That would be unusual, however. Most companies have legal entities that operate several lines of business, with shared accounting support, shared research and development departments, and shared marketing, and so on. At one level, each business may have its own management; at the top, they are overseen by higher level management and the CEO.

Separating the assets that go with the business from those that remain behind requires close scrutiny of the facts. In particular, decisions have to be made about assets that are "shared," that is, used in more than one line of business. In complex organizations, even ones with the best record keeping, it is not possible to identify every asset used to operate a separate line of business.

In most cases, the parties rely on legal drafting solutions to make asset sales work, by identifying categories of assets and transferring them as a group. For example, the seller may agree to generally transfer all "equipment" used in the target business. Legal teams will often argue about whether the buyer should receive, for example, all the equipment used "primarily" by the business, all the equipment used "exclusively" by the business, or all the equipment used to any extent in the business.

Sample Provision

The Sellers shall, or shall cause one or more of their Affiliates to, sell, convey, transfer, assign, and deliver to the Buyer, and the Buyer shall purchase and accept from Sellers or their applicable Affiliates all of the Sellers' and each of their Affiliates' right, title and interest, as of the Closing, in and to the assets, properties, rights, and claims of the Sellers and their Affiliates that are [primarily] [exclusively] [used in or related to] to the Business, whether tangible or intangible, real, personal, or mixed [except for the Excluded Assets], free and clear of all Liens, other than Permitted Liens, including all of such right, title, and interest in and to the following: [litany follows]

Categories of transferred assets may include assignable contracts, accounts receivable, equipment, real estate, and the like. They may also include intangible rights, such as goodwill, contractual claims against third parties, and intellectual property.

Sample Provision

The term "Acquired Assets" shall include all right, title and interest in and to the following:
   a. Assigned Contracts;
   b. Accounts Receivable and Inventory;
   c. Fixtures, Furniture and Equipment;
   d. Leased and Owned Real Property;
   e. Goodwill;
   f. Intellectual Property;
   g. Books and Records;
   h. Credits and prepaid expenses;
   i. Permits (and applications therefor);

> j. Claims, causes of action, lawsuits, and judgments, including insurance claims;
> k. Guaranties, warranties, and indemnities; and
> l. Tax refunds, credits, or similar benefits.

When intellectual property is used in more than one line of business, one side or the other would suffer if it did not retain use of any shared intellectual property. In many cases, one party owns it and licenses it to the other.

Some categories of assets to be sold are over-inclusive. To address this, the parties can specify a list of assets to be carved out and excluded. For instance, if the buyer is acquiring all equipment used in the target business, some shared equipment can be excluded and retained by the seller. Or the list can be used to clarify that cash or other types of assets were intentionally excluded from the list of acquired assets.

Sample Provision

Sellers and their Affiliates shall retain all of their existing right, title and interest in and to, and there shall be excluded from the sale, conveyance, transfer, assignment and delivery to Buyer hereunder, and the Acquired Assets shall not include the following assets, properties, rights and claims of Sellers and their Affiliates (collectively, the "Excluded Assets"): [litany follows].

Third parties may have the right to prevent some assets from being assigned to the buyer. For instance, commercial contracts will normally have an anti-assignment clause, preventing them from being assigned without consent of the counterparty.

On occasion, such anti-assignment provisions include an exception to allow assignment to a buyer of the relevant business. These provisions take on a number of forms. They may simply prohibit assignment, give the third party a right to terminate (which it may or may not elect to exercise), impose "assignment fees" or trigger other economic and contract rights in favor of the third party.

In some cases, anti-assignment and change of control provisions are triggered upon signing the transaction. In most, they will only be triggered by the closing. The parties will seek consent in most cases between signing and closing. Unless consent has been obtained, such contracts are usually not transferred to the buyer at closing.

Sample Provision

To the extent that the sale, conveyance, transfer, assignment, sublease, or delivery to Buyer of any Acquired Asset is prohibited by any applicable Law or would require any Governmental Approvals or third-party Consents, and such Governmental Approvals or third-party Consents shall not have been obtained prior to the Closing, then the Closing shall proceed without the sale, conveyance, transfer, assignment, sublease, or delivery of such asset.

Instead, both parties will normally be required to use their efforts to obtain those consents after closing (or for a period after closing).

Sample Provision

[For a period of __ months] following the Closing, the parties hereto shall use their reasonable best efforts, and cooperate with each other, to obtain promptly such Governmental Approvals or third-party Consents. Once any such Governmental Approvals or third-party Consents are obtained, Sellers shall or shall cause the relevant Affiliates to, sell, convey, transfer, assign, sublease, or deliver such asset to Buyer at no additional cost.

The acquisition agreement may include a fail-safe mechanism if third-party consent is not obtained. The target continues to operate under the contract and must provide the benefits of that contract to the buyer. For instance, the sellers can continue to buy goods under a contract and transfer, at cost, the purchased goods to the buyer.

Sample Provision

To the extent that any such asset cannot be sold, conveyed, transferred, assigned, subleased, or delivered or the full benefits of use of any such asset cannot be provided to Buyer following the Closing, then the parties hereto shall cooperate with each other in any mutually agreeable, reasonable and lawful arrangements designed to provide to Buyer the benefits of use of such asset and to Sellers or their Affiliates the benefits that they would have obtained had the asset been conveyed to Buyer at the Closing.

What liabilities?

In the eyes of the target's creditors, the liabilities of the business represent claims against the target company. An asset sale by the target does not change that fact. Therefore, the target company will need to decide whether it plans to keep and pay particular liabilities, or whether it wants the buyer to assume the target's liabilities when the buyer acquires the target's assets.

The assets and liabilities of the business being acquired are frequently two sides of the same coin. For instance, if the buyer acquires all of the accounts receivable of the business, it typically assumes responsibility for the accounts payable.

Sample Provision

On the terms and subject to the conditions set forth herein, at the Closing, the Buyer shall assume and agree to discharge or perform when due in accordance with their respective terms the Liabilities of the Sellers specifically set forth below (subject, for the avoidance of doubt, to any defenses or offsets against the obligee to whom such Liabilities are owed), in each case solely to the extent [primarily] [exclusively] [used in or related to] the Business and other than the Excluded Liabilities (collectively, the "Assumed Liabilities"). Solely the following Liabilities, in each case other than the Excluded Liabilities, shall be Assumed Liabilities: [litany follows].

Liabilities can be acquired (or not acquired) on a line-item basis or by category, the same as assets. The parties can also define specific liabilities or categories of liabilities that the buyer does not assume. For instance, the parties may agree that the buyer will not assume any product liability claims. In some cases (such as product liability claims and environmental claims), however, underlying law could require that the liability travel with the assets—and thus become the buyer's liability despite any wording in the acquisition agreement to the contrary.

Nevertheless, excluding the liability can still benefit the buyer, because exclusion results in the seller (to the extent it remains a viable entity) being economically responsible for those liabilities under customary indemnity provision that requires the seller to protect the buyer from excluded liabilities.

Sample Provision

Buyer shall not assume, and shall not have any responsibility of any nature with respect to, and shall be deemed not to be a successor in interest to Sellers for any purpose and shall not be liable for any successor liability claims, for any of the following Liabilities of Sellers and their Affiliates (the foregoing, collectively, the "Excluded Liabilities"): [litany follows].

In many cases, there is a practical benefit to the buyer assuming ordinary course liabilities. The buyer will inherit the accounts payable systems and will manage and control the business that generated the liabilities. The buyer may also want to ensure payment of trade creditors if it plans to rely on them for its ongoing business.

On a business level, keeping or taking liabilities is primarily an economic (rather than a legal) issue in the negotiation. If a seller retains a particular liability, it would expect a correspondingly higher purchase price. But liabilities are rarely simple or fixed in value.

War Story ══

When a major equipment manufacturer sold a division to a private equity fund, the parties negotiated over every detail in the acquisition agreement. In particular, they debated for some time how to allocate rights and responsibilities related to so-called "lease residuals."

When equipment is leased, the user pays a monthly fee and returns the equipment at the end of the lease. The manufacturer takes out a loan against the equipment to pay for its manufacturing costs. When the equipment is returned, the manufacturing division then has to resell the equipment as "used" and pay off the loan.

If the price of used equipment falls in the meantime, the manufacturing division loses money, and finds that it made a bad deal on the lease and may even owe extra money to pay off the loan. If used equipment prices go up in the meantime, the manufacturing division pays off the loan and makes a windfall. That upside and downside is called the lease residual.

Eventually, the buyer and seller agreed that the seller would keep the lease residual. It was expected to be a valuable asset, so the buyer paid less for the rest of the business. Unfortunately for the seller, it retained those lease residuals just before energy prices spiked. As users switched their preferences to newer, more energy-efficient equipment, the value of used equipment plummeted.

For several quarters after the sale, rather than taking profits from lease residuals the seller took multi-million-dollar financial charges to cover its lease residual liabilities. Before it was over, the seller had basically made no money on the sale on a net basis.

A variety of substantive laws protect creditors of the target if assets are stripped out of the entity.[2] In limited circumstances, the law forces the buyer of assets to assume related liabilities if the seller does not pay them. This is referred to generally as successor liability. A buyer subject to successor liability could be sued and forced to pay a liability for which it never agreed to assume responsibility.

Successor liability risks fall generally into three categories. The first is statutorily imposed liability. Most notably, environmental liability may be imposed on the buyer of real estate in some cases.[3] Another example is product liability.[4]

The second is fraudulent conveyance statutes and common law rules.[5] Those generally apply if the buyer pays less than fair market value and acquires assets from a seller that is insolvent or that becomes insolvent on account of the transaction with the buyer.

Third, some types of deals can be recharacterized as de facto mergers. If characterized as a merger, the buyer is deemed to have assumed all the seller's liabilities. Although the concept is rejected in Delaware and some other jurisdictions, a recharacterization could occur, for instance, in an asset sale in which the buyer hires the seller's management team and the seller liquidates and distributes the cash to its sellers, leaving no assets behind to satisfy remaining liabilities.

Approvals

In order for a company to sell its assets, it needs to execute an asset purchase agreement. The seller, therefore, needs to obtain normal corporate approvals (e.g., board resolutions) to execute the contract.[6]

As discussed below, a stock purchase to acquire 100 percent of a company requires every stockholder to agree to sell. A merger typically requires a majority of the stockholders to approve the merger. Similar to a merger, state statutes typically require majority shareholder approval if the target sells out its whole business, or enough to constitute what is referred to as "all or substantially all" of its assets.[7]

Sometimes, it is fairly clear that a particular transaction involves the sale of enough assets to constitute all or substantially all of the assets of a company.

Sometimes, it can be difficult to say with any certainty.[8] As is typical for case law, there are a number of factors to consider, and no hard-and-fast rules. In many circumstances, the parties must take some risk that a court will not later second-guess their determination that all or substantially all of the assets were not sold, or they must seek shareholder approval to avoid that risk.

As a rough rule of thumb, selling approximately two-thirds of a business (measured by its assets and revenue, or other relevant tests) can be taken to represent all or substantially all of its assets. If so-called "crown jewel" assets are being sold—such as the only growing and profitable line in an otherwise declining company—the threshold can be crossed at much lower percentage levels—potentially as low as one-third of the assets or revenue.

As noted above, asset sales frequently give rise to the need for third-party consents under anti-assignment provisions. For a seller with thousands of contracts, most of which are by their terms not assignable to the buyer, this can present a significant problem. The significance of the problem depends on the business terms of the nonassignable contract. Some suppliers want nothing more than to continue selling to the new owner of the business on the same terms.

In other cases, a lessor or a licensor of intellectual property may have found just the opportunity to raise prices, or bring the contract payments it receives up to market. The nonassignable contracts may be terminable at will—in which case the business relationship already depends on both parties being interested in continuing the relationship on current terms. If the contract provides the target with below-market rates, then the contract may be viewed as an asset or part of the value being acquired by the buyer. In that case, the buyer would object to the target changing the contract terms in order to obtain consent.

War Story

A small U.S. pharmaceutical company had gotten lucky. It had secured supply contracts for the active ingredient to a drug at long-term, cheap rates long before the drug proved to be a blockbuster. Of course, the supply agreement contained a "boilerplate" anti-assignment clause. There was a badly-worded exception that looked like it was intended to let a buyer of the business take an assignment of the supply agreement, but the lawyers for the U.S. pharmaceutical company were unsure how to interpret it.

A few years later, a large global player proposed to acquire the U.S. company. The buyer's diligence uncovered the anti-assignment clause. They were also not sure whether it would be triggered based on its unusual wording.

There was much discussion as to how the supplier might react to the announcement that the target was being sold. Would the supplier threaten to cut off supply if prices were not renegotiated to blockbuster levels? Would it honor the original bargain without much ado? Would it be possible for the target to stock up on the active ingredient under the current supply agreement terms before announcing the deal?

Eventually, the target and the buyer agreed not to approach the supplier before signing. The buyer decided to take the risk of having to fight it out with the supplier, rather than potentially tipping off the supplier to the issue and risking a leak about the deal talks.

The acquisition eventually fell apart and never closed for unrelated reasons, so the wisdom of their choice was not tested.

"Change of control" provisions also give rise to third-party consents, as discussed below.

Stock Purchase

In a stock purchase, the buyer acquires the stock of the target from its current stockholders. If the buyer acquires 100 percent of the stock, it will own 100 percent of the company that conducts the business.

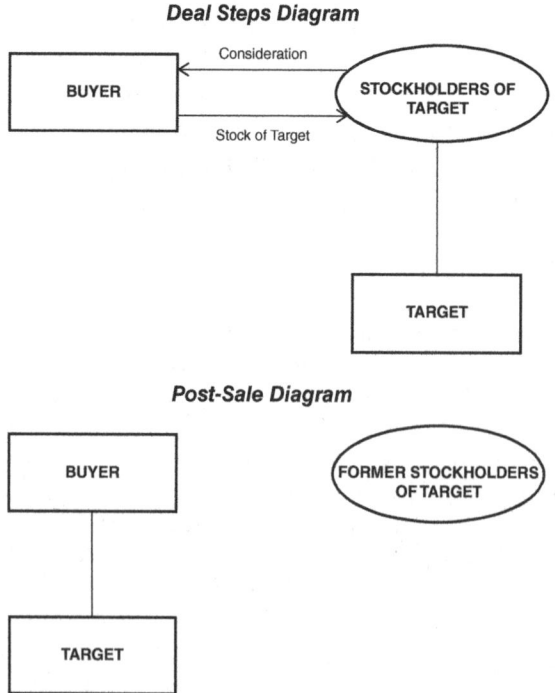

Deal Steps Diagram

Post-Sale Diagram

As noted above, if the target is privately held by a few shareholders, the stock sale is a simple, private transaction. If the target is publicly owned by numerous shareholders, than the stock sale is regulated by the tender offer rules under the federal securities laws. Tender offers are discussed in more detail below.

Who signs?

Each stockholder who sells its shares to the buyer would do so by signing the acquisition agreement and committing to sell its stock. If a single owner sells all the stock of an operating subsidiary, only one seller needs to sign and approve the transaction. This is the simplest form of acquisition.

If numerous small stockholders own the target company, a stock purchase agreement may be cumbersome because of the need to get each individual shareholder to sign. Some shareholders may not be available; some may want to hold out for a higher price or better terms; some may rather not sell at all.

In principle, the target company itself need not be a party to a stock sale agreement. The stockholders, not the target, are doing the selling. If that is the structure, no corporate approval is needed from the target. Sometimes the target is made party to the agreement because the target agrees to some covenants, such as those relating to how the business is operated between signing and closing. (If the target is not a party, the shareholders agree to cause the target to operate in accordance with those covenants.)

Change of control

Anti-assignment restrictions do not generally apply in stock sales. The target company that is party to the contract containing the anti-assignment clause does not actually assign anything to the buyer. Instead, ownership of the target changes.

A change of ownership gives rise to change of control issues, however. Change of control clauses in the target's contracts can take a number of forms. Some are only triggered by a direct change of control (i.e., the direct owner of the target changes).

Some are triggered by an indirect change of control (i.e., the owner of the direct owner changes, or any other controlling party up the chain of ownership above the target). This distinction matters in complicated ownership and control structures, which may involve multiple levels of intermediate holding companies.

Merger

In a merger, one entity merges into another. The combined company has all the assets and liabilities of the two. State merger statutes generally require that one of the two companies be treated as the "surviving" company. The other is treated as having been merged out of existence after it transfers all of its assets and liabilities to the other.[9] The transfer happens by operation of the merger statute.

The owners of the target receive the deal consideration. Technically speaking, the stock in the target is converted into the right to receive the deal consideration from the buyer. Buyers are generally free to convert the target's stock into any form of deal consideration (cash, stock in the buyer, etc.).[10]

The owners of the buyer entity that is party to the merger become the owners of the target. For instance, if the buyer forms a special purpose vehicle to become party to the merger (which is known as a triangular merger, and discussed below) in the stock of the buyer's special purpose vehicle is converted into the stock of the surviving corporation. As a result, the buyer owns the target after the merger.

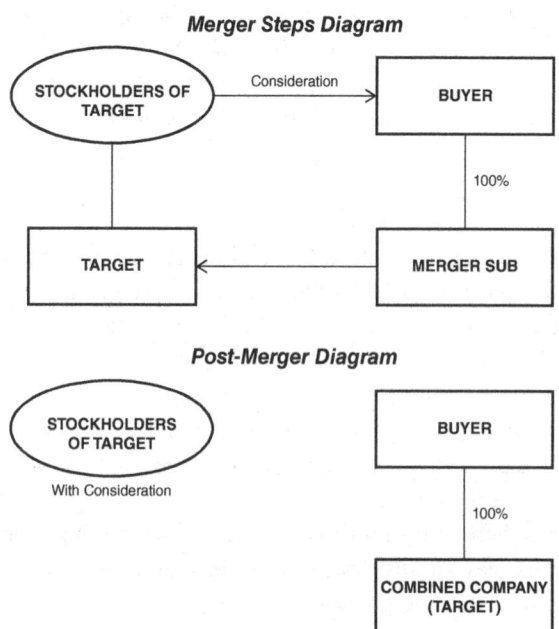

Merger Steps Diagram

Post-Merger Diagram

Shareholder approval

Mergers allow a transaction to be completed with approval of less than all shareholders. The exact approval requirement is governed by the applicable state merger statute; in most states it requires the approval of a majority of the outstanding shares.[11] When numerous shareholders own the stock of a company, a merger can solve the practical problem of obtaining an agreement from each individual stockholder to sell its stock to the buyer. It avoids the potential "holdup" value that an objecting stockholder could have.

Asset sales can avoid the individual shareholder consent problems as well but, as discussed above, they can also create assignment problems (which a merger can, in most cases, avoid). Stock exchange rules require shareholder approval of the buyer's shareholders when a buyer issues 20 percent of its stock in connection with a merger.[12]

Triangular mergers

In most deals, the buyer itself is not party to the merger. Instead, the buyer forms a special purpose merger subsidiary to merge with the target. This is referred to as a "triangular" merger because there are three entities involved.

Buyers use merger subsidiaries primarily so that the buyer itself does not have to seek shareholder approval for the merger. Merger statutes require that both companies merging into each other obtain stockholder approval.[13] If the buyer has a merger subsidiary compete the merger, then the parent buyer entity is not subject to the approval requirement. Instead, the merger subsidiary merely needs to obtain the approval of its stockholder (the buyer), rather than approval of the buyer's shareholders. This three-entity structure also means that, after the merger is done, the buyer owns the target in the form of a separate subsidiary, rather than having the target assets mingled into the buyer's assets.

Triangular mergers can be "reverse" (most common) or "forward," depending on which entity is treated as the surviving company. In a reverse triangular merger, a special purpose merger subsidiary of the buyer is merged into the target. The target company survives the merger; the buyer's merger subsidiary does not. The stock of the buyer's merger subsidiary is turned into stock of the combined company, resulting in the buyer owning the combined company. The stock of the target is turned into the right to receive the deal consideration. The target company is treated as having maintained its existence and, thus, not having assigned its contracts.

A forward triangular merger is almost the same as a reverse triangular merger, except that the target merges into the merger subsidiary and the merger subsidiary remains as the surviving corporation. In a forward triangular merger, the target's assets and liabilities are transformed by operation of the merger statute to the merger subsidiary.

Anti-assignment clauses

Some contract counterparties have argued that the transfer of assets and liabilities from the target to the surviving corporation in a forward triangular merger results in an assignment in violation of the anti-assignment clause. Courts generally find that a forward triangular merger does not trigger anti-assignment clauses.[14] Some draw this conclusion on the basis that the surviving corporation is the successor, not an assignee. Others conclude that customary anti-assignment clauses are not intended to prevent assignment by operation of law. In the context of intellectual property, however, some courts have found this structure to give rise to consent rights by owners who license intellectual property to the target.[15]

Binding share exchanges

A binding share exchange is a stock transfer (as opposed to a merger or asset transfer). Unlike simple stock sales, a binding share exchange can be binding on minority shareholders who do not execute the agreement. Like a merger, this requires majority approval,[16] allowing the deal to be consummated even if unanimous consent is not forthcoming.

Everything else being equal, a merger is used in practice instead of a binding share exchange. A binding share exchange may be used if, for instance, the target is subject to contractual restrictions prohibiting it from engaging in a merger, or third-party contractual rights arise by their terms in a merger but not a binding share exchange. New York and other states have the concept of a binding share exchange, but Delaware does not.[17]

Tender Offer

In a tender offer, the buyer makes a public offer to all of the target's shareholders to acquire their shares.[18] In a private deal with only a few target shareholders, the offer to buy their shares in a stock sale is a private transaction. In a public deal, the offer to the public shareholders is a tender offer. In private deals with a large number of shareholders, whether the offer is a tender offer may depend on the particular facts and circumstances.[19]

A tender offer is subject to a number of legal requirements, such as a requirement for the buyer to hold the offer open for 20 business days.[20] The target must give shareholders withdrawal rights under which they can withdraw their acceptance of the buyer's offer until the tender offer closes. The tender offer rules also require equal treatment of shareholders.

Squeeze-outs

At the close of the offer, the buyer acquires the shares tendered. If successful, those shares will represent at least a substantial majority, but as a practical matter will never result in the buyer acquiring 100 percent of the target's shares. Although allowing a minority stake to remain outstanding is common in many jurisdictions, buyers of U.S. targets generally prefer to acquire 100 percent. This avoids litigation risk from minority shareholders claiming a breach of fiduciary duties.[21]

If a minimum number of shares are acquired at which a squeeze-out may be accomplished, then the buyer may acquire the remaining public shares through a back-end short-form merger. The short form merger is also referred to as a "squeeze-out" merger. In most states, it allows a newly acquired target to enter into a merger with the buyer (its new parent), without having to obtain shareholder approval by the target's remaining shareholders (as a normal merger would require).

In a short form merger, the unaffiliated shareholders receive the same consideration as the other shareholders did in the tender offer and are, thus, squeezed-out. The ownership hurdle, typically required under state law for this squeeze-out rule to apply is 90 percent. Short-form mergers are frequently used in connection with tender offers, in order to squeeze out the remaining equity holders that do not tender into the offer.

Top-up options

Most buyers will worry that they cannot obtain 90 percent acceptances even with an attractive offer because a number of shareholders will not tender. In that case, the buyer may ask the target to grant the buyer a top-up option. The top-up option provides that if the buyer acquires more than an agreed percentage, but less than the squeeze-out threshold, the target will issue shares to the buyer sufficient to result in the buyer owning the minimum squeeze-out amount.

For example, if the buyer is able to acquire only 80 percent in the offer, then the target will issue additional shares to the buyer to bring its percentage ownership up to 90 percent.

Top-up options ensure that the buyer pays a fair price for the additional shares issued to the buyer, equal to the stock price implied in the transaction. The buyer does not actually transfer this sum of money to the target in practice, however. At the instant of closing, the party that is owed the money (the target) is a 100 percent–owned subsidiary of the party that owes the money (the buyer), so there is no one to complain. The third-party equity holders being squeezed out do receive the agreed deal consideration.

THE MARKET

Top-up options are frequently triggered only if the buyer acquires a minimum of 75 percent to 85 percent of the target's stock in a tender offer.

The dilution involved in a top-up option can require an enormous number of shares to be issued. The problem is that the newly issued top-up shares dilute not only the remaining public shareholders but also the shares acquired by the buyer in the tender offer. If a buyer acquires 80 out of a total of 100 shares, then the buyer has 80 percent. It needs to get to 90 percent in order to use the short-form merger.

Getting to 90 percent does not involve simply issuing 10 more shares. That would result in the buyer holding 90 out of 110, or only around 82 percent. To get the buyer up to 90 percent, a total of 100 new shares must be issued to the buyer—doubling the total outstanding shares from 100 to 200. That gives the buyer 180 out of 200, or 90 percent. To take a buyer from 70 to 90 percent requires the outstanding shares to be tripled, and going from 60 to 90 percent requires the shares to be quadrupled.

As a matter of corporate law, the target cannot issue shares unless they are authorized by the target's charter. New shares can only be authorized by the charter with shareholder approval. Most companies have some amount of pre-authorized shares in reserve that can be issued without further shareholder approval, but it is unusual for a company to have pre-authorized shares that are two, three or four times the entire existing shareholder base.

As a result, in many cases issuing a top-up option is not possible without a shareholder vote to authorize new shares to be issued under the option. The need for a shareholder vote requires its own proxy process, which adds to the complexity of achieving a top-up option.

Top-up options have become commonplace in negotiated tender offers, but the negotiated level of ownership the buyer must achieve in order for the option to be triggered varies. As noted above, one reason for the variance is simply the number of available authorized but unissued shares—the top-up option cannot by its terms be triggered at a level that the target cannot fulfill as a matter of underlying corporate law.

The target may, in addition, wish to only override the 90 percent short-form merger standard to a limited extent, and may not be willing as a business matter to offer the top-up option if only slightly more than a majority of the shareholders tender into the offer.

A new Delaware law may put an end to top-up options.[22] The new law permits parties entering into a merger agreement to "opt in" to eliminate a target stockholder vote on a back-end merger following a tender offer as long as the buyer acquires a majority of the shares but less than the 90 percent necessary to effect a short-form merger. The majority standard is increased if the applicable merger vote is higher than a majority.

Tender Offer vs. Merger

Buyers acquire public companies through two primary structures: a merger or tender offer.

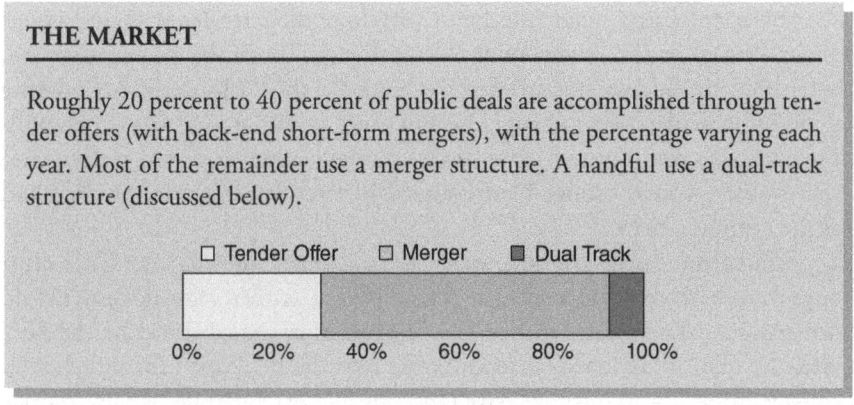

THE MARKET

Roughly 20 percent to 40 percent of public deals are accomplished through tender offers (with back-end short-form mergers), with the percentage varying each year. Most of the remainder use a merger structure. A handful use a dual-track structure (discussed below).

☐ Tender Offer ☐ Merger ■ Dual Track

0% 20% 40% 60% 80% 100%

But how do the parties decide which structure to select? Although other factors are also at play, the buyer has to decide which structure best reduces the risk of a competing bidder disrupting the deal.

A merger requires a merger vote and is subject to the target's fiduciary out rights. The deal is at risk of the target exercising its fiduciary termination right, or a competing bidder convincing the shareholders to vote down the deal. The fiduciary out termination right, expires when shareholder approval is obtained, so both of those risks expire once the shareholder vote is successfully held.

To get to the vote, the parties need to finalize the disclosure documents related to the shareholder vote, including Securities and Exchange Commission (SEC) review, and give the target's shareholders 20 business days to review the disclosure documents once approved by the SEC. The entire process often takes around 10 to 12 weeks from the date of signing.

After the vote, the parties are safe from a competing bidder but cannot close the merger until regulatory approvals are completed (if any remain outstanding). As a result, the critical timing path in a merger is the time required to complete the vote. The path to regulatory approval and closing is not decisive as to whether a competing bidder can top the deal.

In a tender offer, the path to regulatory approval becomes decisive. There is no shareholder vote. Instead, shareholders decide whether to tender their shares for sale to the buyer. The buyer purchases those shares at closing; at which point, the buyer owns a majority of the target. Because closing the tender offer is itself the act that results in the buyer owning the target, the buyer cannot complete the tender offer until all regulatory approvals are satisfied.

The SEC takes the view that shareholders must have withdrawal rights— the ability to change their mind and withdraw their tendered shares—until all conditions to the tender offer are satisfied.[23] Therefore, if regulatory approvals for the deal are not satisfied by the end of the 20-business-day offering period, the tender offer cannot close and must continue to be held open until the approvals are satisfied. As a result, the regulatory approval process and shareholder process cannot be decoupled in a tender offer cannot close and as they can in a merger.

Unlike the disclosure documents for a merger vote that the SEC must approve before they are mailed to shareholders, tender offer documents do not require prior review by the SEC. Instead, they are reviewed by the SEC after the offer is launched. A tender offer must be held open for shareholder consideration for 20 business days (and possibly extended if changes in price or other material changes are made). The entire time frame may take approximately six weeks from signing to closing, as long as all regulatory approvals are satisfied during that period. This makes the tender offer process somewhat faster than the merger process.

Because tender offers can be faster, they may reduce the buyer's deal risk faster than a merger. In particular, a tender offer can lock up a deal by preventing the possibility of a topping bid faster than a merger if regulatory approval is straight-forward. The tender offer will lock up the deal at closing, perhaps six weeks after signing, while a merger will leave the deal vulnerable for 10 to 12 weeks until the shareholder vote can be held.

By contrast, if a deal requires cumbersome regulatory approvals, such as a complicated antitrust review or review by an industry regulator (e.g., the Department of Defense), then a tender offer may be a strategic mistake. In that case, a merger can lock up the deal in 10 to 12 weeks while the parties wait on regulatory approval for closing.

War Story

The deal had started off hostile, so it had to be structured as a tender offer. After some posturing between the parties and a couple of price increases, the target finally agreed to a deal.

Since the target was a multinational defense contractor, the deal needed a wide range of regulatory approvals to close that was just the beginning of the process.

Having reached an agreement, the buyer's counsel simply changed the price in the tender offer to the agreed number, and proceeded to seek the necessary approvals—without ever proposing to change the deal structure to a merger.

Regulators asked questions, but everyone expected approval to come without conditions. Given a number of other pressing priorities at the time for the regulatory, the approval process took longer than anticipated.

Shareholders were happy with the premium, but, of course, the deal could not close until regulatory approval came through. As a result of the regulatory delays, the tender offer had been extended—in two-week increments—over and over again.

Several months into the offer, shortly after the buyer could see the light at the end of the tunnel: a competing bidder with the capacity to offer much more emerged, and topped the original bid price.

Within days, the original bidder saw that pursuing its deal was futile and dropped out. In its place, the new bidder agreed to a deal with the target.

If the original bidder had required the target to sign a merger agreement (rather than staying with its tender offer structure), it could have sealed the deal with the shareholder vote months earlier. If it had done so, the shareholder vote could have been held much earlier, eliminating the risk of an interloper.

Having learned a lesson from the original bidder, the new buyer and the target promptly signed a merger agreement. The new deal closed three months later.

A merger and a tender offer require different levels of support from the target's shareholders in order to obtain 100 percent ownership. A merger normally requires approval of a majority of the outstanding shares.

A tender offer, in contrast, requires at least a majority of the outstanding shareholders to gain control as a legal matter, but requires a higher percentage in practice to get the benefit of a top-up option and ensure that the buyer can acquire 100 percent of the target. If the target is a Delaware corporation, a majority will be sufficient for the short-form merger without the need for a top-up option.

Other Structural Issues

Dual-track structures

Some deals simultaneously pursue a tender offer and a merger. This is meant to achieve the best of both. For instance, in a private equity deal, the parties may expect that a tender offer would be completed four weeks faster than a merger, giving the tender offer the benefit of speed. However, the target may only be able to provide a top-up option if the buyer acquires 80 percent due to the limited number of authorized but unissued shares.

From an approval perspective, that makes the tender offer less attractive than a merger, which only requires majority approval. Absent a dual-track structure, the buyer would have to decide between the timing benefit of the tender offer or the lower approval benefit of the merger. Dual-track structures allow the buyer to take the timing benefit while hedging its risk that it will not achieve the higher approval level.

Under a dual-track structure, the buyer launches a tender offer and the target begins the process for a merger vote at the same time. If the tender offer can close quickly with the required level of tenders, then the parties have achieved the benefit of speed. If the tender offer does not have sufficient tenders, the offer period will simply be extended while the shareholder vote process continues to move forward.

In fact, the existence of the backup shareholder vote process at the majority approval level could improve the chances of the tender succeeding, since shareholders will be more likely to view the deal as inevitable.

Retaining the target as a separate subsidiary

Irrespective of the basic structure (merger, stock sale, or asset sale), the buyer will normally want to ensure that the target becomes a subsidiary at closing and not part of another operating entity of the buyer. This is a matter of good corporate housekeeping, and ensures that creditors of the target do not have claims against unrelated assets of the buyer.

In order to achieve this result in an asset sale, the buyer will form a new entity into which it acquires the target's assets. In a stock sale, no new entity is needed, since the buyer acquires the target entity itself. In a merger, the buyer will form a new merger subsidiary that merges with the target entity (a triangular merger). After the merger, either the merger subsidiary or the target survives, but, in either case, the surviving corporation ends up being a subsidiary of the buyer.

Complex structuring

Large corporations have complex internal corporate structures, which may include multiple levels of intermediate and top-level holding companies. Structuring complexity can also be generated by multiple transaction steps, which may arise due to tax considerations.

A Reverse Morris Trust structure is a good example of how simple structural building blocks can be pieced together in novel ways. It basically combines each major structure type in a sequence: an asset sale to a new subsidiary, followed by a stock transfer to public shareholders, followed by a merger with the buyer.

A Reverse Morris Trust transaction allows a public company to sell a business "tax free" in circumstances where typical deal structures would be taxable to the seller. The Reverse Morris Trust structure even allows the seller to take cash out of the target business on a tax-free basis, by levering it up the instant before closing—the seller keeps the cash proceeds and passes the debt along to the buyer. Even in tax-free stock-for-stock deals with mixed cash/stock consideration, at a minimum the cash component is always taxable: but not so in a Reverse Morris Trust deal.

Such a deal plays out in a sequence of transaction steps, which combine elements of several basic structures.

- *Internal segregation of the target.* A public company seller transfers its target business into a separate, stand-alone subsidiary. This includes the intellectual property and related assets that are going with the target in the deal.
- *Levering up the target.* The new target subsidiary takes on debt and distributes the cash proceeds up to its parent. The trick is that the public company seller keeps the cash proceeds, without guaranteeing the debt. The cash stays with the seller, while the obligation to repay the debt stays with the

target subsidiary on its path through the next steps of the transaction, and ultimately to the buyer. There are tax-based limits on how much cash can be taken out of the target.

- *Split-off of the target.* The target company is spun off or split off to the owner's public shareholders. In a split-off, the seller makes an offer to its public shareholders to swap out some of their stock in the seller for stock in the target subsidiary (and, ultimately, the buyer). Since the public company takes back part of its own equity in the process, this structure allows it to retire stock (which boosts earnings per outstanding share and is perceived as a positive influence on its stock price). In a spin-off, the seller dividends to its public shareholders the stock in the target subsidiary.

  An economic incentive is usually offered to the seller's shareholders to encourage them to tender into the split-off. For example, the seller may offer its shareholders the right to exchange $1.00 worth of stock in the seller for $1.10 worth of stock in the target (and, ultimately, the buyer). This premium carries relatively little risk, since the buyer's stock can be immediately sold in the market or shorted in advance of closing. Such premium tenders are usually heavily oversubscribed.

  After the split-off or spin-off, the target business is a stand-alone public company, owned by the public shareholders of the seller who participated in the split-off—but only for an instant.

- *Merger of target/buyer.* The target company is merged into the buyer. The buyer assumes the target company's debt. As part of the merger, the stock in the target is exchanged for publicly traded stock in the buyer.

All of these steps occur on paper in an instant, at the closing of the deal. As a result, the seller has retained cash proceeds of the target's debt and has retired a portion of its equity (equal to a little less than the leveraged equity value of the target business in the deal). The seller's stockholders who participated in the split-off own at least a majority of the buyer's outstanding equity. The buyer owns the target business.

The use of this structure is limited by its complexity and specific tax requirements. The seller's shareholders need to own a majority of the combined target/buyer business (in order for the distribution of the stock by the seller to its shareholders to remain tax free). As a result, such transactions can only be accomplished where the buyer is smaller than its target in terms of equity value. Despite that imbalance, the buyer's senior management team normally continues as the combined company's senior management.

Appraisal Rights

Generally speaking, shareholders of a private target company may have so-called "appraisal" rights if the deal is structured as a merger.[24] These rights generally provide the target company's shareholders who do not vote to approve the deal with a right to opt out of the deal consideration and, instead, pursue a claim in state court to receive the fair value of their shares.

Shareholders exercising appraisal rights give up their right to the deal consideration in exchange for "fair value" as determined by the court. That value may be more or less than what the shareholder would have gotten from the merger. As a result, pursuing appraisal rights can result in risk for both the shareholder (who may get less) and the buyer (who may have to pay more).

Most states grant appraisal rights in the case of a merger. With respect to asset sales, Delaware does not grant appraisal rights to target shareholders.[25] New York provides appraisal rights to the target's shareholders in asset sales if the buyer is offering equity consideration, but not if the deal consideration consists of cash.[26] Other states offer appraisal rights to target shareholders if the deal is structured as a sale of all or substantially all of the target's assets (whether or not the deal consideration is cash).[27] Appraisal rights do not apply in the case of a stock sale, because shareholders must individually agree to the sale and are not being forced out.

Even if the deal structure calls for appraisal rights, those rights may not be available under a so-called "market out" exception. This exception applies in Delaware, for instance, if the target's shares are traded on a U.S. stock exchange.[28]

Litigation Endnotes

1. Pennsylvania and Texas have unique provisions that could permit the sale of one line of business. In Texas, an asset sale can be completed by a merger because Texas permits multiple surviving companies from a merger, each with the package of assets the parties decide to give it. *See* Tex. Bus. Orgs. Code §§ 1.002(14), 10.002. Pennsylvania has the concept of a division in which a company splits itself into two parts, with each part having a portion of the business. *See* 15 Pa. Cons. Stat. § 1951.

2. For example, certain states have adopted "bulk sales" laws, which are intended to prevent a seller from selling a company's assets, disappearing with the money, and leaving the company's creditors unpaid for the company's liabilities. Most state laws are based on Article 6 of the Uniform Commercial Code, and may apply upon the sale of a division or the sale of substantial assets of a business. Among other things, prior to closing, the buyer is required to give notice to the seller's trade creditors. This can be difficult or impossible, and in practice the parties typically do not comply with the bulk sales law notice procedures. A buyer's noncompliance does not render the sale ineffective or otherwise affect the buyer's title to the assets. Rather, the buyer is liable for damages caused by noncompliance. *See* U.C.C. §§ 6-107(1), 6-107(8).

3. Environmental liability may be based on federal or state law. For example, federal law imposes successor liability for environmental clean-up costs under the Comprehensive Environmental Response Compensation and Liability Act of 1980 (CERCLA). *See* 42 U.S.C. § 9601 et seq. Various states have enacted similar statutes imposing liability for cleanup costs as well. *See, e.g.,* Conn. Gen. Stat. § 22a-452a; N.J. Rev. Stat. § 58:10-23.11f.

4. With respect to product liability claims, state courts have developed the "product-line" exception in cases involving third-party claims over defective products, whereby a successor buyer may be held liable for defects in the predecessor's products. California courts, for example, have imposed strict liability upon a successor to a manufacturer based on: (1) the virtual destruction of the plaintiff's remedies against the original manufacturer caused by the successor's acquisition of the business, (2) the successor's ability to assume the original manufacturer's risk spreading role, and (3) the fairness of requiring the successor to assume a responsibility for defective products that was a burden necessarily attached to the original manufacturer's good will being enjoyed by the successor in the continued operation of the business. *Ray v. Alad Corp.,* 560 P.2d 3, 9 (1977). In *Knapp v. North American Rockwell Corp.,* the Third Circuit ruled that social policy considerations required that a transaction, while structured as an asset sale in exchange for stock consideration, should be treated as a merger for the purpose of imposing tort liability on the buyer for injuries caused by a defective machine manufactured by the selling corporation and distributed prior to the date of acquisition. 506 F.2d 361 (3d Cir. 1974). By contrast, in *Bernard v.*

Kee Manufacturing Co., Florida's highest court refused to impose liability on the purchaser of a manufacturing firm that continued under the same name and with the same product line, reasoning that the purchaser had not created the risk, only remotely benefited from the product, and was never in a position to eliminate the risk. 409 So. 2d 1047, 1050 (Fla. 1982).

5. The traditional common law rule of corporate successor liability applicable in most states provides that where one corporation purchases the assets of another, the purchasing or successor corporation can take the assets free of the liabilities of the first corporation unless one of four limited exceptions applies: (1) the successor expressly or impliedly agrees to assume the liabilities; (2) a de facto merger or consolidation occurs; (3) the successor is a mere continuation of the predecessor; or (4) the transfer to the successor corporation is a fraudulent attempt to escape liability. *See United States v. Mex. Feed & Seed Co.,* 980 F.2d 478, 487 (8th Cir.1992); *Shane v. Hobam, Inc.,* 332 F. Supp. 526, 527–528 (E.D. Pa. 1971).

6. In the case of a sale of all or substantially all the assets, approval by the board of the seller is usually required by statute. *See, e.g.,* 8 Del. Code Ann. § 271; N.Y. Bus. Corp. Law § 909.

7. *See, e.g.,* 8 Del. Code Ann. § 271 (requiring majority shareholder approval). *See also* N.Y. Bus. Corp. Law § 909(a)(3).

8. Courts have held that if the "sale is of assets quantitatively vital to the operation of the corporation and is out of the ordinary and substantially affects the existence and purpose of the corporation," then the sale is of "all or substantially all" of the corporation's assets. *Gimbal v. Signal Cos.,* 316 A.2d 599, 606 (Del. Ch.), *aff'd,* 316 A.2d 619 (Del. 1974). Some Delaware courts have focused on the significance of the assets that remain after the sale, noting that if the retained portion of the business constitutes a substantial, viable, ongoing component of the corporation, the sale does not constitute all or substantially all the assets. *See, e.g., Hollinger Inc. v. Hollinger Int'l, Inc.,* 858 A.2d 342 (Del. Ch. 2004). Delaware law also states that, for purposes of asset sales, "the property and assets of the corporation include the property and assets of any subsidiary of the corporation." 8 Del. Code Ann. § 271(c).

9. State laws also generally permit two companies to merge into each other with a third newly created company acting as the surviving entity (rather than having one of the two parties to the merger be the surviving entity). The corporate existence of both parties to the merger ceases in that case. This is rarely used in practice.

10. *See* 8 Del. Code Ann. § 251(b)(5); N.Y. Bus. Corp. Law § 902(a)(3); Model Bus. Corp. Act § 11.02(c)(3).

11. Delaware law requires that a majority of the outstanding stock entitled to vote on the merger must vote in favor of a merger transaction. *See* 8 Del. Code Ann. § 251(c). *See also* N.Y. Bus. Corp. Law § 903(a)(2) (majority of votes of shares entitled to vote, but only for companies incorporated after February 22, 1998). In other states, approval may require the vote of a higher percentage of outstanding

shares in certain situations. For example, Ohio law requires the affirmative vote
of at least two-thirds of the voting power (or such different proportion as the
articles may provide, but not less than a majority). *See* Ohio Rev. Code Ann.
§ 1701.78(F). The Model Business Corporation Act requires merely a majority
of the shares voting, so long as a quorum is present. *See* Model Bus. Corp. Act
§ 11.04(e).

12. For example, § 312.03*l* of the New York Stock Exchange (NYSE) Listed Company Manual requires that shareholders of an acquirer approve an acquisition in
which it issues to the target's shareholders common stock of the acquirer having
voting power equal to or in excess of 20 percent of the voting power outstanding
before the issuance of such stock. *See also* NASDAQ Marketplace Rule § 4350(i)
(1)(C); AMEX Company Guide § 712(b).

13. *See, e.g.*, 8 Del. Code Ann. § 251; N.Y. Bus. Corp. Law § 902; Model Bus. Corp.
Act § 11.04(a).

14. The official comments to § 11.06(a)(2) of the Model Business Corporations
Act note that a "merger is not a conveyance or transfer," and does not give rise
to claims based on prohibited conveyances or transfers. Model Bus. Corp. Act
§ 11.06(a)(2) cmts. (2010).

15. For example, in *PPG Industries, Inc. v. Guardian Industries. Corp.*, the Sixth Circuit ruled that a merger constituted a transfer under the applicable state statutes
and, therefore, violated an anti-transfer clause in a nonexclusive parent license.
597 F.2d 1090 (6th Cir. 1979). Subsequently, a number of courts have cited
PPG Industries in support of a general proposition that intellectual property
licenses are not assignable absent an express provision to the contrary. *See* Elaine
D. Ziff, *The Effect of Corporate Acquisitions on the Target Company's License Agreements*, 57 Bus. Law. 767, 785 (2002). Copyright assignments may vary depending on whether the license is exclusive or not. If exclusive, some courts treat the
holder of the license as the owner, with the free right to transfer. If the copyright
is nonexclusive, courts are more likely to restrict assignment without the consent
of the licensor. *See, e.g., In re Golden Books Family Entm't*, 269 B.R. 309, 316–19
(Bankr. D. Del. 2001); *Gardner v. Nike, Inc.*, 279 F.3d 774, 780 (9th Cir. 2002).
For patents, whether or not the patent license is assignable, some courts have
found that no assignment is permitted without the consent of the patent holder.
See, e.g., In re Hernandez, 285 B.R. 435, 439–440 (D. Ariz. 2002).

16. Under the Model Business Corporation Act, a binding share exchange requires
the majority vote of shares at a meeting in which a quorum consisting of at least
a majority of the votes entitled to be cast is present. *See* Model Bus. Corp. Act
§ 11.04(e).

17. *See* N.Y. Bus. Corp. Law § 913.

18. In friendly deals, the buyer makes the tender offer under an agreement with the
target.

19. Although neither the Williams Act nor SEC rules define the term "tender offer,"
courts have provided some guidance as to how to distinguish between public

tender offer solicitations and privately negotiated stock purchases. In a decision that has been endorsed by the SEC, one federal district court focused on eight common characteristics of tender offers: (1) an active and widespread solicitation of public shareholders for the shares of an issuer; (2) the solicitation is made for a substantial percentage of the issuer's stock; (3) the offer to purchase the shares is made at a premium over the prevailing market price; (4) the terms of the offer are firm rather than negotiable; (5) the offer is contingent on the tender of a fixed number of shares; (6) the offer is open only for a limited period of time; (7) the offeree is subject to pressure to sell his stock; and (8) public announcements of a purchasing program concerning the target company precede or accompany a rapid accumulation of large amounts of the target company's securities. *Wellman v. Dickinson,* 475 F. Supp. 783, 823–24 (S.D.N.Y. 1979), *aff'd on other grounds,* 682 F.2d 355 (2d Cir. 1982), *cert. denied,* 460 U.S. 1069 (1983). *See also* Commission Guidance on Mini-Tender Offers and Limited Partnership Tender Offers, 65 Fed. Reg. 46,581, 46,582 (July 31, 2000).

20. The primary federal rules governing tender offers are Regulations 14D and 14E under the Exchange Act. *See, generally,* 17 C.F.R. §§ 240.14d-1 et seq., 240.14e-1 et seq. The requirement to keep an offer open for at least 20 business days is found in Exchange Act Rule 14e-1(a). 17 C.F.R. § 240.14e-1(a).

21. *See Perlman v. Feldmann,* 219 F.2d 173 (2d Cir. 1955), *cert. denied,* 349 U.S. 952 (1955) (applying Indiana law); *Insuranshares Corp. v. N. Fiscal Corp.,* 35 F. Supp. 22 (E.D. Pa. 1940); *Brown v. Halbert,* 271 Cal. App. 2d 252 (1969). *See also Weinberger v. UOP, Inc.,* 457 A.2d 701 (Del. 1983); *Sinclair Oil Corp. v. Levien,* 280 A.2d 717 (Del. 1971).

22. *See* 8 Del. Code Ann. § 251(h).

23. SEC guidance states that "security holders have withdrawal rights and may withdraw tendered shares during the entire period the equity tender offer remains open." *Equity Tender Offer FAQs,* Exh. 99.6, Pilgrim's Pride Corp., Schedule TO-C: Form 8-K (Sept. 28, 2006).

24. *See, e.g.,* 8 Del. Code Ann. § 262 (providing for appraisal rights under Delaware's general corporation law).

25. *See id.*

26. *See* N.Y. Bus. Corp. Law § 910(a)(1)(B).

27. *See, e.g.,* Tex. Bus. Orgs. Code § 10.354 (providing for appraisal rights where shareholders dissent to "a sale of all or substantially all of the assets" of a company). *See also* Model Bus. Corp. Act § 13.02(a).

28. *See* 8 Del. Code Ann. § 262(b)(1)(i).

Index